Bertolt Brecht Collected P[lays]

The Antigone of Sophocles, [The Days of the Commune,] Turandot or The Whitewashers' Congress

Volume Eight of Brecht's *Collected Plays* contains his last completed plays, from the eight years between his return from America to Europe after the war and his death in 1956. Brecht devoted his energies at this time to the establishment of a new, post-fascist literature and theatre. He founded the Berliner Ensemble with his wife, Helene Weigel, and created models of production practice for future generations.

Brecht's *Antigone* (1948) is a bold adaptation of Hölderlin's classic German translation of Sophocles' play. A reflection on resistance and dictatorship in the aftermath of Nazism, it was also a radical new experiment in epic theatre. The play was first staged in Switzerland, in collaboration with associates from the pre-Nazi years and the production formed the basis for Brecht's first *Model-Book*.

The Days of the Commune, a semi-documentary account of the Paris Commune of 1871, was originally planned to be the first production by the new Berliner Ensemble in 1949. Partly for political reasons, it was not in fact premièred until after Brecht's death. His most serious and ambitious historical play, it sticks closely to the historical sources; ideologically, it is an exercise in thinking beyond defeat.

In *Turandot or the Whitewashers' Congress*, Brecht returned to a long-running plan to write a grand satire of the bourgeois intellectual class. He developed a bizarre comic variation on the old Turandot story, dressed up as a farcical review of the flailing left-wing intelligentsia of the Weimar Republic, the Nazi bureaucracy, the ineffectual anti-fascist exiles, and the calcified civil service of the young GDR. It was his last completed play.

The plays are accompanied by an introduction and notes by Tom Kuhn and David Constantine, including variants and relevant texts by Brecht.

Bertolt Brecht was born in Augsburg on 10 February 1898 and died in Berlin on 14 August 1956. He grew to maturity as a playwright in the frenetic years of the twenties and early thirties, with such plays as *Man equals Man*, *The Threepenny Opera* and *The Mother*. He left Germany when Hitler came to power in 1933, eventually reaching the United States in 1941, where he remained until 1947. It was during this period of exile that such masterpieces as *Life of Galileo, Mother Courage* and *The Caucasian Chalk Circle* were written. Shortly after his return to Europe in 1947 he founded the Berliner Ensemble, and from then until his death was mainly occupied in producing his own plays.

Brecht's Plays, Poetry and Prose

Series Editors: John Willett, Ralph Manheim and Tom Kuhn

BRECHT COLLECTED PLAYS: ONE

Baal; Drums in the Night; In the Jungle of Cities; The Life of Edward II of England; A Respectable Wedding; The Beggar or The Dead Dog; Driving Out a Devil; Lux in Tenebris; The Catch

BRECHT COLLECTED PLAYS: TWO

Man equals Man; The Elephant Calf; The Threepenny Opera; The Rise and Fall of the City of Mahagonny; The Seven Deadly Sins

BRECHT COLLECTED PLAYS: THREE

Lindbergh's Flight; The Baden-Baden Lesson on Consent; He Said Yes/He Said No; The Decision; The Mother; The Exception and the Rule; The Horatians and the Curiatians; St Joan of the Stockyards

BRECHT COLLECTED PLAYS: FOUR

Round Heads and Pointed Heads; Fear and Misery of the Third Reich; Señora Carrar's Rifles; Dansen; How Much Is Your Iron?; The Trial of Lucullus

BRECHT COLLECTED PLAYS: FIVE

Life of Galileo; Mother Courage and her Children

BRECHT COLLECTED PLAYS: SIX

The Good Person of Szechwan; The Resistible Rise of Arturo Ui; Mr Puntila and his Man Matti

BRECHT COLLECTED PLAYS: SEVEN

The Visions of Simone Machard; Schweyk in the Second World War; The Caucasian Chalk Circle; The Duchess of Malfi

BRECHT COLLECTED PLAYS: EIGHT

The Antigone of Sophocles; The Days of the Commune; Turandot or The Whitewashers' Congress

Poetry

POEMS 1913–1956

POEMS AND SONGS FROM THE PLAYS

BAD TIME FOR POETRY: 152 POEMS AND SONGS

FURTHER POEMS*

Prose

BRECHT ON THEATRE, VOL. 1

BRECHT ON THEATRE, VOL. 2*

DIARIES 1920–1922

JOURNALS 1934–1955

LETTERS 1913–1956

SHORT STORIES 1921–1946

BRECHT ON ART AND POLITICS

BRECHT ON FILM AND RADIO (*edited by Marc Silberman*)

**in preparation*

BERTOLT BRECHT

Collected Plays: Eight

The Antigone of Sophocles
translated by David Constantine

The Days of the Commune
translated by David Constantine

Turandot or The Whitewashers' Congress
translated by Tom Kuhn

Edited and introduced by Tom Kuhn and David Constantine

Methuen Drama

METHUEN WORLD CLASSICS

10 9 8 7 6 5 4 3 2 1

First published in Great Britain in hardback in 2003
by Methuen Publishing Ltd
215 Vauxhall Bridge Road, London SW1V 1EJ
by arrangement with Suhrkamp Verlag, Frankfurt am Main

First published in paperback in 2004

A CIP catalogue record for this book is available from the British Library

ISBN 0 413 77352 3

Typeset by Deltatype Ltd, Birkenhead, Wirral
Printed and bound in Great Britain by Cox and Wyman Ltd, Reading, Berkshire

Published with the support of the International Goethe Institute, Bonn

This volume, the last in the series of Brecht's Collected Plays, is dedicated to the memory of John Willett, who initiated this edition and did more than any other to bring Brecht to the English language.

Contents

TURANDOT OR THE WHITEWASHERS' CONGRESS

Introduction

THE LAST PLAYS, 1948–56

The three plays in this volume date from the last years of Brecht's life, when he returned from the United States and tried to establish a career in Europe once again. He had had six somewhat frustrating years in America, in which he had failed to make much impact where it might have mattered most to him – in Hollywood and on Broadway – and he had already started to plan his return by the end of 1946. His summons in the following year to appear before the House Committee on Un-American Activities (investigating 'Communist infiltration of the motion picture industry') can only have served to convince him that there was no future for him there. The day after testifying, on 31 October 1947, Brecht boarded a flight to Paris. A few days later he was on his way to Zurich, where he was hoping to stage *Mr Puntila and his Man Matti* at the Zurich Schauspielhaus (a theatre which had played an extraordinary role in keeping an oppositional German theatre alive during the Nazi years). 'The old continent is shabby and impoverished,' he wrote to Ruth Berlau, 'but I think you'll like it, as I do. We'll be able to work' (*Letters*, p.440). Europe was clearing up after the war, and the competition between the Western powers and the Soviet Union for political influence over central Europe was in full swing. Germany was divided into four separately administered zones, its people exhausted and mistrustful – if also cautiously inquisitive for the European and American culture which they had been denied over the past dozen years. Brecht himself was stateless, a suspect subversive, but without much else of a reputation. Next to nothing of his writings since 1938 was published, and nothing was in print. There was a serious paper shortage. Many of the theatre buildings were in ruins. It was not going to be easy.

It is sometimes maintained that these last nine years of Brecht's life were comparatively unfruitful, and it's true, he wrote less than in the apparently far more difficult circumstances of exile in Scandinavia and the United States. On the other hand, whereas the plays he wrote for European and American exile were designed to be accessible to bourgeois audiences internationally, and have duly become popular theatrical hits, the three major plays of Brecht's post-war years are, in their different ways, more uncompromising and more challenging works. *The Antigone of Sophocles* was conceived as a new experiment in the epic theatre, and is linguistically an extraordinary composition. *The Days of the Commune* is Brecht's only real excursion in historical drama, an attempt to write an adequate Marxist account of a key moment in revolutionary history, and a huge play. And *Turandot or The Whitewashers' Congress* is part of a grand satire of the bourgeois intelligentsia which engaged him intermittently for over twenty years. All three were important works for Brecht.

In other ways too, the years 1948 to 1956 were productive. Brecht had to establish a position in a German-speaking cultural context, in the institutions of the theatre, with the audiences and critics, and, in due course, with the cultural and political bureaucracies of the Soviet sector and subsequently the GDR (founded in 1949). Besides, one of his pre-eminent concerns was to consolidate his considerable achievements of the previous decades. He was extremely active in organising and promoting productions of his plays, visiting and corresponding with theatres all over Europe, offering opinions and advice. He prepared texts for publication, or re-publication, continuing the *Versuche* (*Experiments*) series of the pre-1933 years, and subsequently initiating a Collected Works edition. And he wrote new texts: poems (including the *Buckow Elegies*), prose sketches, political and cultural commentaries, and the all-important synthesis of his theoretical ideas in the *Short Organum for the Theatre*, his 'description of a theatre for the scientific age'. Perhaps most importantly, in terms of Brecht's subsequent reputation in the European theatre, he and Helene Weigel founded a theatre company, devoted to promoting Brecht's own works, method and theatrical style, and schooling a whole new generation of directors and actors. Given the state of German theatre and cultural life after National Socialism, that entailed the rediscovery of a repertoire and a whole new justification of the social role of the theatre. It was no small undertaking.

In their different ways the three plays presented here were all conceived as contributions to that larger task: not just efforts to relaunch Brecht's career, but investigations into the appropriate culture for a post-war, post-Fascist Europe.

Interestingly, given the debates at the time about the value of the cultural heritage, they all take some existing literary text as a basis or model. *Turandot* obviously has its roots in earlier versions of that story, even if it has become something rather different in Brecht's hands; one might say that, in this case, the existing fable was a peg on which to hang a brand new drama with quite new concerns. *The Days of the Commune* is a more purposeful counter-design, provoked (as much as inspired) by Nordahl Grieg's play about the Paris Commune, *Defeat*. Only the first of the three, *Antigone*, is akin to what one might normally understand as a conscientious literary adaptation. Brecht's dramatic output is full of adaptations of some sort or another, derived from a startlingly wide range of sources. One of his enduring preoccupations was with the culture of the past, and the uses to which it could, and should, be put. It is a matter which becomes particularly urgent in these last years, partly as a consequence of that mission to rediscover the repertoire and to create a cultural tradition for a Germany after Nazism.

As editors, we have sought to maintain a distinction: between, on the one hand, plays, such as those of this volume, which were independent literary projects, initiated and undertaken by Brecht (abetted by the customary collaborators), and, on the other hand, the stage adaptations of the Berliner Ensemble, which are clear examples of teamwork by the directors and dramaturgs of the Ensemble, and in which Brecht's own contribution, although he was the team-leader, may sometimes have been quite small. The Ensemble's engagement with the repertoire, in critical dialogue with the culture of the past, is a separate, important strand in Brecht's late work in the theatre.[1]

* * *

Arrived in Zurich, Brecht's first real contact was with Caspar Neher, the old schoolfriend who had designed the sets for many of his most successful pre-1933 productions and who had stayed in Germany. Together (and with the Austrian composer Gottfried von Einem, and the dramaturg of the Schauspielhaus Kurt Hirschfeld, amongst others), they hatched a whole range of plans and re-established contact with an array of friends and colleagues in the theatre world. The letters and diaries of these first months back in Europe are bursting with names.

Amongst their initial schemes in 1947/48 were the translation back into German of the new version of *Galileo*, the productions of *Puntila* in Zurich and of *Mother Courage* in Berlin a year later, as

---

[1] Some of the most important of the Berliner Ensemble adaptations, all given out as the work of their original authors and not published in Brecht's lifetime as 'his', have been published separately in English: J.M.R. Lenz's *The Tutor*, Shakespeare's *Coriolanus*, Anna Seghers's *The Trial of Joan of Arc*, Molière's *Don Juan*, and George Farquhar's *Trumpets and Drums*.

well as various translations and productions in non-German-speaking countries. But the very first project came about rather more unexpectedly. In November 1947 Brecht chanced to meet Hans Curjel, a Berlin theatre director whom he had got to know in 1929, working on *Mahagonny*. Curjel immediately mooted the possibility of a new venture at the theatre in Chur, of which he was now director. Within a few weeks, Brecht and Neher had mapped out an adaptation of Hölderlin's translation of Sophocles' *Antigone* and visited the old cinema in Chur which served as a theatre. In several ways, this must have seemed a return to the circumstances prior to 1933. It was to be Brecht's first job as a director back in the professional German-speaking theatre, it marked the beginning of renewed collaboration with Neher (who did the costumes, stage set and more) and, perhaps most enticingly, it was to be Helene Weigel's first real speaking part in ten years. Brecht was excited to be working in German again; the fact that this was a text which strained the language to its utmost merely added to the pleasure and the sense of importance (evidenced in the *Journal* entries quoted in the Notes). But the other great attraction was to be able to work experimentally again with his theories of epic and of *Verfremdung*. This is a play which employs a chorus and masks, and a decisive amount of reported action. So it is significant that the practical work on the *Antigone* adaptation coincided with Brecht's preparation of the summary of his theatre-theoretical ideas which became the *Short Organum*. One must imagine him working simultaneously on these projects.

After some postponements, the première of *The Antigone of Sophocles* came eventually on 15 February 1948. The attendance of friends and guests from Zurich and elsewhere ensured that Brecht's return to German-language theatre enjoyed some resonance. All the same, it was not a great success. The production has retrospectively achieved a particular reputation by virtue of the painstaking documentation in text and photographs of the *Antigone-Model* (see pp.203–15), but at the time it saw only five performances, one a matinée in Zurich. Contemporary reviews praised the Prelude, set in Berlin in April 1945, for its compelling updating of the myth, and it was recognised that the epic presentation – the actors showing, rather than impersonating their roles – marked this out as a significant theatrical event. Nonetheless, the critics struggled with the text and with Brecht's efforts to manoeuvre the story away from its familiar moral battleground (of individual conscience and the demands of the state). The publication a few months later of the *Antigone-Model*, including the complete play-text, was even more disappointing; only some five hundred copies were sold initially. There was to be just one further full production of the play in Brecht's lifetime, in the small German town of Greiz in November 1951. This was understood as an opportunity to test out the model. Although the conclusions were again generally favourable, it was still a minor event in a decidedly modest theatre. The experience of *Antigone* may have been a crucial test for the participants, but it would take more than this to re-establish Brecht's position. For the time being, he returned to the *Short Organum* and to *Puntila*, which had its opening night on 15 June 1948. *Puntila* was the fourth of his Scandinavian plays to have its première in Zurich, but it was the first which Brecht was to direct himself.

Brecht's adaptation remains a fascinating chapter in the life of the Antigone story: a paradoxical attempt to rationalise and update the story according to Brecht's own social philosophy (with none of the psychological baggage of other modern treatments of classical myth), while at the same time apparently allowing the extraordinary dramatic and poetic language of his predecessors (both Sophocles and Hölderlin) to derail his own project. It seems evident that his interest in the material was increasingly linguistic and theatrical, rather than moral or political. Besides, Brecht's literary adaptations are seldom wholesale appropriations, designed to obliterate the original. Instead they seek, self-consciously, to allow the history of a text to show through, in order to imply the possibility of a future evolution too. For Greiz, Brecht deleted the 'Berlin 1945' Prelude, with its powerful yet ambiguous invocation of anti-Fascist resistance, and replaced it with a speech (see 'New Prologue', p.218) which simply enjoins the audience to

> Search in your own hearts and minds for similar deeds
> In the recent past or for the absence
> Of any such deeds.

So it may be quite appropriate that, in the 1960s, critics of this deliberately and transparently adapted play heard and saw hints of contemporary events in Vietnam, Pakistan and India. The epic method is meant to encourage just such an open, re-evaluative approach. Despite its difficulty, Brecht's *Antigone* remains an intriguing text and a provocative play, whose day is not done as long as there are wars and the moral and social conflicts they entail.

* * *

In the meantime, there were plans afoot to bring Brecht back to Berlin, led by Herbert Ihering, the critic who had championed him in the 1920s and who had remained in Germany. Brecht himself hoped to be able to return to the Theater am Schiffbauerdamm, where he had worked in the last years of the Weimar Republic. Early in 1948 Wolfgang Langhoff staged a successful production of *Fear and Misery of the Third Reich* at the Deutsches Theater, and then offered that theatre for Brecht's and Erich Engel's own production of *Mother Courage*. Later in the year there were productions of *Puntila* in Hamburg and of *Mother Courage* in Vienna. But Brecht himself was still in Zurich, waiting for his papers to come through. Contemplating the risk of future travel restrictions, he discussed with Neher and von Einem the possibility of working as house playwright at the Salzburg Festival, of which von Einem was a director, and of acquiring Austrian citizenship.

Eventually, Brecht and Weigel made a first visit to Berlin, in October 1948. Thanks to the efforts of Ihering, Langhoff and others, and with the support of the Communist Kulturbund and senior figures in the Central Committee of the Socialist Unity Party (Wilhelm Pieck, soon to be the first President of the GDR, and Otto Grotewohl, the equivalent of Prime Minister), they were given an official welcoming reception. But negotiations and discussions about a company, and about the availability of a suitable theatre, remained mired in nervous uncertainty. Then, quite suddenly, the success of *Mother Courage* in Berlin in January 1949 lent momentum to the matter. The couple were offered what was in the circumstances an extraordinary opportunity: to set up their own ensemble. They moved quickly. In February 1949 the constitution of the Berliner Ensemble was agreed, and by April its funding was approved. Weigel became its able and strong-willed intendant (and was to give defining performances as Courage and Pelegea Vlassova in *The Mother*); Brecht was its artistic director and, in the first years, the director, or co-director with Engel, of its most famous productions; Dessau and Eisler were its composers; and Neher was for years its exemplary designer. From now on, the composition of this Ensemble and its repertoire became Brecht's overriding concerns.

This was the context of *The Days of the Commune*. Brecht had returned to Zurich alone in late February, in order to recruit actors and other theatre professionals, to collect his daughter, and to settle his affairs there (including setting up a Swiss bank account, just in case). It was presumably the new Ensemble's commitment to a 'progressive' programme that induced him, despite his reservations about the author's political insight, to look once more at Nordahl Grieg's play, *Defeat* (see Editorial Notes). The appraisal of the Paris Commune by Marx and Engels (and subsequently Lenin) had established the Commune as the first 'proletarian revolution' and the earliest example of a 'Soviet'-style social organisation by democratic council. It must have seemed ideal material for the new company's opening production. If it didn't work out, the other play Brecht was considering was Büchner's French Revolutionary drama, *Danton's Death*. In Zurich Ruth Berlau joined him and, with Caspar Neher, they worked together on the evidently recalcitrant material, resolving soon to depart quite decisively from Grieg's play. By the end of April 1949 the manuscript of the new play was finished. But it had been a rush-job and it is clear that Brecht still had his misgivings. He resolved to launch the Ensemble with the far less controversial *Puntila*, and *The Days of the Commune* was scheduled instead as the third production (after *Puntila* and Maxim Gorki's *Vassa Shelesnova*). In December he decided to postpone it still further, in favour of a new adaptation of J.M.R. Lenz's *The Tutor* – 'because the Volksbühne with about 60,000 members, which makes up the bulk of our audience, has only about 0.3% workers' (*Journals*, p.425). Preliminary preparations for a production continued, but other new projects kept intervening. It was not in fact until 17 November 1956, three months after Brecht's death, that *The Days of the Commune* had its première, in Karl-Marx-Stadt (Chemnitz), under the joint direction of two of Brecht's young protégés, Benno Besson and Manfred Wekwerth.

In his interpretation of the Paris Commune Brecht adhered closely to the 'classical' line established by Marx and represented in Brecht's most important historical source-book, Hermann Duncker's edited collection of documents and other material, *Pariser Kommune 1871* (Berlin, 1931): that the outcome of the siege of Paris after the Franco–Prussian War could only have been different if the ruling class had been prepared to align themselves behind the National Guard, but that the French bourgeoisie were terrified at the thought of an armed labour force, and so initiated the betrayal of the French people by its government and the capitulation of Paris. He defended his account in November 1949 in a letter to Eric Russell Bentley, his American translator and an early champion of the Brechtian theatre:

> It's probably true that the play cannot be accepted unless one accepts the Marxist point of view. But to take a classical example: To accept *Hamlet* or *Troilus and Cressida* mustn't one accept the attitudes of Montaigne or Bacon? [. . .] What the play can show is only that the proletariat cannot counter the force of its adversaries unless it is prepared to use force. I've made no attempt to bring out parallels between Paris in 1871 and Berlin in

> 1949, not even where they might have greatly simplified the play. (*Letters*, p.482)

Some of the possible objections to the play are anticipated, even before it had been published or produced. But the debate is clearly not just about the interpretation of distant historical events. The reference to Berlin in 1949 is to a tense political situation. In response to economic reform in the West and the perceived threat of a strong new currency, the USSR had severed land communications to the Western sectors of the city, leading to the blockade. As Brecht saw it, the new Communist regime was seeking to protect itself against the capitalist West, rather as the Paris Commune had erected the barricades against the bourgeois government and its new Prussian friends. Under the circumstances, it is hardly surprising that the play seemed too party-political for commentators in the West. Correspondingly, for the Communist world it was insufficiently politically resolute: an internal report for the Central Committee condemned Brecht's new piece as a depressing account of a failed revolution.

The première seven years later (with Neher's stage set and Eisler's music) met with considerable interest, partly because it was the first production of a Brecht play after his death. But the critics were still uncertain what to make of it. They were divided in their assessments of its historical value and of possible contemporary analogies (now to the uprising in Hungary), they wondered if Brecht had abandoned *Verfremdung* in favour of Socialist Realism, and Alfred Kurella opined that it was one of Brecht's weakest works, for it spoke to neither heart nor head. The atmosphere of the Cold War invaded the responses in the West: this was a celebration of terror, an incitement to political murder, and so on. Arthur Adamov riposted with his own Commune-play *Le Printemps 71* (1960), an effort to set the record straight in both historical and artistic terms. A second Berliner Ensemble production, in 1962, of a radically revised version by Wekwerth and Tenschert, was evidently conceived to imply an analogy between the Paris barricades and the erection of the Berlin Wall (in August 1961). It was quietly but positively received in the East; in the West the perfection of the staging was admired, while the political implications (that such brutal measures might be necessary) were deplored. Since then *The Days of the Commune* has been one of the least performed of Brecht's plays, and at the same time one of the most contentious. Its reception in the theatre has been, more than of any other play, entangled in the changing political contexts: a first West German production soon after the 1968 unrest, a Frankfurt production at the time of the RAF terrorist attacks, and so on. The

Commune has been made to serve as a symbol both of the endangered Communist revolution and of anti-Communist revolt. Directors and critics have repeatedly exploited the claim that the play is supposedly unfinished.

The accusations sometimes levelled at the play, of a crude realism, historical naivety and, worse, of political propagandism and Stalinism, are misplaced. Brecht may insist on violence for the preservation of the good cause, but his determined move back to Marx's own critique of the Commune implies very much a revolutionary history carried on the back of the working masses, and not a Leninist Party, let alone a Stalinist one. Brecht creates a class of representative individuals, and above all a family (Madame Cabet and her circle), as both objects and potentially powerful subjects of history. And the play employs familiar Brechtian strategies: relatively self-contained 'gestic' scenes, moments of *Verfremdung* and 'play-within-play'. In one particular way, however, the technique does perhaps represent an interesting variation. Although Grieg's play is obviously an important point of departure, *The Days of the Commune* also proceeds – in an exceptionally documentary manner for Brecht (see Editorial Notes) – from the stuff of history (and from that one canonical interpretation, by Marx). So, whereas he is elsewhere inclined to confront the fables and the fictions with social and historical reality (and it is out of that that a critical, *verfremdet* reception is derived), here the contradictions have to be discovered between the historical facts themselves and the historical truth (in Brecht's sense of a 'useful' insight) – between the real mistakes of the Commune and the interpretations of those mistakes, in their turn historically determined.

In his work on the *Antigone-Model* Brecht had suggested that the choice of material depended on its capacity both to set interesting formal problems and to achieve a certain contemporary resonance. Writing later about *Coriolanus* he argued that the discovery of new and 'relevant' readings was part of 'the fun of dealing with a slice of illuminated history' (*Brecht on Theatre*, p.265). Klaus Detlef Müller has argued that *The Days of the Commune* is just such a slice.[1] The dialectical negotiations between the historical material and its changing relevance in different historical periods and contexts are a key to a continuing engagement with Brecht's drama. Rather like the

---

[1] In the *Brecht-Handbuch*, edited by Jan Knopf, vol.1 (Stuttgart/Weimar, 2001), p.557. This is a valuable reference work, which we have used alongside the standard, commentated German edition of Brecht's works, the *Berliner und Frankfurter Ausgabe* (abbreviated as BFA).

process of transparent adaptation (in *Antigone*) which invites the continual re-evaluation of a text, so the process here is conceived to reveal what we might call 'the history of a history': from Marx (whom Brecht treats as a base), through Lenin, to the divided Germany of 1949. It is a small step to develop this trajectory beyond Brecht's own lifetime: to the uprisings of 1956, the crisis of 1961/62, the eruptions of the later 1960s, and after. Although the vision of a proletarian state may have faded in our own time, it is still possible to see in Brecht's play shadows of more recent political phenomena, such as the collapse of the very Communist state for which it was originally conceived, or the corruption of social democracy by global capitalism. Above all, *The Days of the Commune* is a conscientious exercise in thinking beyond defeat.

* * *

So, in November 1949, the Berliner Ensemble began its career not with a new play, but with the Brecht-Engel production of *Puntila*, once more with Leonard Steckel (a former Piscator actor from Zurich) as Puntila, and now with music by Dessau and sets by Neher. The early history of the remarkable institution of the Berliner Ensemble – a state company of the GDR under the auspices of the Ministry of Education – belongs elsewhere: its array of old talents from the Left theatre of the Weimar Republic, the exceptional performers and directors of the younger generation who were trained here, the controversies over programmes, the adaptations and excursions into old and new repertoires, its move back into the Schiffbauerdamm Theatre, its struggles at home and its triumphant tours to Paris and London. The outline is given in the *Letters* volume (pp.431–39), and the political context and Brecht's response discussed in more detail in *Brecht on Art and Politics* (pp.273–81).

For Brecht's own last play we turn away, in the first instance, from the broader history of this literary field, and even from the 1950s. For the first mention of the title *Turandot* is in a notebook of 1922/23, in a list of literary works and figures that had attracted Brecht's interest. As far as we know, he only came back to the story in the 1930s. Drafts and sketches from the next twenty years are reviewed briefly in the Editorial Notes.

There are a handful of projects like this, that occupied Brecht's energies intermittently over a very long period. His first play *Baal* was revisited in three subsequent decades; the first sketches for what was to become, in the 1940s, *The Good Person of Szechwan* date from the mid-1920s; and *Life of Galileo* went through three very different versions over the course of nearly twenty years. In each case, these were concepts which were allowed to evolve, to shed old concerns and to accrue new ones, as the context of writing and reception moved on. In each case, the later versions are supported as though on a layered skein of allusions and points of reference. The concerns of the older drafts are still visible through the later texts. Rather as *Antigone* and *The Days of the Commune*, by their very structure, encourage re-evaluations, here the texts themselves are changeable, for a changeable world. Contradictions are allowed, even encouraged, to survive the process. So *Turandot or The Whitewashers' Congress* manages to be 'about' the role of the intellectual in the Weimar Republic, and in Nazi Germany, and in the GDR. It is vain to search for a single integrated reading which can easily embrace all its terms of reference. All sorts of allusions, again to over twenty years of contemporary history, are allowed to rub up, one against the other.

In *Turandot*, all this is made easier by the extremely free treatment of the traditional Turandot story, and by the use of an obviously *verfremdet*, almost fairy-tale setting. Brecht's China only very occasionally stands in for the real contemporary China (where Kai Ho takes his bow as Mao Tse-tung). More often it is the poetic fiction of 'Chima', as Brecht sometimes called it: a simplified model of social, economic and political structures, part feudal, part monopoly-capitalist, into which he attempts to interleave a bit of Chinese and a lot of European history. In the 1930s Brecht specifically noted that the costumes for this play should be half European and half Chinese.

The genesis (or perhaps better: evolution) of the play is further complicated by its relation to a far larger project, the so-called *Tui-Novel*. In the mid-1930s Brecht began gathering material for what Walter Benjamin described as 'an encyclopaedic overview of the idiocies of the Tellectual-Ins (the intellectuals)'. In the first place, the object was a satirical account of the role of the intellectuals in Imperial Germany and the Weimar Republic – who had pretended that their spirit might shape society, when in fact they were in the pay of the ruling class. This was the 'Golden Age of the Tuis', before their banishment by the Nazis. The Tuis' teahouse in *Turandot* is distinctly reminiscent of the Viennese coffee-houses in Brecht's 'Unpolitical Letters' of 1933 (*Brecht on Art and Politics*, pp.126–9). The archive contains a vast chaos of further material, sketches, plans and fragmentary drafts. But the ambitious project failed to cohere. Brecht started to discover Tuis almost wherever he looked. The whole notion of the Tuis as a class began to slip out of focus. The conflict between Stalin and Trotsky and the subsequent trials suggested, for example, that the Tuis were still very much a force in the Soviet Union. His experience of America, on the other hand, seemed to imply that the whole thrust of his satire had been misplaced – in this variety of capitalism, prostituting the intellect had become entirely socially acceptable. Gradually the plan metamorphosed: the Tuis became the excuse-mongers, the intellectual lackeys and henchmen of the powers-that-be in every ideological camp. Intellectual enquiry itself, which in the early modern age, had been a productive force, liberating the emergent bourgeoisie (as portrayed in *Galileo* and represented in the Baconian Tui-motto 'knowledge is power'), had not only become unproductive, it had actually fallen into the service of the repression of further social development. Still, the novel remained a series of fragments, and the plan for a play was not, for the time being, pursued.

By the 1950s, Brecht's perspective on all of this had changed quite radically. Whereas in the past he had always conceived of himself as in opposition, now the status of the Berliner Ensemble, and of Brecht as one of the new state's pre-eminent cultural figures, meant that he was himself a member of the establishment, communicating with ministers, contributing to the development of policy, and making public statements. He was, moreover, genuinely committed to the future of the GDR, and particularly to its younger generation. Especially in the early years, he wrote a number of Laureate-like poems, and took an active part in the work of the new Academy of Arts, of which he was a founding member. So the problem had become a much more urgent and personal one: how should the creative intellectual, how should the artist conduct himself in the service of a state of which he broadly approved? There may be hints even in the 1930s that Brecht recognised himself, ironically, as a Tui; but in the GDR he was unquestionably implicated with the organs of political power. The difficulty of this quite new situation should not be underestimated. For, although he was clearly no distantly critical dissident, the differences between Brecht and his political masters were considerable too. Despite his general loyalty to the Socialist Unity Party (the SED), the defensive nationalism of the new state contradicted Brecht's fundamentally open, internationalist attitudes. Moreover, there were serious arguments about aesthetics and the cultural heritage. These surfaced intermittently throughout the period, but perhaps most damagingly over Brecht's and Dessau's opera version of *Lucullus*, which was compulsorily withdrawn in March 1951 on account both of its modern idiom and of its pacifism (cf. *Collected Plays: 4*). The reprise of the old formalism debates of the 1930s was a particularly depressing experience for Brecht. Differences flared up again in 1953, over a production of the *Urfaust* and over Eisler's intended Faust opera, both of which the authorities considered an affront to the cultural heritage (cf. *Turandot*, scene 9, and see *Brecht on Art and Politics*, pp.309–30).

Nowhere were the agonised contradictions of Brecht's situation clearer than in his response to the events of 17 June 1953. On that day workers in East Berlin rose up against the government's demands for increased productivity, and were joined in violent demonstrations by a mixed crowd from West Berlin. The disturbances were brutally swept aside by Soviet intervention. Brecht's instant reaction was to assure the Party that, whatever its mistakes in the recent past, he was on its side. His letter to Walter Ulbricht, First Secretary of the SED, was swiftly exploited. The official newspaper, *Neues Deutschland*, published just the final sentence, implying all Brecht's support, but none of his criticism. Despite Brecht's anger, the initial outcome was a boost to his status and to that of his theatre. In private, he complained that events had 'alienated the whole of existence' (*Journals*, p.454). To his assistant, Käthe Rülicke, he wrote, 'Difficult days. The whitewashers are hard at it. Then again: what a chance to be a good Communist!' (BFA 30, p.180). There is no question that, from this point on, Brecht found it more difficult to lend the regime his wholehearted support.

This was the moment then, in response to the new Tuism of the German Democratic Republic, to the tensions between Moscow and East Berlin, and specifically in reaction to the workers' uprising, that Brecht got out the old files and disentangled his *Turandot* once more from the complex of Tui-material. Now the play was relatively quickly written. One of the primary objects had become to illuminate the role of the intellectual 'whitewashers' of a regime which was becoming increasingly bureaucratic and dictatorial. As he writes in the Preface to *Turandot*, 'unconvinced but cowardly, hostile but cowering, ossified officials began again to govern against the population' (see p. 247). The material also offered Brecht an opportunity to point up traumatic continuities with the Nazi past, a matter which was very much in his mind if we are to judge by the poems of the *Buckow Elegies* which date from these years. At the same time, he could gesture across to the recent success of the Chinese Revolution, which he understood as the outcome of a genuinely popular movement, and so a salutary contrast to the imported Stalinist bureaucracy of the GDR. The German people had not risen up and overthrown their criminal regime, and Brecht was mistrustful of their ability to act as a basis for the development of Socialism.

There was a time
When all was different here.
The butcher's wife knows.
The postman has too erect a gait.
And what was the electrician?
('Eight Years Ago', *Poems*, p.443)

Turandot or The Whitewashers' Congress is Brecht's last (more or less) completed play. He contemplated publishing it in the *Versuche* (*Experiments*) series, and even planned a production, first under Harry Buckwitz, then under Benno Besson in Rostock (with Regine Lutz as Turandot, Helene Weigel as the Dowager, Ernst Busch as A Sha Sen, and Ekkehard Schall as Wang, the Secretary of the Tui Academy). There was even a brief flurry of rehearsals in spring 1954, when Brecht revised the text. According to Käthe Rülicke he was, however, still dissatisfied, and would have returned to it in 1955 had not the preparation of publications and of productions at the Berliner Ensemble and elsewhere intervened. In the event, Brecht died without ever coming back to the play. It was not published in German until 1967.

The première of *Turandot* took place on 5 February 1969 at the Zurich Schauspielhaus under the direction of Benno Besson and Horst Sagert, with music by Yehoshua Lakner. It had a mixed reception. No one seemed quite sure what the targets of the satire were. Subsequent productions in Cologne (1971), East Berlin (1973) and elsewhere provoked similar confusion. The confrontation of exuberant popular theatre styles with the complex political ambiguities of the parable has left generations of critics groping for a clear line. To this day it remains a difficult work, full of richly associative satirical material and wonderfully lively farce, but unwieldy on the stage. It invites revision by a firm hand.

* * *

1953 was a crucial year, both for the GDR and for Brecht. The year began with the death of Stalin in March, provoking wild turns in the Soviet attitude to the GDR. Meanwhile, the East German Academy of Arts promoted a major conference on Stanislavsky, the theorist of an emotional theatre, who seemed to represent everything Brecht opposed. Brecht did not attend. Then came the workers' uprising in June, and all the political tensions consequent upon that. The state was struggling to assert its legitimacy, not on the basis of popular support (which it did not enjoy), but rather on the basis of a particular interpretation of German history. That is why the cultural debates were so vehement. Brecht's adaptations of Lenz's *The Tutor*, his work with *Faust*, *Turandot*, and even *The Days of the Commune*, were all designed to some extent to develop a critique of the class of teachers, public servants and bureaucrats, who, according to Brecht, had provided key support for Nazism, and were now to blame for the ills of the Socialist Republic. The particularly craven behaviour of this middle-class intelligentsia was seen as a long-term product of the failure of Germany's progressive social forces in the eighteenth century. The SED, by contrast, sought to uphold the idea of the GDR as the legitimate heir to the best progressive traditions – while all the worst aspects of the past, including the Fascist past, could be located in the West. In the spirit of dialectics, Brecht appears at times to have relished the ferocious ideological exchanges with the authorities which resulted from these differences, but the continuing experience of criticism and censorship by what he saw as the lesser cultural functionaries was taking its toll. His insistence on the 'German Misere' interpretation of history was seen as treasonous, and even *Mother Courage* was attacked for its 'pacifism, decadence and negativity'. Amongst the very sparse diary entries for 1953, Brecht noted that 'our performances in Berlin have almost no resonance any more', and later that, if there were free elections, the Nazis might well be returned (*Journals*, pp.454 and 455).

Nevertheless, the end of 1953 saw a relative upturn in Brecht's situation. He moved into a new flat in central Berlin, and the German collected works edition began with his *Plays One*; there were several interesting productions in hand. The political unrest had in fact given force to his own arguments and strengthened the hands of his allies. At the beginning of 1954 the various commissions for the arts were replaced by a new Ministry for Culture, partly in response to Brecht's vigorous campaigning. The new Minister was an old colleague, Johannes R. Becher, and Brecht served on an advisory committee. Gradually, the old 'formalism' arguments were allowed to wither away. In March 1954 some of the pressures on the Berliner Ensemble were relieved when at last, after extensive building-works, they were able to move into the old Schiffbauerdamm Theatre (where they opened with Molière's *Don Juan*). Brecht himself directed the première of *The Caucasian Chalk Circle* in June. He became vice-president of the Academy in July, and in December 1954 was awarded the Stalin Prize (the ceremony took place in Moscow in May 1955). Brecht chose to interpret the award as encouragement for his work for peace, and for a peaceful unification of Germany. At the same time, work on the many productions of the Berliner Ensemble, and on films and productions of his own plays by other companies, continued. He participated in the hugely successful Berliner Ensemble tours to Paris, with *Mother Courage* in 1954 and with *The Caucasian Chalk Circle* in 1955. In 1956 he began preparing *The Caucasian Chalk Circle* for London.

Also from about 1954, however, an elegiac tone begins to enter Brecht's poems and an unmistakable air of disappointment and exhaustion invades his sparse journal entries and letters. 'This country still gives me the creeps,' one note reads. To Becher he ended up complaining, 'the era of collectivism has become largely an era of monologue' (*Journals*, p.458, *Letters*, p.559). He was suffering from minor ailments, worried about his eyesight and his heart. Early in 1956 he had a brief stay in hospital, where he was treated for the after-effects of a bout of influenza. He died of a heart attack on 14 August 1956, shortly before the London season opened.

His early death, aged 58, spared him much of the recrimination within the Communist Party following upon Krushchev's revelation of Stalin's 'crimes' at the Twentieth Party Congress. He did not live to see either the Soviet suppression of the Hungarian Uprising, or the hardening of political attitudes which was to lead before long to the building of the Berlin Wall. Nevertheless, Brecht's years in the GDR had been dominated by the escalating Cold War and by the many conflicts between his engagement with the ideas of Socialism and their far from perfect realisation in the difficult world of a divided post-Fascist Germany. It is hardly surprising that he had not had all that much time for original compositions. Instead, his priority had been to devote himself to cultural politics, and to the promotion of his vision of the role of the arts and of the theatre in the newly Socialist half of the country.

The three plays in this volume are nonetheless challenging literary documents of those negotiations, important experiments in textual adaptation and quotation and in the epic mode, and models of a new political drama, able to respond allusively to historical change. Despite some similarities in the working methods behind them, they are also astonishingly different. One would hardly imagine that this serious verse adaptation from Sophocles, this semi-naturalistic historical drama, and this funny, sprawling comedy could all be by the same author. The range of Brecht's interests and the variety of his responses to his situation continue to surprise.

Increasingly also, Brecht had been giving his energies as a mentor to new writers and to the younger members of the Ensemble. He had developed projects for and with them, bequeathing a whole generation of Brechtian directors, writers and actors to the theatres of both East and West. It was they who were to continue the struggles of the creative intellectual, wrestling with the details of commitment: to Communism, to the East German state, and to the discipline of dialectics. To theatre and to song.

THE EDITORS

Chronology

1898 10 February: Eugen Berthold Friedrich Brecht born in Augsburg.

1917 Autumn: Bolshevik revolution in Russia. Brecht to Munich university.

1918 Work on his first play, *Baal*. In Augsburg Brecht is called up as medical orderly till end of year. Elected to Soldiers' Council as Independent Socialist (USPD) following Armistice.

1919 Brecht writing second play *Drums in the Night*. In January Spartacist Rising in Berlin. Foundation of German Communist Party (KPD). Rosa Luxemburg murdered. April–May: Bavarian Soviet. Summer: Weimar Republic constituted. Birth of Brecht's illegitimate son Frank Banholzer.

1920 May: death of Brecht's mother in Augsburg.

1921 Brecht leaves university without a degree. Reads Rimbaud.

1922 A turning point in the arts. End of utopian Expressionism; new concern with technology. Brecht's first visit to Berlin, seeing theatres, actors, publishers and cabaret. He writes 'Of Poor BB' on the return journey. Autumn: becomes a dramaturg in Munich. Première of *Drums in the Night*, a prize-winning national success. Marries Marianne Zoff, an opera singer.

1923 Galloping German inflation stabilised by November currency reform. In Munich Hitler's new National Socialist party stages unsuccessful 'beer-cellar putsch'.

1924 'Neue Sachlichkeit' exhibition at Mannheim gives its name to the new sobriety in the arts. Brecht to Berlin as assisant in Max Reinhardt's Deutsches Theater.

1925 Field-Marshal von Hindenburg becomes President. Elisabeth Hauptmann starts working with Brecht. Two seminal films: Chaplin's *The Gold Rush* and Eisenstein's *The Battleship Potemkin*. Brecht writes birthday tribute to Bernard Shaw.

1926 Première of *Man equals Man* in Darmstadt. Now a freelance; starts reading Marx. His first book of poems, the *Devotions*, includes the 'Legend of the Dead Soldier'.

1927 After reviewing the poems and a broadcast of *Man equals Man*, Kurt Weill approaches Brecht for a libretto. Result is the text of *Mahagonny*, whose 'Songspiel' version is performed in a boxing-ring at Hindemith's Baden-Baden music festival in July. In Berlin Brecht helps adapt *The Good Soldier Schweik* for Piscator's high-tech theatre.

1928 August 31: première of *The Threepenny Opera* by Brecht and Weill, based on Gay's *The Beggar's Opera*.

1929 Start of Stalin's policy of 'socialism in one country'. Divorced from Marianne, Brecht now marries the actress Helene Weigel. May 1: Berlin police break up banned KPD demonstration, witnessed by Brecht. Summer: Brecht writes two didactic music-theatre pieces with Weill and Hindemith, and neglects *The Threepenny Opera*'s successor *Happy End*, which is a flop. From now on he stands by the KPD. Autumn: Wall Street crash initiates world economic crisis. Cuts in German arts budgets combine with renewed nationalism to create cultural backlash.

1930 Nazi election successes; end of parliamentary government. Unemployed 3 million in first quarter, about 5 million at end of the year. March: première of the full-scale *Mahagonny* opera in Leipzig Opera House.

1931 German crisis intensifies. Aggressive KPD arts policy: agit-prop theatre, marching songs, political photomontage. In Moscow the Comintern forms international associations of revolutionary artists, writers, musicians and theatre people.

1932 Première of Brecht's agitational play *The Mother* (after Gorky) with Eisler's music. *Kuhle Wampe*, his militant film with Eisler, is held up by the censors. He meets Sergei Tretiakov at the film's première in Moscow. Summer: the Nationalist Von Papen is made Chancellor. He denounces 'cultural bolshevism', and deposes the SPD-led Prussian administration.

1933 January 30: Hitler becomes Chancellor with Papen as his deputy. The Prussian Academy is purged; Goering becomes Prussian premier. A month later the Reichstag is burnt down, the KPD outlawed. The Brechts instantly leave via Prague; at first homeless. Eisler is in Vienna, Weill in Paris, where he agrees to compose a ballet with song texts by Brecht: *The Seven Deadly Sins*, premièred there in June. In Germany Nazi students burn books; all parties and trade unions banned; first measures against the Jews. Summer: Brecht in Paris works on anti-Nazi publications. With the advance on his *Threepenny Novel* he buys a house on Fyn island, Denmark, overlooking the Svendborg Sound, where the family will spend the next six years. Margarete Steffin, a young Berlin Communist, goes with them. Autumn: he meets the Danish Communist actress Ruth Berlau, a doctor's wife.

1934 Spring: suppression of Socialist rising in Austria. Eisler stays with Brecht to work on *Round Heads and Pointed Heads* songs. Summer: Brecht misses the first Congress of Soviet Writers, chaired by Zhdanov along the twin lines of Socialist Realism and Revolutionary Romanticism. October: in London with Eisler.

1935 Italy invades Ethiopia. Hitler enacts the Nuremberg Laws against the Jews. March–May: Brecht to Moscow for international theatre conference. Meets Kun and Knorin of Comintern Executive. Eisler becomes president of the International Music Bureau. At the 7th Comintern Congress Dimitrov calls for all antifascist parties to unite in Popular Fronts against Hitler and Mussolini. Autumn: Brecht with Eisler to New York for Theatre Union production of *The Mother*.

1936 Soviet purges lead to arrests of many Germans in USSR, most of them Communists; among them Carola Neher and Ernst Ottwalt, friends of the Brechts. International cultural associations closed down. Official campaign against 'Formalism' in the arts. Mikhail Koltsov, the Soviet jounalist, founds *Das Wort* as a literary magazine for the German emigration, with Brecht as one of the editors. Popular Front government in Spain resisted by Franco and other generals, with the support of the Catholic hierarchy. The Spanish Civil War becomes a great international cause.

1937 Summer: in Munich, opening of Hitler's House of German Art. Formally, the officially approved art is closely akin to Russian 'Socialist Realism'. In Russia Tretiakov is arrested as a Japanese spy, interned in Siberia and later shot. October: Brecht's Spanish war play *Señora Carrar's Rifles*, with Weigel in the title part, is performed in Paris, and taken up by antifascist and amateur groups in many countries.

1938 January: in Moscow Meyerhold's avant-garde theatre is abolished. March: Hitler takes over Austria without resistance. It becomes part of Germany. May 21: première of scenes from Brecht's *Fear and Misery of the Third Reich* in a Paris hall. Autumn: Munich Agreement, by which Britain, France and Italy force Czechoslovakia to accept Hitler's demands. In Denmark Brecht writes the first version of *Galileo*. In Moscow Koltsov disappears into arrest after returning from Spain.

1939 March: Hitler takes over Prague and the rest of the Czech territories. Madrid surrenders to Franco; end of the Civil War.

Eisler has emigrated to New York. April: the Brechts leave Denmark for Stockholm. Steffin follows. May: Brecht's *Svendborg Poems* published. His father dies in Germany. Denmark accepts Hitler's offer of a Non-Aggression Pact. August 23: Ribbentrop and Molotov agree Nazi-Soviet Pact. September 1: Hitler attacks Poland and unleashes Second World War. Stalin occupies Eastern Poland, completing its defeat in less than three weeks. All quiet in the West. Autumn: Brecht writes *Mother Courage* and the radio play *Lucullus* in little over a month. November: Stalin attacks Finland.

1940 Spring: Hitler invades Norway and Denmark. In May his armies enter France through the Low Countries, taking Paris in mid-June. The Brechts hurriedly leave for Finland, taking Steffin with them. They aim to travel on to the US, where Brecht has been offered a teaching job in New York at the New School. July: the Finnish writer Hella Wuolijoki invites them to her country estate, which becomes the setting for *Puntila*, the comedy she and Brecht write there.

1941 April: première of *Mother Courage* in Zurich. May: he gets US visas for the family and a tourist visa for Steffin. On 15th they leave with Berlau for Moscow to take the Trans-Siberian railway. In Vladivostok they catch a Swedish ship for Los Angeles, leaving just nine days before Hitler, in alliance with Finland, invades Russia. June: Steffin dies of tuberculosis in a Moscow sanatorium, where they have had to leave her. July: once in Los Angeles, the Brechts decide to stay there in the hope of film work. December: Japanese attack on Pearl Harbor brings the US into the war. The Brechts become 'enemy aliens'.

1942 Spring: Eisler arrives from New York. He and Brecht work on Fritz Lang's film *Hangmen Also Die*. Brecht and Feuchtwanger write *The Visions of Simone Machard*; sell film rights to MGM. Ruth Berlau takes a job in New York. August: the Brechts rent a pleasant house and garden in Santa Monica. Autumn: Germans defeated at Stalingrad and El Alamein. Turning point of World War 2.

1943 Spring: Brecht goes to New York for three months – first visit since 1935 – where he stays with Berlau till May and plans a wartime *Schweik* play with Kurt Weill. In Zurich the Schauspielhaus gives world premières of *The Good Person of Szechwan* and *Galileo*. November: his first son Frank is killed on the Russian front.

1944 British and Americans land in Normandy (June); Germans

driven out of France by end of the year. Heavy bombing of Berlin, Hamburg and other German cities. Brecht works on *The Caucasian Chalk Circle*, and with H. R. Hays on *The Duchess of Malfi*. His son by Ruth Berlau, born prematurely in Los Angeles, lives only a few days. Start of collaboration with Charles Laughton on English version of *Galileo*.

1945 Spring: Russians enter Vienna and Berlin. German surrender; suicide of Hitler; Allied military occupation of Germany and Austria, each divided into four Zones. Roosevelt dies; succeeded by Truman; Churchill loses elections to Attlee. June: *Private Life of the Master Race* (wartime adaptation of *Fear and Misery* scenes) staged in New York. August: US drops atomic bombs on Hiroshima and Nagasaki. Japan surrenders. Brecht and Laughton start discussing production of *Galileo*.

1946 Ruth Berlau taken to hospital after a violent breakdown in New York. Work with Auden on *Duchess of Malfi*, which is finally staged there in mid-October – not well received. The Brechts have decided to return to Germany. Summer: A. A. Zhdanov re-affirms Stalinist art policies: Formalism bad, Socialist Realism good. Eisler's brother Gerhart summoned to appear before the House Un-American Activities Committee. November: the Republicans win a majority in the House. Cold War impending.

1947 FBI file on Brecht reopened in May. Rehearsals begin for Los Angeles production of *Galileo*, with Laughton in the title part and music by Eisler; opens July 31. Brecht's HUAC hearing October 30; a day later he leaves the US for Zurich.

1948 In Zurich renewed collaboration with Caspar Neher. Production of *Antigone* in Chur, with Weigel. Berlau arrives from US. Summer: *Puntila* world première at Zurich Schauspielhaus. Brecht completes his chief theoretical work, the *Short Organum*. Travel plans hampered because he is not allowed to enter US Zone (which includes Augsburg and Munich). Russians block all land access to Berlin. October: the Brechts to Berlin via Prague, to establish contacts and prepare production of *Mother Courage*.

1949 January: success of *Mother Courage* leads to establishment of the Berliner Ensemble. Collapse of Berlin blockade in May followed by establishment of West and East German states. Eisler, Dessau and Elisabeth Hauptmann arrive from US and join the Ensemble.

1950 Brecht gets Austrian nationality in connection with plan to involve him in Salzburg Festival. Long-drawn-out scheme for

Mother Courage film. Spring: he and Neher direct Lenz's *The Tutor* with the Ensemble. Autumn: he directs *Mother Courage* in Munich; at the end of the year *The Mother* with Weigel, Ernst Busch and the Ensemble.

1951 Selection of *A Hundred Poems* is published in East Berlin. Brecht beats off Stalinist campaign to stop production of Dessau's opera version of *Lucullus*.

1952 Summer: at Buckow, east of Berlin, Brecht starts planning a production of *Coriolanus* and discusses Eisler's project for a *Faust* opera.

1953 Spring: Stalin dies, aged 73. A 'Stanislavsky conference' in the East German Academy, to promote Socialist Realism in the theatre, is followed by meetings to discredit Eisler's libretto for the *Faust* opera. June: quickly suppressed rising against the East German government in Berlin and elsewhere. Brecht at Buckow notes that 'the whole of existence has been alienated' for him by this. Khrushchev becomes Stalin's successor.

1954 January: Brecht becomes an adviser to the new East German Ministry of Culture. March: the Ensemble at last gets its own theatre on the Schiffbauerdamm. July: its production of *Mother Courage* staged in Paris. December: Brecht awarded a Stalin Peace Prize by the USSR.

1955 August: shooting at last begins on *Mother Courage* film, but is broken off after ten days and the project abandoned. Brecht in poor health.

1956 Khrushchev denounces Stalin's dictatorial methods and abuses of power to the Twentieth Party Congress in Moscow. A copy of his speech reaches Brecht. May: Brecht in the Charité hospital to shake off influenza. August 14: he dies in the Charité of a heart infarct.

1957 *The Resistible Rise of Arturo Ui*, *The Visions of Simone Machard* and *Schweyk in the Second World War* produced for the first time in Stuttgart, Frankfurt and Warsaw respectively.

The Antigone of Sophocles

A version for the stage after Hölderlin's translation

Collaborator: Caspar Neher

Translator: David Constantine

Characters:

TWO SISTERS
SS MAN

ANTIGONE
ISMENE
CREON
TIRESIAS
HAEMON
GUARDS
THE ELDERS OF THEBES
MESSENGER
MAIDS

PRELUDE

Berlin. April 1945.

Daybreak.
Two sisters come back to their home from the air-raid shelter.

FIRST SISTER:
And when we came up from the air-raid shelter
And the house was whole and in a brighter
Light than dawn from the fire opposite
It was my sister who first noticed it.
SECOND SISTER:
Sister, why is our door open wide?
FIRST SISTER:
The draught of the fire has hit it from outside.
SECOND SISTER:
Sister, what made the tracks there in the dust?
FIRST SISTER:
Nothing but someone who went up there fast.
SECOND SISTER:
Sister, the sack in the corner there, what's that?
FIRST SISTER:
Better that something's there than something's not.
SECOND SISTER:
A joint of bacon, sister, and a loaf of bread.
FIRST SISTER:
That's not a thing to make me feel afraid.
SECOND SISTER:
Sister, who's been here?
FIRST SISTER:
How should I know that?
Someone who's treated us to something good to eat.
SECOND SISTER:
But I know! We of little faith! Oh luck

Is on us, sister. Our brother is back.

FIRST SISTER:

Then we embraced each other and were cheerful
For our brother was in the war, and he was well.
And we cut and ate of the bacon and the bread
That he had brought us to feed us in our need.

SECOND SISTER:

Take more for yourself. The factory's killing you.

FIRST SISTER:

No you.

SECOND SISTER:

It's easier on me. Cut deeper.

FIRST SISTER:

No.

SECOND SISTER:

How could he come?

FIRST SISTER:

With his unit.

SECOND SISTER:

Now
Where is he, do you think?

FIRST SISTER:

Where they are fighting.

SECOND SISTER:

Oh.

FIRST SISTER:

But there was no noise of fighting to be heard.

SECOND SISTER:

I shouldn't have asked.

FIRST SISTER:

I didn't want you scared.
And as we sat there saying nothing a sound came
In through the door that froze the bloodstream.
A screaming from outside.

SECOND SISTER:

Sister, there's someone screaming. Let's see who.

FIRST SISTER:

Sit still. You go and see, you get seen too.
So we did not go outside the door

To see what things were happening out there.
But we ate no more either and we did not
Look at each other again but we stood up and got
Ready to go to work as we did daily
And my sister took the plates and I bethought me
And took our brother's sack to the cupboard
Where his old things are stored.
And I felt, so it seemed, my heartbeat stop:
In there his army coat was hanging up.
Sister, he isn't in the fight
He's run for it, he's cleared out
His war's over, he has quit.

SECOND SISTER:
Those still there, he's left them to it.

FIRST SISTER:
They had death lined up for him.

SECOND SISTER:
But he disappointed them.

FIRST SISTER:
There was still an inch or two . . .

SECOND SISTER:
That was where he crawled through.

FIRST SISTER:
Some still in, he's left them to it.

SECOND SISTER:
His war's over, he has quit.

FIRST SISTER:
And we laughed and we were cheerful:
Our brother was out of the war and he was well.
And as we stood there such a sound came
It felt like ice in the bloodstream.
A screaming from outside.

SECOND SISTER:
Sister, who is it screaming outside our door?

FIRST SISTER:
Again they are tormenting folk for pleasure.

SECOND SISTER:
Sister, should we not go and find out who?

FIRST SISTER:

Stay in. You go and find out, you get found out too.
So we waited a while and did not go and see
What the things that were happening outside might be.
Then we had to leave for work and I was the one who saw
What it was outside our door.
Sister, sister don't go out.
Our brother is home but he is not
Safe and sound but hanging there
From a meat hook. But my sister
Went out of the door
And screamed herself at what she saw.

SECOND SISTER:

They have hanged him, sister. That was
Why he cried out loud for us.
Give me the knife, give it here
And I'll cut him down so he won't hang there
And I will carry his body in
And rub him back to life again.

FIRST SISTER:

Sister, leave the knife.
You'll not bring him back to life.
If they see us standing by him
We'll get what he got from them.

SECOND SISTER:

Let me go. I didn't while
They were hanging him. Now I will.

FIRST SISTER:

And as she made for the door
An SS man stood there.
Enter an SS man.

SS MAN:

We know who he is. Say who you are.
He came out of here.
Seems to me very probable
You know that traitor to his people.

FIRST SISTER:

Sir, we are not the ones to question.
We do not know the man.

SS MAN:

So what's she doing with the knife, her there?

FIRST SISTER:

Then I looked at my sister.
Should she on pain of death go now
And free our brother who
May be dead or no?

Outside Creon's palace. Daybreak.

ANTIGONE *collecting dust in an iron pot*:

Sister, Ismene, twin shoot
From the stem of Oedipus, do you know any thing
Error, sad travail, any disgraceful thing
Not visited by the Father of the Earth
On us who have lived to here?
In a long war, one man among many
Eteocles fell, our brother. In the tyrant's train
He fell young. And younger than him Polynices
Sees his brother pulped under horses' hooves. Weeping
He rides from an unfinished battle, for this to one
And that to another the battle spook deals when he comes at him hard
With his just deserts and smashes his hands. Headlong
Already the fugitive
Had crossed the streams of Dirce and breathing again
He sees the seven gates of Thebes still standing, then Creon
There at the rear lashing them into the fight
Seizes him splashed with the blood of his brother and hacks him to pieces.
Have they told you or have they not told you
What more shall be heaped on Oedipus'
Dwindling breed?

ISMENE:

I did not show myself in the marketplace, Antigone.
No further word has come to me of loved ones
No kind word and no sad one either.
I am not happier and not more troubled.

ANTIGONE:

Hear it from me then. And whether your heart's
Beat stops or beats
Deeper in misery, show me that.

ISMENE:

You with the dust in your collecting hand, you seem
To dye your words with red.

ANTIGONE:

This then: our two brothers
Dragged both into Creon's war for the grey metal
Against remote Argos and slaughtered both
Shall not be covered both of them with earth.
The one who did not fear the fight, Eteocles
He, it is said, shall be wreathed and buried as is the custom.
Of the other's though, who has died wretchedly,
Of Polynices' corpse they say they have
Broadcast it in the city he shall not
Be hidden in any grave and not lamented.
He shall be left unwept without a grave
Sweet dish for the birds. But whosoever
Does anything about this will be stoned.
So tell me then what you will do about it.

ISMENE:

Sister, are you testing me?

ANTIGONE:

Would I have your help?

ISMENE:

In what dangerous endeavour?

ANTIGONE:

To cover him.

ISMENE:

Whom the city has abjured?

ANTIGONE:

Whom they have failed.

ISMENE:

The man in rebellion.

ANTIGONE:

Yes. My brother and also yours.

ISMENE:

Sister, you will be caught in lawlessness.

ANTIGONE:

But not
In faithlessness.

ISMENE:

Unlucky girl, are you impelled
To gather us all below now
Of Oedipus' stock?
Let be what's past.

ANTIGONE:

You are younger, you have seen
Less horror. What is past, let be
Does not stay past.

ISMENE:

Think of this too: we are women
And must not make a quarrel against men
Not being strong enough and thus in thrall
In this and much else harsher too. Therefore
I beg them down below whom only earth oppresses
They will forgive me. Under this duress
I will follow the ruler. For doing
Things in vain is unwise.

ANTIGONE:

I shall not go on asking. You
Follow whoever gives the orders and do
Whatever he orders. But I
Will follow the custom and bury my brother.
And if I die in it, so what? I will be quietened
Lying with the quiet ones. Behind me I will have
Accomplished what is holy. Then a longer time
I shall be liked by those down there than here
For there I'll dwell for ever. But you
Laugh at disgrace and live.

ISMENE:

Antigone, it is bitter
To suffer a wild disgrace, but also
There is a limit on the salt of tears, they do not spring
From the eyes inexhaustibly. The edge of the axe
Ends sweet life but it opens
The veins of pain in the ones it leaves behind. They must lament
Without rest but even lamenting they hear
Above them the twittering of birds and again
Through the veil of their tears appear

The ancient elms and the roofs of home.

ANTIGONE:

I hate you, shamelessly showing me
A lap of skirt full of holes and in it your
Dwindling stock of grief. Meanwhile
On bare stones flesh of your flesh is lying
Served up to the birds of the far and wide skies, he is to you
Already a yesterday thing.

ISMENE:

Only
To raise myself in revolt I am not good enough, and clumsy
And fear for you.

ANTIGONE:

Don't counsel me. Come out with your own life!
But let me do the very least and honour what is mine
Where it has been reviled. I am in all things
Not so delicate, I hope, that I could not
Die an unlovely death.

ISMENE:

Go then with your dust. But listen: your speech
Is all awry, but lovely on what we love.

Exit Antigone with her jug. Ismene goes indoors. Enter the Elders.

ELDERS:

But victory big in booty has come
And favoured the numerous chariots of Thebes
And after the war
Now let there be a forgetting.
Into all the gods' temples
With choirs through the night
Come and let Thebes whose nakedness laurels have clothed
Be shaken with the stamp and dancing of Bacchus!
But the bringer of victory
Creon, Menoeceus' son, must have hurried here
From the battlefield to proclaim
Booty and at last the return of the soldiers
Since he has called and commanded this gathering of the Elders.

Creon comes out of the palace.

CREON:
Sirs, share this with everyone: there is
No Argos any more. The settling up
Was total. From eleven townships
Few got away, oh very few!
As it is said of Thebes: you bear to Good Luck
Twins in a trice, and Bad Luck
Does not flatten you, it
Itself is flattened. Your spear's thirst
Was quenched at the first drinking. And was not denied
Repeated drinking. Thebes, you laid to rest
The people of Argos on a hard place. Now without town or tomb
What mocked you lies in the open air.
And looking where
Their city was
What you see are dogs
With glistening countenances.
The noblest vultures wing their way to her, they tread
From corpse to corpse
And from the rich servings there
They cannot lift into the air.

ELDERS:
Sweet picture, sir, of vast and terrible things.
And it will please the city when it comes to them
If shrewdly mixed with something else: chariots
Climbing the streets here carrying our own.

CREON:
Soon, friends, soon. But now to business. Not yet
Will you see me hang my sword up in the temple.
There are two reasons why I summoned you
From among all. For one, because I know
You don't keep count how many wheels the war god's
Foe-crushing chariots need and don't begrudge him
Your sons' blood in the battle, but when he comes
With losses home under the well-defended roof
There is much reckoning up in the market place. Swiftly
Therefore make clear to Thebes the blood-spillage
Does not exceed the usual. Then this, because

All too forgiving Thebes, being saved
Again, will hurry as always to wipe the gasping home-
comers'
Sweat off their brows and will not especially note
Whether the sweat is the sweat of the angry fighter or
Only the sweat of fear and with it mixed
The dust of flight. Therefore I covered
And you are to approve it, Eteocles
Who died for the city, with wreath and grave
But the poltroon Polynices, to him
And to me related and a friend to the people of Argos
Will lie unburied as they lie. Like them
He was an enemy, to me was and to Thebes.
My wish therefore is no one mourn him, also
That he be left unburied and on show
A meal, a meat torn up by birds and dogs.
For who rates higher than his native city
His life, I count him nothing.
Who means my city well though, dead or alive
Equally always he has my esteem.
I hope that you approve that.

ELDERS:
We do approve it.

CREON:
Be overseers then in the aforesaid.

ELDERS:
Fill suchlike posts with young men.

CREON:
Not that. The corpse already has a watch out there.

ELDERS:
And we're the watchers on the living, are we?

CREON:
Yes. There are certain people it displeases.

ELDERS:
There's no such fool here he will gladly die.

CREON:
None openly. But many a one there is
Goes on shaking his head till it falls off.
And that brings me to this: more still needs doing, alas.

The city must be cleansed . . .
Enter a guard.

GUARD:
Sir!
My führer, breathlessly
I hurry to hand in the swiftest news, don't ask why not
Even swifter, my feet
Ahead of my head or else
It tugging them after, for
Wherever I am going and how long
Still in the sun and out of breath
Going I am at least nevertheless.

CREON:
Why so out of breath or
So hesitant?

GUARD:
I hush nothing up. Why, say I
Not say straight out what wasn't done by me?
And don't know either for I do not even know
Who did this thing to you. Harsh sentence
On one so ignorant would be
Discouraging.

CREON:
Taking no chances are you? The eager messenger
Of your own misdeed you want the prize
For good legwork.

GUARD:
Sir
You laid a vast thing on your watchers. But
Vast things do also give a lot of trouble.

CREON:
Speak, will you, finally, then go again.

GUARD:
I'll speak then. Somebody who got away
Just now has buried the dead man, sprinkling
His skin with dust so the vultures would not spy him.

CREON:
What's that you say? Who was it dared do this?

GUARD:

I do not know. A spade had not dug there
Nor any shovel flung. And smooth the ground
Not ridden over by wheels. No sign
Who did it. Not a burial mound
Only a gentle dust as though someone had shied
Before the ban and had not brought much dust.
And nowhere prints of any beasts
Nor dogs that had come and torn.
When first light showed us this it had
To all of us an eerie feel. And I
Was chosen by lot to tell you, führer
And no one loves the bearer of dire words.

ELDERS:

Oh Creon, son of Menoeceus, might not
The gods be in this happening?

CREON:

Enough of that. Don't make me angrier still
And say the spirits are gentle on the coward
Who coldly would have let be violated
The groups of columns of their temples and the offerings.
No
Some in the city take some things amiss
And mutter and in the harness will not bow
Their necks for me. I know for sure
These got this up, with bribes.
For among all things ever stamped for use
None is so bad as silver. Whole towns
It leads astray and goads men from their houses
To know the knack of every godless work.
Hear this though, if you do not bring me in
Earthly and alive, whoever did it
Yoked and guilty, you'll be hanged and go
With a rope around your neck to the underworld.
Then see where you can draw your profit from
Share out the spoils with one another and learn
Not everything is there to buy and sell.

GUARD:

Sir, our kind have a lot to be afraid of.
The place, the down-below place, you allude to

For us has far too many entrances. I'm less
Not to say not at all, afraid this minute that
I was given any silver – but if you think so
I'd better turn my pockets out twice more
In case there's something in there after all –
Than that I'll make you cross by contradicting.
But what I fear more is when I start looking
It's rope I might be given, in high hands
There being more of rope for such as us
Than silver. If you take my meaning.

CREON:
You, so transparent, are you setting me conundrums?

GUARD:
The high-up dead man had his high-up friends.

CREON:
Catch them around the shins if you can't reach higher
Up them. There are, I know, one place or another
Malcontents. Some hear of my victory
Quaking with joy and put the laurel on
With fearful haste. I'll find them out.
Exit into the palace.

GUARD:
Unhealthy place this where the high
Are scrapping with the mighty. I'm
So it seems, still here. To my surprise.
Exit.

ELDERS:
Monstrous, a lot. But nothing
More monstrous than man.
For he, across the night
Of the sea, when into the winter the
Southerlies blow, he puts out
In winged and whirring houses.
And the noble earth of the gods in heaven
The unspoilable tireless earth
He rubs out with the striving plough
From year to year driving
The race of horses to and fro.
And the breed of the lightly made birds
He ensnares and hunts

And the tribe of wild beasts
And Pontus' nature that thrives in salt
With ropes slyly slung
This knowing man.
And catches the game with his arts
That sleeps and roams on the mountains.
And over the rough-maned horse he flings
The yoke on its neck, and over the mountain-
Wandering and untamed bull.
And speech and the airy flight
Of thought and statutes to order a state
He has learned and to flee the damp airs
Of ill-blowing hills and
The bolts of rain. All-travelled
Untravelled. He comes to nothing.
Always he knows what to do
Nothing nonplusses him.
In all this he is boundless but
A measure is set.
For when he wants for an enemy
He rises up as his own. Like the bull's
He bows the neck of his fellowmen but these fellowmen
Rip out his guts. When he steps forth
He treads on his own kind, hard. By himself alone
His belly will never be filled but he builds a wall
Around what he owns and the wall
Must be torn down. The roof
Opened to the rain. Humanity
Weighs with him not a jot. Monstrous thereby
He becomes to himself.
  But it stands before me now like God's temptation
  That I should know and yet shall say
  This is not the child. Antigone
  O unhappy girl of the unhappy
  Father Oedipus, what is this bearing
  Over you and where is it leading you
  For disobeying the statutes of the state?

Enter the guard, leading Antigone.

GUARD:

She did it. She did. We seized her
Making the grave. But where is Creon?

ELDERS:

Here, even as you ask, back from the house.
Creon comes out of the palace.

CREON:

How is it you fetch her here? Where did you seize her?

GUARD:

She made the grave. Now you know everything.

CREON:

Your word is clear but was it you who saw her?

GUARD:

As she mounded the grave, which you forbade.
A man in luck is clear at once as well.

CREON:

Give your account.

GUARD:

The affair was so. When I had gone away
From you, from your colossal threats
And we had wiped the dust off the dead man
Lying already rotting, we sat up in the air
On a high hill because a stink
Came off the dead man strongly. We agreed
In case of sleep to jab each other in the ribs
With the elbow. Suddenly then we opened
Our eyes wide, and why? Because a warm wind
Suddenly lifted up the mist from the ground
Covering the valley in a twisting storm
Tearing the hair out from the valley's trees and all
The vast ether was full of it so we were blinded
And rubbed our eyes, just so, and after that
Then she was seen and stood and wept out loud
With a sharp voice the way a bird will grieve
Seeing the empty nest and no young in it.
So she lamented, seeing the dead man bare
And gathered dust on him again from the iron jug
Three times with waterings so burying over
The dead man. Quickly we ran and seized her
Who seemed unabashed and charged her with

The present and with the already happened.
But she denied nothing and was at once
A sweet and an unhappy thing before me.

CREON:
Do you say or deny it that you did it?

ANTIGONE:
I say I did it and do not deny it.

CREON:
Then tell me now, not lengthily but briefly
Do you know what was given out in public
Concerning that particular dead man?

ANTIGONE:
I knew. How shouldn't I? Was it not clear?

CREON:
You dared to break my statute in this way?

ANTIGONE:
Because it was yours, because a mortal made it.
A mortal then may break it and I am
Hardly less mortal than you are. But if I die
Before the time I think I will, that is
I say, even a gain. Who lives like me
With many ills surely receives
Some small advantage, dying? Further, had I left
Lying without a grave my mother's other dead
That would have saddened me. But this
Saddens me not at all. But if you think it foolish
That I should fear the heavenly gods who from above
Have no wish to observe uncovered that piecemeal man
And so do not fear you, now let a fool
Pass judgement on me.

ELDERS:
The wild father's ilk shows wildly in the child:
Under a bad fate she has never learned compliance.

CREON:
But even the strongest iron
Cooked in the furnace still its obstinacy
Will break and fail. You see this every day.
But she discovers a delight in muddying
The laws prescribed. And having done it

Her second impudence is to boast and laugh
That she did it. I hate a person caught in the wrong
And making out the thing is something beautiful.
But you, insulting me although my blood-relation
Because my blood-relation I will not condemn at once
But ask you: since you did this thing in secret
That now is in the open, will you say
And so avoid a heavy punishment, you are sorry?
Antigone remains silent.

ELDERS:
Say then why you are obstinate.

ANTIGONE:
For an example.

CREON:
Do you not care that I have you in my hands?

ANTIGONE:
What more can you do than kill me now you have me?

CREON:
Nothing. But having that I have it all.

ANTIGONE:
Why wait? Of all your words
None pleases me, none will please me
And so myself I am not agreeable to you
Although I am to others for what I did.

CREON:
So you think others see it as you see it?

ANTIGONE:
These see it too, these too are smitten by it.

CREON:
Aren't you ashamed to interpret them unasked?

ANTIGONE:
Surely we honour humans of one flesh?

CREON:
He's also of one blood who died for the country.

ANTIGONE:
One blood. Child of the selfsame man and wife.

CREON:
And the one who spared himself you rate him with the
other?

ANTIGONE:
Though he was not your serf he is still my brother.
CREON:
True if you count all one, godless and godly.
ANTIGONE:
Nor is death one and the same for the country or for you.
CREON:
So there's no war?
ANTIGONE:
Yes, yours.
CREON:
Not for the country?
ANTIGONE:
A foreign country. It did not content you
Ruling over my brothers in Thebes
A city of our own and sweet
Not living in fear, the life beneath its trees. You
Had to drag them to distant Argos to rule
Over them there too. And the one you made into a butcher
Of peaceful Argos and the terrified other
Him you lay out now, quartered, a terror to his own.
CREON:
I advise you, you'll say nothing, to her there
Speak nothing, if you know what's good for you.
ANTIGONE:
But I appeal to you to help me in my trouble
And help yourselves, so doing. Who seeks power
Drinks of a salty water, he cannot desist but must
Drink it and drink it. My brother yesterday, today it's me.
CREON:
And I am waiting
To see who sides with her.
ANTIGONE *when the Elders remain silent*:
So then you let it be and keep your mouths shut for him.
Let that not be forgotten.
CREON:
She notes it against you.
At odds she wants us under the roof of Thebes.

ANTIGONE:
Screaming for unity you live on discord.

CREON:
So first in discord here and then in the field against Argos!

ANTIGONE:
Of course. Exactly. When you have need of violence abroad
Then you'll have need of violence at home.

CREON:
And me, so it seems to me, in her goodness she'll give to the vultures
And never mind then if Thebes, so at odds
Falls as a feast to foreign rule?

ANTIGONE:
You, the rulers, threaten and threaten the city will fall
At odds, will founder and feast on it others and foreigners
And we bow our necks and fetch you the sacrifices and thus
Weakened our city founders and foreigners feast on it.

CREON:
Do you tell me I am throwing the city to foreigners to feast on?

ANTIGONE:
She throws herself to them, bowing her neck to you
For bowing the neck nobody sees what's coming
But only the earth and, alas, the earth will have him.

CREON:
Slander the earth in your wickedness, slander the homeland!

ANTIGONE:
Wrong there. The earth is travail. The homeland is not just
Earth, nor the house. Not where a man poured his sweat
Not the house that helplessly watches the coming of fire
Not where he bowed his neck, he does not call that the homeland.

CREON:
You however the homeland no longer calls her own
But you are cast out like a biting filth that pollutes.

ANTIGONE:
Who casts me out? There are fewer in the city now
That you rule and fewer will be still.
Why do you come here alone? You went out with many.

CREON:
You dare say that?
ANTIGONE:
Where are the youths, the men? Are they not coming back?
CREON:
How she lies! When everyone knows they are out still
Only to cleanse the battlefield wholly of the axes left.
ANTIGONE:
And to do your last misdeeds
And to be a terror until their fathers
No longer recognise them when at the end
Like animals run amok they are slaughtered finally.
CREON:
She defiles the dead!
ANTIGONE:
Fool of a man, I've no desire
To be proved right.
ELDERS:
She is unhappy. Don't hold her words against her.
But you, do not forget in your folly and because
Of your own grief Thebes' splendid triumph in battle.
CREON:
But she does not want
The people of Thebes to be seated in the houses of Argos. She
Would rather see Thebes broken and beaten.
ANTIGONE:
Better we'd be sitting in the ruins of our own city
And safer too than with you
In the enemy's houses.
CREON:
Now she has said it. And you heard it.
Going beyond the measure she breaks every statute, she is
Like a guest not staying much longer, not wished to be seen again
Who packing his bags in his insolence cuts through the guy-ropes.
ANTIGONE:
But all that I took was mine and I had to steal it.

CREON:
Always all you see is the nose in front of you. The state's
Order, that is from God, you do not see.

ANTIGONE:
From God it may be but I'd rather have it
Human and humane, Creon, Menoeceus' son.

CREON:
Away now! You were our enemy and will be it still below
Like him I hacked, and forgotten. There he is shunned as
well.

ANTIGONE:
Who knows? Perhaps down there the custom's different.

CREON:
An enemy, even dead, will never be friend.

ANTIGONE:
One thing is sure: I live for love not hatred.

CREON:
Go down below then if you want to love
And love down there. I'll not have ones like you
Living for long up here.
Enter Ismene.

ELDERS:
But Ismene is coming from indoors
Sweet girl, who is for peace.
But tears are washing
Washing a face bloodshot with suffering.

CREON:
Yes, you, squatting in there at home. I've brought
Two torments up, snake sisters.
Tell us forthwith
You shared the deed at the grave
Or are you thick with innocence?

ISMENE:
I did it, if my sister will agree.
I took my part, I take the blame on me.

ANTIGONE:
Her sister will not let that be however.
She would not do it. I did not take her with me.

CREON:
You settle it. I won't be petty in a petty matter.

ISMENE:
I'm not ashamed to share my sister's trouble
And beg her now to have me for a comrade.

ANTIGONE:
By those who have gone through with it
And talk with one another down below
I don't like anyone who loves with words.

ISMENE:
Sister, revolt not everyone is good for
But one like her it may fall to to die.

ANTIGONE:
Don't die in common. What's no concern of yours
Don't make it yours. My death will be enough.

ISMENE:
My sister is too severe, I love you.
Have I, if she is gone, a love left in my life?

ANTIGONE:
Creon, love him. Stay his, I leave you both.

ISMENE:
Perhaps it is my sister's pleasure to mock me.

ANTIGONE:
Perhaps her grief as well, and I desire my cup of suffering full.

ISMENE:
But what I said to you is also part still.

ANTIGONE:
And that was good. But so I have decided.

ISMENE:
Is it because I failed I'm no loss to you now?

ANTIGONE:
Be of good cheer, and live. My soul has died
And now I'm servant only to the dead, sister.

CREON:
These women, I tell you, one is losing
Her wits right now, the other did long ago.

ISMENE:
I cannot live without her.

CREON:
The talk is not of her now. She is done with.
ISMENE:
You are killing your own son's bride-to-be as well.
CREON:
A man has more than one field he can plough in.
Get ready to die. But so that you will know
When it will be: it will be when for Bacchus she,
My drunken Thebes, joins me dancing. Now take
The women away.
Exit the guard into the palace with Antigone and Ismene. Creon orders his bodyguard to give up his sword.
AN ELDER *taking the sword*:
Dolling yourself for the victory revels don't stamp
On the ground too hard and not where it's greening.
But strong as you are, whoever has angered you
Now let him praise you.
AN ELDER *handing Creon the staff of Bacchus*:
Don't fling him too deep
Where you lose sight of him.
Down there and when no falling further is possible
A man stripped naked has no more to fear. He sheds
All his shame. Terrified, terrible
The man flung down rises up. Made less than human
He remembers a shape his life had once and arises, new.
ELDERS:
In their charred house the sons of Lachmeus sat and suffered it
Mouldering, feeding on lichens, forever the winters
Tipped ice on them and their women
Were absent at nights and sat in the day
In secret crimsons. And over their heads
Always the threatening rockface tilted.
But not before Pelias
Entered among them, dividing them with his staff and only
Touching them lightly, did they arise and
Slaughter all their tormentors.
This was the worst to them but often the least thing
Rounds up the sum of misery. The unseeing
Sleep of the wretched, as though in exhaustion

They lay in an ageless time, has an end.
The moons wax, slowly, swiftly, unevenly
Dwindle and all the time long
The evil is growing and already
Upon the last root left the light is trained
In Oedipus' houses.
And greatness does not fall in on itself
But on much besides. As when down there
When the Thracian winds
Blow evilly on the sea
The night under the salt
Befalls a little dwelling
And turns the dark sand inside out and upside down
Dishevelling it
And all the thrashed coast groans.
  Haemon is coming, of your sons
  The lastborn, troubled
  That the young Antigone should perish
  The wedding woman
  Sick that their bed will evade him.
Enter Haemon.

CREON:
Son, there was talk you might be coming to me
For that young woman's sake, not to the ruler
Rather to the father and if that were so
You'd come in vain, wholly. Returning from the battle
Which went our way by the bloody self-sacrifice of many
I found her alone undutiful, begrudging
Our house its victory, and bothering only with her own affairs
And worse besides.

HAEMON:
It is in this affair nevertheless
That I have come and hoping to the father
The familiar voice of him he got
Will not sound ill when to the ruler
It brings ill rumours.

CREON:
True, if a man got insolent children

Of him what could be said but that he got
Trouble for himself and made his enemies gleeful? Sour things
Sear the palate. So they are necessary.

HAEMON:

Much is under your governance. If what you like
Is only listening to what you like to hear
Then take things easy: slacken
Your sails like a man who has given up steering and drift.
The people quail at your name. So if great things
Flare up, the most they will ever report to you is small things.
But one advantage of the family is
Not everything goes by deserts. Many a debt
Is never called in and so sometimes
We may hear truth from family because
Though angry we curb ourselves for them.
Now clearly it cannot be Megareus, my brother
Who fought at Argos and is not back yet
And knows no fear, who tells you. So I must.
Be told: the city is full of inner disaffection.

CREON:

And you be told: when family goes bad
It is my enemies I feed. Who are not definite
Who are unknown to one another, never meet, and even
In their grievances are not united, being sick of taxes these
And those of serving in the war
And all held under me and held apart
By the power of my spear. But when
There are gaps there and government itself appears
At odds and wavers and is not definite then
The pebbles gather and become a slide and press
Against the house that let itself go. Speak
But I hear the one I fathered and the one
I set before the storms of spears, the son.

HAEMON:

Amid it all is truth. Do we not say
Steel your tongue on the unlying anvil? She
Who did not want her brother left to be eaten

By merciless dogs, the city
Is with her in that although condemning
The misdeed of the dead man.

CREON:
Isn't enough. I call that spinelessness.
Isn't enough that I hack off what's rotten –
It must be in the marketplace, to other rottenness
Quite unforgettable that I hack off what's rotten.
And my hand demonstrate that it never misses.
But you, knowing nothing of the situation
So knowing nothing, counsel: look around uncertainly
Adopt the thoughts of others, speak their language
As if authority could engage
The many bodies on a difficult commission
If all it is is a little ear and a cowardly.

ELDERS:
But it eats much strength up pondering cruel punishments.

CREON:
Pressing the plough to earth so that it ploughs takes strength.

ELDERS:
Mild government works wonders and with ease.

CREON:
Governments are many. But: who does the governing?

HAEMON:
Even if not your son I'd answer: you.

CREON:
If it were laid on me I'd have to do it my way.

HAEMON:
Your way, but let that be the right way.

CREON:
Not knowing what I know you couldn't know it.
Are you my friend however I choose to act?

HAEMON:
I wish you'd act so that I were your friend
But don't say you are right and no one else.
For anyone who thinks alone he has
No thoughts and speech and soul like any other
If such a man were ever opened up

He would appear empty. It is no shame
If someone there is someone wise, to learn
A lot and not push anything too far.
See by the stream in spate that's hurtling past
The trees give way, and all of those
Leaf up warmly but the strugglers against
Are gone at once. Likewise a prosperous ship
That throws its weight around and will give way to nothing
All falling backwards from the banks of rowers
Its certain course is wreck.

ELDERS:

Give way where your mind is, allow us change
And have from us a creaturely hesitation.
Hesitate with us.

CREON:

And have the horses
Steer the charioteer. That's what you want?

HAEMON:

And the horses
When they get a whiff of cadavers
From the knacker's yard might rear up wondering
Where they are being driven, being driven so hard
And fling themselves in the abyss with wheels and driver.
Be told: the city at war is maddened already worrying
What peace may bring.

CREON:

There is no war now. Thanks for the advice.

HAEMON:

Then this, that you, parading for victory
Intend a bloody cleaning out of everyone
At home who ever crossed you
Often the suspicion has been voiced to me.

CREON:

Who by? You might do some good there. Much more
Than only being the mouth of them
There so suspiciously gabbing about suspicion.

HAEMON:

Forget them.

ELDERS:
Of all a ruler's virtues
The healthiest, they say, is: know how to forget.
What's old, let it stay old.

CREON:
Since I'm so old
I find forgetting hard. But you
Could you not, if I asked you to
Forget her for whose sake you have gone so far out
That all who wish me ill mutter
He, so it seems, fights on the woman's side?

HAEMON:
On the side of right, wherever it shows itself.

CREON:
And has a hole.

HAEMON:
Even insulted my concern
For you will not be silent.

CREON:
Your bed would still be empty.

HAEMON:
Did that not come from the father I'd call it stupid.

CREON:
I'd call that brash if not from a woman's lackey.

HAEMON:
Who's happier hers than being your lackey.

CREON:
Now it is out and won't be got back in.

HAEMON:
Nor should it be. Say everything, that's you
And listen to nothing.

CREON:
Rid of the brood, and quickly!

HAEMON:
And I'll get rid of me so you need see
No one upright, and tremble.
Exit Haemon.

ELDERS:
Him leaving in anger, sir, he is your lastborn.

CREON:
Still he'll not save the women from their deaths.

ELDERS:
You think of killing both of them now, do you?

CREON:
Her who kept out of it, not that one, there you're right.

ELDERS:
Thinking of the other, how will you do the killing?

CREON:
Conduct her from the city where my people now
Are lifting their feet for Bacchus, she however
The guilty one, be stored where human tracks are lonely
Alive in a pit of rock with only millet and wine
The due of the dead, as though buried herself.
So I decree it
So that the city will not wholly be disgraced.
Exit Creon into the city.

ELDERS:
But like a mountain of clouds it stands before me now
That this is the hour when Oedipus' child in her chamber
Hears Bacchus in the distance and prepares for her last way.
For now he summons his own and as ever still thirsting for joy
Our wasted city gives him a joyful answer.
For victory is great and Bacchus cannot be resisted
When he approaches our anxious city and hands her the drink of forgetting.
Then the black she was sewing, the mourning black for her sons
She flings it away and hastens to the orgies of Bacchus, seeking exhaustion.
The Elders fetch themselves Bacchic staves.
Spirit of lusts of the flesh but always
Winner in any quarrel. Even the tied by blood
He flings all awry, so strongly he pleads.
He is never worsted, whoever he comes on
Are not themselves, they are seized, they rave
And under the yoke they stir and
Offer new necks, not fearing
The breath of the salt mine nor on

The black waters the thin-walled ship. Skins
He mixes with others and flings
Them all together but does not lay waste
The kingdom of earth with violent hands but is
From the first for peace and joins in the making
Of great ends. For in them unwarlike
Heavenly beauty plays her part too.

Enter Antigone led by the guard and followed by maids.

AN ELDER:

But now myself I lose
The measure and can no longer stop
The spring of tears for now
Antigone must receive the gifts
Of the dead, the millet and wine.

ANTIGONE:

My fellow citizens of home, oh see
Me going the final way
And seeing the sun's
Last light.
That never again? For he
Who will bed us all one day, the god of death
Is leading me living
To the banks of Acheron.
No wedding will be mine
No bridal song will be sung for me
I am the bride of Acheron.

ELDERS:

But you go famous and accompanied by praise
Away to that chamber of the dead
Not carried off by sickness nor given
The iron wages of iron
But living the life of your own
You go down alive
Into the world of the dead.

ANTIGONE:

Oh alas they are mocking me
Not yet gone below
Still in the daylight.
Oh city, oh you my city's

Men of plenty! And yet one day
You must be my witnesses how I
Unwept by loved ones and in accordance with
What sort of laws
Must enter the opening dug for me
The unheard of grave. I am
Not joined with mortals
Nor with the shades
With life nor death.

ELDERS:

Power, when power is the issue
Never gives. In the angry knowing herself
She has destroyed herself.

ANTIGONE:

Oh my father, oh unhappy mother
From whom with a darkened mind I came
To them I am coming cursed
To live with them without a man.
Alas, alas my brother
Sweet to live and fallen
Me too who was still here
You drag down with you.

AN ELDER *setting a dish of millet before her*:

But Danaë too she had to have
On her body instead of the light of the sky
The iron grid, and bear it. She lay in the dark.
But, child, her birth was lofty.
And she counted the strokes of the hours
The golden strokes, for the author of time.

ANTIGONE:

Lamentably, so I have heard, she died
Who came from Phrygia
Tantalus' daughter
On Sipylus' peaks
She is crouched and shrunk
To a slow stone, they put her in chains
Of ivy and winter is with her
Always, people say, and washes her throat
With snow-bright tears

From under her lids. Like her exactly
A ghost brings me to bed.

AN ELDER *setting down a jug of wine before her*:
Named among the holy however, holy
In her birth, is she but we are earth and born earthly.
True, you perish, but as one of the great. And not
Unlike our offerings to the gods.

ANTIGONE:
Already, with sighs, you are giving me up.
You are gazing into the blue and never
Into my eyes. But all I did was do
In holiness what is holy.

ELDERS:
And the son of Dryas, when his mouth ran over
Scolding the wrong, by Dionysus
He was swiftly seized and buried under chutes of stone
And groping in madness, with a scolding tongue
He got to know the god.

ANTIGONE:
And better it would be if you
Collected together all the scolding of wrong and dried
It of tears for me and put it to use. You are not
Farseeing.

ELDERS:
But on chalky rocks
Where at both ends sea is, on the Bosporus shores
Close to the city, there the god of battle
Watched while the eyes of the sons of Phineus
For seeing too far, the eagle eyes
Were stabbed with spears and it grew dark
In the brave orbs of their eyes.
For the force of fate is terrible.
Not wealth nor the god of battle
Or tower escapes it.

ANTIGONE:
Do not, I beg you, speak of fate.
I know it. Speak of him
Who lays me out, innocent, for death. Knit him
A fate! For do not think

Unhappy souls, you will be saved.
Other bodies, hacked
Will lie in heaps unburied around
That one unburied. You having dragged the war
For Creon over zones beyond our homeland
However many battles he is lucky in, the last
Will swallow you up. Calling for spoils
It won't be chariots full you see coming but
Empty. I weep for you, the living
What you will see
When my eyes are already filled with dust. Sweet Thebes
My native city! And oh, you springs of Dirce
And all around Thebes, where the chariots
Parade, oh you groves of trees! It tightens my throat
To think what will happen to you. Inhuman
Human beings have come forth from you and so
You must come to dust. Tell
Whoever asks for Antigone we
Saw her flee to the grave.
Exit Antigone with the guard and the maids.

ELDERS:
Turned and with long strides walked as though she
Were leading her guard. Over the square
She went where the victory columns
Are raised already, brazen. There she walked faster;
Vanished.
But she also once
Ate of the bread that was baked
In the stony dark. And while unhappiness
Harboured in the towers
In their shadow she sat at ease until
The deadly things that went forth from Labdacus' home
Returned deadly. The bloody hand
Dealt them among its own and they
Did more than receive, they grabbed at it.
Only after that did she
Lie angrily in the open air and was also
Flung into the good!
The cold woke her.

Not until the last
Patience was consumed and measured out the last
Criminal act, did the child of unseeing Oedipus
Remove the long since threadbare blindfold from her eyes
To look into the abyss.
Now just as unseeing
Thebes lifts her heels and staggering tastes
The drink of victory that is mixed
Of many herbs in the dark
And gulps it down and exults.
  Tiresias is coming, the blind man, the seer, impelled
  For sure by the stench of waxing discord
  And revolt boiling below.
Enter Tiresias led by a child and followed by Creon.

TIRESIAS:
Easy, child, go always and steadily
Unshaken by the dancing, you
Are the leader. The leader
Must not follow Bacchus.
A fall is certain for anyone lifting
His heels too high from the ground.
And don't hit against
The victory columns. In the town
They are shrieking victory
In the town full of fools
And the blind man
Follows the sighted child but after the blind man
Comes one blinder still.

CREON *who has followed him mockingly*:
What's that you're mumbling
Moaner, about the war?

TIRESIAS:
This, that you are dancing
Fool, before the victory.

CREON:
Old and troublesome
Seer of things that are not but you do not see
Columns set up all around
And towering high.

TIRESIAS:

I do not. And my wits
Are not addled. And therefore I have come
Dear friends. For even the leaves
Of the laurel when they are fleshy I rarely know them
But only when dry, when they rustle for me
Or I bite them and taste
Bitterness in them and know: that is laurel.

CREON:

You dislike festivities. Then at once
Your mouth's more terrible when you speak to us.

TIRESIAS:

I have seen terrible things. Hear what the birds
Mean for Thebes so drunk
With early victory and deaf
With the droning din of the Bacchic dancing: I sat
In the ancient chair and had before me a haven of all the birds.
I heard a stirring in the air then, murderous
And came a raging, tearing with claws at one another
And slaughter among the winged creatures. In fear
I tried the altars that were swiftly lit. And
In no place did I come upon a good fire. Only smoke
Writhed upwards thickly and the thighs
Of the sacrifices looked open from the fat that covered them.

ELDERS:

A very bad sign on the victory day
And news that cankers our enjoyment.

TIRESIAS:

Creon, the signless orgies' deadly interpretation
Would be that you are why the town is sick
Because the altars are and fire places
Defiled by dogs and birds who have fed full
On the unseemly fallen son of Oedipus.
Therefore the birds' wellmeaning cry no longer
Comes rushing here for it has eaten of
A dead man's fat. But the gods
Can't stomach smoke like that. Therefore

Yield to the dead man, do not persecute
One who has gone.

CREON:

Old man, your birds
Fly how you like. I know that. Haven't they
Flown for me too? I am not that unschooled
In dealing and the arts of prophecy
Never having stinted. So pocket
Electrum from Sardis and gold from India
But don't think I will let the coward be buried.
I'm not afraid of sicknesses from heaven.
No human moves the gods. I know that much.
But among mortal men
Old man, even some very mighty fall
A very grievous fall if they speak sweetly
Words that desolate, for their own profit.

TIRESIAS:

I am too old to place myself to gain
A small time more.

CREON:

No one is so old
He would not like to live longer.

TIRESIAS:

I know.
But I know more besides.

ELDERS:

Say it, Tiresias.
Sir, let the seer be heard.

CREON:

Say it however you like. But leave off haggling.
All the clan of seers love silver, as we know.

TIRESIAS:

And tyrants offer it, so I have heard.

CREON:

And a blind man
Bites into the coin and knows
That's silver.

TIRESIAS:

And I'd rather you offered me none.

For no one knows in war what he'll hold on to.
Be it silver, be it sons, or be it power.

CREON:

The war is over.

TIRESIAS:

Is it?
I asked you something?
Since I, as you have said, know nothing
Our kind must ask. Since I, as you have said
Can't see into the future
I have to look into the present and the past and so
Maintain my art and am a seer. True, I see
Only what any child can see. That the bronze
On the victory columns is very thin. I say: because
Spears are being made still, many spears. That for the army
Fleeces are being sewn. I say: as though autumn were coming.
And fish being dried, as though for winter quarters.

ELDERS:

I thought that was before the victory in battle
And cancelled now? And booty coming
With bronze and fish from Argos now?

TIRESIAS:

And there are guards in plenty but whether it's much
Or little they guard, nobody knows. But there is great
Loggerheads in your home and no forgetting
As there is usually after happy business. And it is said
That your son Haemon went from you distressed
Because you flung Antigone, betrothed to him
Into a pit of stone when for her brother
For Polynices, she wished to open a grave
Because you struck him down and left him graveless
When he rose up opposing you because
Your war lost him his brother Eteocles.
So I know you to be cruelly entwined in cruelty
And since my wits have not been spoiled by silver
I ask the second question. Why are you cruel
Creon, Menoeceus' son? I'll make it easier:
Is it because you want bronze for your war?

What is it you've done, what foolish thing or evil
That now in evil things you must go on and foolish?

CREON:
You two-tongued villain!

TIRESIAS:
Worse would be half a tongue.
But I've my twofold answer which is: none.
And I knit nothing with nothing and I say:
Misrule cries out for great men and finds none.
War goes forth from itself and breaks a leg.
From pillage pillage comes and harshness needs harshness
And more needs more and comes in the end to nothing.
And now I have looked back and all around me
You: look ahead, in terror.
Lead me from here, child.
Exit Tiresias, led by the child.

ELDERS:
Sir, had my hair
Just now been black still, now
It would be white. The man in anger
Said bad things
And worse things did not say.

CREON:
So I say what
Has not been said, why utter it?

ELDERS:
Creon, son of Menoeceus, when
Are the young men coming home
To the city empty of men and how
Fares your war, Creon, son of Menoeceus?

CREON:
Since he malevolently has directed
The gaze at this, I'll tell you: the war
Treacherous Argos made against us, the end
Of it is not yet now nor is
It going very well. When I decreed the peace
Only a little was still wanting and that
Because of Polynices' treachery.

But he lies chastised
And with him she who wept for him.

ELDERS:

And this too is not
Yet at an end, for he
Has turned himself away from you who leads
The storms of spears for you here, the younger born
Son, Haemon.

CREON:

Nor do I want him any more
At all. Out of my sight and yours
With him who abandoned me
For the petty bother of his bed.
Megareus still fights for me
My son incessantly pitching
In waves against the tottering walls of Argos
The bronze-clad youth of Thebes.

ELDERS:

Which is not inexhaustible.
Creon, son of Menoeceus
We always followed you. And there was
Good order in the city and you kept off our throats
Our enemies here under the Theban roof
A rapacious populace that has nothing and is provided for in war
And those who live on discord, the loud mouths
Lean and hungry, long in the wind, in the marketplace
Speaking because they are paid to or not paid to.
Now they are loud in the mouth again and have
A dubious subject too. Son of Menoeceus, have you perhaps
Broached an enormity?

CREON:

When I went against Argos
Who was it sent me? Metal in the spears
Went after metal in the mountains
At your bidding. For Argos
Is rich in metals.

ELDERS:

And therefore rich in spears, it seems. We heard
Many a bad thing from there and dismissed it with
The messengers, trusting you, and stopped our ears
Fearful of fear. And shut our eyes when you drew in
The reins tighter. Only one more
Drawing in of the reins and one more battle
You said, does it need, but now
You are beginning to treat with us
As with the enemy. And cruelly
Waging a double war.

CREON:

Yours!

ELDERS:

Yours!

CREON:

Once I've got Argos
No doubt it will have been yours again. Enough.
So she, in her revolt
Has muddled you and those who listened to her.

ELDERS:

Certainly the sister had a right to bring home her brother.

CREON:

Certainly the captain had a right to chastise a traitor.

ELDERS:

Asserted to the bone, this right and that flings us into the abyss.

CREON:

War makes new rights.

ELDERS:

And lives on the old.
War eats itself not given what it needs.

CREON:

Ungrateful, all of you. You eat the meats but
Don't like the bloody aprons of the cooks. I gave you
Sandalwood for your houses which the din
Of swords never enters, but it grew in Argos.
And no one has sent me back the ore
I fetched from Argos, but bending over it
You blather of butchery there and lament my brutality.

I'm used to greater indignation if the loot is late.

ELDERS:

How long, tell us, will you have Thebes go without her men?

CREON:

Until her men have won rich Argos for her.

ELDERS:

Unlucky man, before they are lost, recall them.

CREON:

Empty-handed? You answer for it then.

ELDERS:

With empty hands or none, whatever's still flesh and blood.

CREON:

So I will. Soon Argos will fall. Then I will call them.
And my firstborn, Megareus, will bring them to you.
And be sure that your doors and portals are not too small –
High enough only for such as are low in their ways –
Or the shoulders of men of a larger stature might stave in
Here the gates of a palace and there a treasury door.
And perhaps their joy when they see you again will be such
When they grip you they'll shake your hands and your arms
Right out of the sockets. And when the armour presses
Boisterously against your fearful hearts beware of your ribs.
For on that joyful day you will see more naked iron
Than you did in the days of grief. Many a hesitant victor
Has gone in garlands of chains and danced with collapsing knees.

ELDERS:

Wretch, are you theatening us with our own? Are you goading
Our own on us now?

CREON:

I will
Discuss it with my son, with Megareus.

Enter a messenger from the battle.

MESSENGER:

Stiffen your neck, sir. I am sent here
By disaster. Stop the hasty celebrations

Of victory too soon credited. In another battle
Your army is beaten before Argos, and in flight.
Your son Megareus is done with. He lies
In pieces on the hard ground of Argos. When you
Acted to punish Polynices' flight
And seized and hanged in public the many in the army
This aggrieved and you yourself
Had hurried back to Thebes, thereupon
Your firstborn drove us forward once again.
Our stormtroops, not having slept enough after
The bloodbath in their own ranks, raised only wearily
Their axes wet still with the blood of Thebans
Against the people of Argos. And there were all too many
Faces turned back on Megareus who
To be more terrible to them than the enemy
Goading them on, his voice was perhaps too harsh.
And yet the luck of battle seemed with us at first.
Fighting begets, of course, the love of fighting
Blood smells the same, yours or another's blood
And makes you drunk. What bravery can't do
Fear can. But the terrain
And gear and rations count for something.
And, sir, the people of Argos fought a crafty fight.
The women fought, also the children fought.
Long since with nothing to eat in them
From burned-out roof-timbers with boiling water
Cooking pots fell on us. Even the unharmed houses
Were fired behind us as though nobody
Thought to house anywhere again. For the utensils
And rooms of home were weaponry and stuff for barricades.
But on and always on your son drove us and drove
Us deeper into the city which so laid to waste
Became a grave. The rubble heaps
Began to cut us off from one another. Smoke
From all the taken districts, seas of fire
Veiled out our vision. Fleeing fires
And looking for enemies we struck upon our own.
And no one knows whose hand your son fell by.

The flower of Thebes, all vanished
And Thebes herself cannot abide much longer for over her
The people of Argos are coming now with men and chariots
On all the streets. And I who have seen this
Am glad I am already done for.
He dies.

ELDERS:
Alas for us.

CREON:
Megareus! My son!

ELDERS:
Waste no
Time on laments. Gather the stormtroops.

CREON:
Gather the nothings. In a sieve.

ELDERS:
Drunk on victory
Thebes is jigging and all upon us
The enemy is advancing with grey iron.
Deceiving us
You gave the sword away. Now
You may wish to remember your other son.
Fetch the younger.

CREON:
Yes, Haemon, the last! Yes, my latest born!
Come and be a help now in the great collapse. Forget
The things I said for when I was master
I was not master of my senses.

ELDERS:
To the stony ground
Hurry and quickly release the grave maker
Release Antigone.

CREON:
If I dig her out
Will you stand by me then? You, if not always
The movers, were always compliant. That
Implicates you.

ELDERS:

Go now.

CREON:

Axes! Axes!

Exit Creon.

ELDERS:

Stop the dancing.

ELDERS *clashing the cymbals*:

Spirit of joy, pride of the waters
That Cadmus loved
Come if you long to see her again
Your city, and travel fast and come
Before nightfall for later
She will not be there.

For here, O god of joy
In the mother city, in bacchantic
Thebes you were at home, at the cold beck of Ismenus.
By the smoke of sacrifices sweetly shaped
Over the shoulders of the roofs you have been seen.
Of her many houses you may meet with
Not even the fire nor the smoke of the fire
Nor of the smoke the shadow. Her children
Who for a thousand years to come
Saw themselves seated already by remotest oceans
They will tomorrow, they have today
Scarcely a stone to bed their heads upon.

On the Cocytus in your day
God of joy, you sat with the lovers
And in Castalia's woods. But also
You visited the smiths and tested
Smilingly with your thumb the sharpness of the swords.
Often according to the undying
Songs of Thebes
You walked in the streets where they were still rejoicing.

Alas, the iron hacked into its own
But exhaustion will eat the arm nevertheless.
Oh violence needs a miracle
And mercy only a little wisdom.

So now the often
Beaten enemy stands
Over our palaces and shows
Full of bloody spears all around
The seven mouths and gates
And from there he will not depart
Till he has filled
His cheeks full of our blood.

But there one of the maids comes
Parting the throng and press of those in flight
Surely with a message from Haemon whom the father
Set at the head of the stormtroops who will save us.

Enter a maid as messenger.

MESSENGER:

Oh so much all used up! Oh last sword broken!
Haemon is dead, bleeding by his own hands.
I am an eyewitness, what happened before
I had it from the servants going with their lord
To the high field where, its flesh being torn by dogs
The poor dead body of Polynices lay.
They washed him, no one speaking, and laid him
What was left, among new leafy sprays
And of the homeland's earth
Carefully they raised a little hill.
With others hurrying ahead the lord approached
The grave in the stony hollow where we, the maids, were standing.
But one among us heard a voice and loud
Lament and crying in the chamber
And ran to meet the lord, to tell him.
He hurried then, and as he neared the more
In him he felt that dark and troubled voice
And all around until, up close, he screamed
And pitiably lamenting saw the bolt
Torn from the wall and said with difficulty but as if
He did believe himself: 'That is not Haemon's
My child's voice.' We searched after
The frightened master's words. Thereupon
Back furthest in the graves we saw

Her, hanging by the neck, Antigone
A noose of linen around her throat
And him outstretched below her lifted feet
Wailing over the bridebed and the abyss below
And his father's work. He, seeing this
Went in to him and spoke to him, saying:
'Come out my child, I beg you on my knees.'
But looking coldly, saying nothing back
The son stared back at him
And drew his sword, two-edged against him first.
And when the father, frightened into flight
Turned, he failed. Then saying nothing further
He stood and into his own side
He thrust the swordpoint, slowly. Fell without a word.
Death lies with death now, shyly they came to
Their wedding's consummation in the houses of
The world below. The lord comes now himself.

ELDERS:

Our city is finished, used to reins and now
Without any. Leaning on women
Comes the man who is all in vain now and
He is bearing in his hands a large memorial
Of stupid raging . . .

Enter Creon carrying Haemon's cloak.

CREON:

See what I have here. It is the cloak. I thought
It might have been a sword I went to fetch. The
Child died on me early. One more battle
And Argos would be in the dust. But all
The bravery and uttermost that was mustered
Was only against me.
So now Thebes falls.
And let it fall, let it with me, let it be finished
And there for the vultures. That is my wish now.

Exit Creon with maids.

ELDERS:

And turned around and in
His hands from all the house
Of Labdacus only a bloodstained cloth

Into the foundering city he went away.
But we
Even now all follow him still and the way
Is down. Our biddable hand
Never to strike again
Will be hacked off. But she who saw everything
Could help nobody but the enemy who now
Is coming and quickly will wipe us out. For time is short
And disaster all around and never enough of time
To live on thoughtlessly and easily
From compliance to crime and
Become wise in old age.

The Days of the Commune

Collaborator: RUTH BERLAU

Translator: DAVID CONSTANTINE

Characters:

Mme Cabet, seamstress · Jean Cabet, her son · Babette Cherron, his girlfriend · François Faure, seminarist, National Guard · Philippe Faure, his brother, Government Forces · Geneviève Guéricault, a young teacher · Papa, a National Guardsman · Coco, his friend · Portly gentleman · Waiter · Two children · Wounded German cuirassier · Pierre Langevin, a worker · Mme Pullard, the baker · Three women · Thiers · Jules Favre · Manservant · Bismarck · Beslay, Varlin, Rigault, Delescluze, Ranvier, delegates of the Commune · Four mayors · Delegates of the eleventh arrondissement · Tax-collector · His wife · Newspaper seller · Functionary · De Plœuc, Governor of the Bank of France · An aristocratic woman · Her niece · Servants · Street trader · Sergeant · Porter · Fat churchman · Old beggar · Officer in the National Guard · Wounded woman · Stretcher-bearers · Guy Suitry, Geneviève's fiancé · A nun · Ladies and gentlemen · National Guardsmen · Commune delegates · Government Forces

I

Around 19 January 1871. A little café in Montmartre in which a National Guard recruiting station has been set up. Outside the café a portly gentleman in a thick coat is sitting at a table in conversation with the waiter. Two children carrying a cardboard box are conferring together. Noise of artillery.

WAITER: Monsieur Bracque was here three times asking for you.

PORTLY GENTLEMAN: What, Bracque here, in Paris?

WAITER: Not for very long. Here's a message, monsieur.

PORTLY GENTLEMAN *reading*: There's no peace and quiet in Paris these days. Prices, percentages, commission! Well, that's war, everyone contributes in his own way. Do you know anybody who would be willing to run certain errands for me? Somebody with nerve, but reliable. They rarely go together, eh?

WAITER: We'll find someone. *The portly gentleman gives him a tip.* And monsieur really prefers to wait out here in the cold?

PORTLY GENTLEMAN: The air in your place has got very bad lately.

WAITER *glancing at the notice, 'Citizens, your country is in danger, join the National Guard'*: I understand.

PORTLY GENTLEMAN: Do you? If I pay 80 francs for my breakfast I don't want the sweat of the slums up my nose while I'm eating it. And kindly remain where you are and keep that vermin – *he points at the children* – away from me.

Enter a poorly dressed woman and a young worker, carrying a basket between them. The children approach the woman.

MME CABET: No, I don't want anything. Yes, I do. Later

perhaps. Rabbit, you say? Jean, what about a Sunday dinner?

JEAN: That isn't rabbit.

MME CABET: But he wants 14 francs 50 for it.

CHILD: The meat is fresh, madame.

MME CABET: First of all I have to see what they'll pay us today. Wait here, children. I might take the meat. *She makes to move on and a few cockades fall out of the basket.* Be a bit more careful, Jean. I'm sure we've lost some already along the way. Then I'll have to talk ninety to the dozen so they won't notice when they count.

PORTLY GENTLEMAN: Business all around! Business, business, while the Prussians make war.

WAITER: Small scale and large, monsieur.

Noise and the tread of marching men in the background.

PORTLY GENTLEMAN: What's that? You, run and see what's happening now. I'll give you five francs.

One of the children runs off.

MME CABET: We've brought the cockades, Emile.

WAITER: The gentleman has a little errand for your Jean, Madame Cabet.

MME CABET: Oh how kind of you! Jean has been out of work for two months. He's a stoker and of course the trains aren't running any more. What do you say, Jean?

JEAN: I'm not one for errands, mother. You know that.

MME CABET: I'm very sorry. Jean is the kindest person in the world. But he has opinions. He's a bit like his late father.

They carry the basket into the café.

PORTLY GENTLEMAN: This war won't last much longer. Aristide Jouve says so. All the business that could be done with this war has been done. There's nothing left in it.

Three National Guardsmen come limping down the street from the fighting at the forts. The first, Papa, is a building worker in his middle years; the second, Coco, a watchmaker; the third, François Faure, a young seminarist with his arm in a sling. They are escorting a captured German cuirassier with a dirty bandage around his chin.

CHILDREN: A Fritz! Did you get a thrashing, Fritz? Can we tug his epaulettes?

PAPA: Why not?

CHILDREN: Is it going well at the front?

PAPA: Yes, for the Prussians.

CHILD: But the Governor won't capitulate, so they say.

PAPA: At least not to the French, my son. How does it go? Down with the Gov . . .

CHILDREN: . . . vernor!

PAPA *to the waiter*: Three Pernods. No, four.

WAITER: Very good. But the *patron* insists you pay in advance. Four Pernods, that's twelve francs.

COCO: Man, can't you see we've been in the battle?

WAITER *softly*: Twelve francs.

COCO: They're out of their minds.

PAPA: No, they're not out of their minds. We are, Gustave. You'd have to be to fight for one and a half francs a day. That's exactly half a Pernod in this place, isn't it? And what do we fight with? And how? *He thrusts his weapon under the portly gentleman's nose.* That's a breech-loader from the forties. Good enough for the new battalions. A decent chassepot, that cost the state seventy francs, would cost two hundred now. But we'd hit the mark with it, monsieur.

COCO: Fetch the Pernod, you swine. Or there'll be trouble. We're defending Paris and you cut-throats are making a killing on the drinks.

PAPA: Monsieur, we didn't get rid of the Stinker, declare a republic and form the National Guard so that you could make money on our efforts.

PORTLY GENTLEMAN: There we have it! Anarchy! You're not interested in defending Paris, you people. You want to conquer her.

COCO: Oh really? And you and your sort own her, do you? *To Papa*: Nice, isn't he? Nice and fat. He doesn't look bad on the siege, does he?

PORTLY GENTLEMAN: Messieurs, you seem to be forgetting where the front is.

The child that ran off now returns.

PAPA: What's that? *To the third National Guardsman, a young man with a bloody bandage round his head:*

François, the gentleman thinks you've forgotten where you got your scratch.

COCO: The gentleman thinks we should keep our minds on Fritz when we can't get any beer. Fritz, what do you think? You're not a fat man, that's for sure. Waiter, a Pernod for Fritz or we'll wreck the place. Four Pernods for two francs, do you hear?

WAITER: Very good. *Exit.*

PORTLY GENTLEMAN: Stay where you are, do you hear?

CHILDREN *singing*: Fritz is not a fat man! Fritz is not a fat man!

CHILD *who returned*: Monsieur, what you can hear is the 207th Battalion. They are very discontented and are marching to the Hôtel de Ville, to hang the generals.

PORTLY GENTLEMAN: Messieurs, while the Prussians . . .

PAPA: Oh yes, while the Prussians . . . The siege! The ring of iron! Break out, beat the Prussians and you'll have potatoes again. We're beginning to see who's really besieging us. You and your ilk most of all. Or is it the Prussians putting up the price of potatoes?

PORTLY GENTLEMAN: Messieurs, I hear you discussing the price of potatoes even as men are fighting on the ramparts . . .

PAPA: Fighting! Dying, you mean! Do you know what's going on? We lie all night in the rain and the muck in the fields around Mont Valérien. Me with my rheumatism! The attack begins at ten o'clock. We take the fort at Montretout, the park at Buzenval, we take St Cloud, we advance to Garches. Of 150 guns only thirty are in use, we take Garches without artillery cover, we're through, the Prussians are running for their lives. Then come orders from the rear: Halt! We wait two hours. Then come orders from the rear: Fall back! And Trochu evacuates Montretout and all the positions we took. What is the meaning of that, monsieur?

PORTLY GENTLEMAN: I assume your generals know where the enemy will concentrate his fire.

COCO: They know all right. That's where they send the National Guard, monsieur.

PORTLY GENTLEMAN: Enough. Have you any idea what you are saying? Are you accusing your commanding officers, France's generals, of treason? May I perhaps ask you for proof?

PAPA: He wants proof, Gustave. And we have none. Except death. Except that we die like flies. Fine, you are dead, Monsieur Whatsyername. Be so kind as to prove you've been hit over the head. Say the word and we'll open proceedings. Ah, nothing to say? I politely enquire what your demands might be, Monsieur Whatsyername, and you don't move a muscle.

PORTLY GENTLEMAN: We know all about your demands and your demonstrations at the Hôtel de Ville. The Commune and its extortions!

COCO: Carry on, carry on. We've got time. We're still waiting for the 101st. It won't start till then.

PORTLY GENTLEMAN: The long and short of it is you don't want to pay your rents. France is fighting for her life and all you think about is your pay and your pensions. Butter's too dear! But be warned: Paris is losing patience.

The National Guardsmen stand in silence.

PORTLY GENTLEMAN: *You* are the traitors. But take note: We don't find your newspapers amusing any more. We've had enough selfishness from the mob. Quite enough.

The waiter comes back with four Pernods and a casserole covered by a serviette. The portly gentleman waves him away.

WAITER: Your chicken, monsieur.

COCO: Monsieur, your chicken!

PORTLY GENTLEMAN: I'll have you thrown out. I've had enough of you and the whole National Guard. Don't you dare . . .

The portly gentleman exits hastily.

CHILDREN: Monsieur, the five francs! *They chase after him.*

WAITER: Messieurs, permit me to offer you some refreshment.

COCO *offering the cuirassier a glass*: There you are, Fritz. Oh damnation, you can't, can you? Poor devil. Your good health then. *They drink.*

Mme Cabet and her son come out of the café, still carrying the basket.

JEAN *to the waiter*: Where's the man who had an errand for me?

The waiter motions him to be silent. Then the young Guardsman who has been wounded recognises the Cabets.

FRANÇOIS: Madame Cabet!

JEAN: François!

MME CABET: François, are you wounded? I must ask you to pay your share of the rent on the room. You know the government is making us pay all the arrears. And in there now they won't take my cockades. I'm ruined, we'll be on the streets.

FRANÇOIS: But Madame Cabet, I haven't been paid for three weeks. Things are a bit tight for me as well at the moment.

MME CABET: But when will you pay? Messieurs, it's no laughing matter. He's my lodger.

COCO: Yes, François, when will you pay? Madame, we understand your worries. All we can say is that two battalions, back from two days' fighting outside the walls, are just on their way to the Hôtel de Ville, to put a few ticklish questions to the government.

PAPA: And one among them might well be the remission of all our rents. Meanwhile all we can offer you, as a small mark of our sympathy, is the gift of this chicken here that a gentleman ordered but did not eat. *They conduct Mme Cabet to the table in front of the café, take the casserole from the waiter's hands and serve up the chicken elegantly to Mme Cabet.* Garçon, the *patron* would do well in future to insist that the better class of customer pay in advance. It might be that circumstances will arise which make it impossible for them to breakfast satisfactorily. Will you get into trouble?

WAITER: Indeed I will, monsieur. Serious trouble. I shall be obliged to decide to join you. Perhaps the government will pay for Madame Cabet's chicken? Two battalions of the National Guard should surely be enough to push through such a demand.

COCO: Your good health, madame.

PAPA: Bon appétit! The 101st are honoured to entertain you.

MME CABET: Messieurs, you are very kind. As it happens, I don't have all that much in my belly today. Chicken is my favourite dish. Will you allow me to share it with my son Jean?

JEAN: Present company might be interested to know why they've stopped taking cockades in there. The officials inside, after new directives from above, consider recruitment to the new battalions of the National Guard to be at an end.

COCO: What's that? Did you hear that, Papa?

PAPA: I'm not too bothered. She'll come with us to the Hôtel de Ville.

COCO: Do you understand, madame? Papa wants you to come with us to the Hôtel de Ville to show your cockades that are not needed any more. Put your chicken with them in the basket.

FRANÇOIS: And now here come the 101st!

Behind and above the wooden fence the 101st Battalion can be seen passing. Bayonets with loaves of bread impaled. Flags. The National Guardsmen help Mme Cabet to her feet and take her with them.

PAPA *pointing to Jean*: What's the matter with him? Why isn't he fighting? Are we too far to the left for him in the new battalions?

MME CABET: Oh no, monsieur. I'd say a bit far to the right, I do beg your pardon.

PAPA: Ah!

JEAN: And consider me one of yours from now on, messieurs. I like the way you're heading.

Papa takes François' képi and puts it on Jean Cabet's head.

FRANÇOIS: I've been very bored without you.

They leave. The waiter flings the serviette on to the little table, turns out the lamp and is about to follow them when he catches sight of the cuirassier, who has been forgotten. He shoos him away, driving him after the National Guards.

WAITER: Quick march, Fritz, quick march!

2

25 January 1871. Bordeaux. Thiers and Jules Favre in conversation. Thiers, still in his dressing gown, is testing the temperature of his bath water and directing his manservant to add hot or cold.

THIERS *drinking his morning milk*: This war must end, it is becoming an abomination. We fought it and we have lost it. What are we waiting for?

FAVRE: But the Prussian demands! Herr von Bismarck speaks of five billion in reparations, the annexation of Alsace-Lorraine, the retention of all prisoners-of-war and the continuing occupation of the forts until everything is concluded to his satisfaction. It will be our ruin!

THIERS: But what the Parisians are demanding, won't that be our ruin?

FAVRE: Certainly.

THIERS: Will you take coffee? *Favre shakes his head.* Then milk, like me? Not allowed even that? Ah, Favre, would that we still had stomachs! For we do still have appetites. But back to Herr von Bismarck. A student of the bierkeller, now demented. He racks up his demands because he knows we must accept them, all of them.

FAVRE: Must we really? What about the iron and tin mines in Lorraine? They are the future of French industry.

THIERS: What about our secret agents? They are being thrown in the Seine. What use are iron and tin mines to France if the Commune is in Paris?

FAVRE: Five billion! All our trade!

THIERS: It is the price of order and stability.

FAVRE: And Prussia's lead in Europe for three generations.

THIERS: And the securing of our rule for five.

FAVRE: We shall be a nation of peasants, in these modern times.

THIERS: I'm counting on the peasants. They are the cornerstone of peace. What do they care about Lorraine? They don't even know where it is. Favre, you ought at least to take a glass of water.

FAVRE: Is it really necessary, I ask myself.

THIERS: Even a sip of water is a sign of life. Just the swallowing of it. Oh, I see. Yes, the other is necessary too, absolutely. The price of order and stability.

FAVRE: The National Guard will be France's downfall. We made a patriotic sacrifice and armed the mob against the Prussians. Now they have weapons for use against us. That is the truth. But is it not also the case, can it not also be said that these people are defending Paris, that they are actually fighting?

THIERS: My dear Favre, what is this thing Paris? They speak of Paris in those circles as a holy place that they'd rather burn than surrender. They forget that Paris consists of valuables, they forget because they have no valuables themselves. The scum are quite prepared to blow everything up. But it doesn't belong to them. They are screaming to be given petroleum, but for the authorities, for us, Paris is not a symbol but a possession. You don't defend it by setting fire to it.

Sound of marching men. Thiers and Favre freeze. Thiers, too agitated to speak, waves his manservant to go to the window.

MANSERVANT: A company of the marine, monsieur.

THIERS: If they suppose I could ever forget those humiliations . . .

FAVRE: Bordeaux is quiet, is it not?

THIERS: What does quiet mean? Perhaps quiet is too quiet. Such a bad example! Favre, we must exterminate them. We must smash their unwashed faces on the cobbles, in the name of culture. Our civilisation is founded on property. Property must be protected at all costs. They have the nerve to dictate to us what we must give up and what we can keep? Get me sabres, get me cavalry! If it takes a sea of blood to wash Paris clean of its vermin then let us have a sea of blood. My towel!

The manservant hands him his towel, Thiers wipes the foam from his lips.

FAVRE: You are becoming agitated, think of your health, so precious to us all.

THIERS *choking*: And you armed them! From that moment

on, from the morning of 3 September on, I've had only one thought in my head: how to end the war, quickly, at once.

FAVRE: But they fight like devils, alas. Our good friend Trochu is right: the National Guard won't see reason until ten thousand of them have bled to death. Dear, dear. He sends them into the fight like cattle, to dampen their ardour. *He whispers into Thiers' ear.*

THIERS: No, no, he is free to listen. Hippolyte is a patriot.

FAVRE: I can assure you, Monsieur Thiers, that in this matter at least you have Herr von Bismarck's entire sympathy.

THIERS *drily*: Delighted to hear it since he thinks me, so I am told, less capable than the average horsetrader, and that after meeting me in person.

FAVRE: Mere boorishness, not at all his real opinion of you.

THIERS: I think I may say that I have risen above the personal, my dear Favre. What interests me is how Herr von Bismarck proposes to help us.

FAVRE: He suggested to me personally that as soon as there is a ceasefire he might permit some provision of foodstuffs to the people, but would then put them back on half-rations until they give up their weapons. He thought such a procedure might be more effective than a continuation of hunger.

THIERS: Not bad. We remind our Parisians what meat tastes like. I've never denied that Herr von Bismarck has talent.

FAVRE: He will even restrain the firms in Berlin who are looking to supply Paris with food.

THIERS: Talent and courage go together, do they not, Favre? And by the way, the Prussians must undertake to occupy those *quartiers* in which the National Guard have placed their guns.

FAVRE: A very good point. Excellent.

THIERS: I daresay Herr von Bismarck is not the only one with talent. We shall, for example, also get it written into the capitulation treaty that the first instalment of reparations, 500 million, won't fall due until after the pacification of Paris. That will give Herr von Bismarck an interest in our victory. And incidentally, I should be glad if the word pacification were used more often. It is one of those words that make everything perfectly clear. Ah yes, the reparations. Hippolyte, you can leave us now.

MANSERVANT: Your bath is at the right temperature, monsieur. *Exit.*

THIERS: What is their thinking about these sums of money?

FAVRE: It has been proposed that certain German firms, especially Herr von Bleichröder, Herr von Bismarck's own banker, should finance the reparations. Commission was mentioned ... As a member of the government I did of course refuse to accept any percentages.

THIERS: Of course. Did they give figures?

Favre writes a figure on a scrap of paper which Thiers takes and reads.

THIERS: Impossible.

FAVRE: As I said.

THIERS: We must have peace. France needs it. I hope I shall have the power to carry it through.

FAVRE: Your election is absolutely secured, Monsieur Thiers. Twenty-three departments are for you, all the rural ones.

THIERS: I shall need that power. The forces of disorder are armed.

FAVRE: Monsieur Thiers, France trembles for your health. Only you can save her now.

THIERS *matter-of-factly*: I'm aware of that. That is why you see me drinking milk, which I detest, my dear Favre.

3

Night of 17–18 March in the rue Pigalle. There is a cannon on the street.

a

One o'clock in the morning. François Faure and Jean Cabet, seated on cane chairs, are guarding the cannon. Babette Cherron is just getting up from Jean's lap.

BABETTE *stroking the barrel of the gun*: Good night, my love.

Makes her way slowly to a house at the lower end of the street and enters there.

JEAN: Girls have to be given things. They are materialists, it excites their senses. It used to be a pretty dressing table, nowadays it's a cannon that Monsieur Thiers wanted to give to Herr von Bismarck.

FRANÇOIS: And he'd have it now if we hadn't fetched it here. – Geneviève isn't a materialist.

JEAN: The little teacher girl? No, she's pure spirit and that's why you want to go to bed with her.

FRANÇOIS: I don't want to go to bed with her.

JEAN: Babette says she's got a nice body.

FRANÇOIS: How can you two discuss her?

JEAN: They live together, don't they? Incidentally, she's engaged. He's a prisoner-of-war, a lieutenant. Her breasts are her best bit.

FRANÇOIS: You're trying to annoy me, aren't you?

JEAN: The way you talk about girls no one would ever guess you're from the country. But you'd surely had it with a dairymaid by the time you were fourteen.

FRANÇOIS: You won't annoy me.

JEAN: Won't I? Well anyway I told Babette to tell Geneviève you're interested. It might amuse her to wind a priest around her little finger.

FRANÇOIS: I'm a physicist.

JEAN: OK, a physicist. Isn't physics the science of bodies?

FRANÇOIS: But you said yourself she loves a lieutenant.

JEAN: I said she's engaged to him.

FRANÇOIS: Same thing.

JEAN *laughing*: You've got the wrong idea. As though you only want to go to bed with a person because you love them! Truth is, some days you know first thing when you get up: I've got to have a woman today. Why should it be any different for women? It's a need. Not necessarily brought about by the sight of a particular pair of breasts, but just so. And thereupon you find her breasts particular. It's the same for women. In a word, seize hold of such a day, and you are Mr Right. Even with Geneviève.

FRANÇOIS: Quite wrong. And now I'm off to bed. *He stands up.* I'm very glad I've got my little room with you again.

JEAN *likewise standing up*: I don't think we need keep guard any longer either. If they were going to raid us it would have to be in the middle of the night. White bread tomorrow, so I hear.

FRANÇOIS: By the way, Jean, since we were talking about physics: I suppose my microscope and my Lavoisier are safe at your uncle's?

JEAN *in embarrassment*: At my uncle's? At Langevin's?

FRANÇOIS: Your mother gave them to him, to look after.

JEAN: Oh yes. Yes, of course. They're absolutely safe at Langevin's.

FRANÇOIS: It's just that I could do with the Lavoisier.

JEAN: Of course.

They carry the chairs into the house.

b

Five in the morning. Women, among them Geneviève Guéricault and Babette, are queuing outside a baker's not yet opened.

WOMEN: White bread from Papa Thiers! That's supposed to make his sell-out taste better. – Paris for ten tons of flour! – And no trains come in either. The flour was here all along. – But they took my old man's leg off just last week. Shrapnel. At the same time they were already doing a deal. – Now they must have something else up their sleeves. They never give us anything for nothing. Lady Muck that I used to do the washing for, if she ever gave me a pair of her old knickers I knew she'd reported my Emile for remarks he'd made. – My old man told them he'd take his leg home with him or they'd tell him at the pensions place he never did have two. – Thiers is getting five million from the Germans. – And how much from some Frenchmen I could name? – They're capitulating though there's more than 300,000 National Guard in Paris alone. – *Because* there's 300,000! – And they're quite happy to let the Prussians keep our prisoners till we've paid. – To hell with their filthy war! Good thing it's over. – But who'll pay for the peace? – We will, citizen. Who else? The ones with nothing pay. – So we've got nothing? We've got 200,000 bayonets, madame. – I tell you it's only a ceasefire, they'll never take our streets, the Prussians won't and neither will Thiers. – He didn't risk coming into Paris, Herr von Bismarck, did he? Paris wasn't for sale. – Well, you're up early! The old lady wanted to be on her own, I suppose. Someone else putting it up for a change? *A man has arrived with a poster. He puts it up and goes away again. Babette leaves the queue and reads it out.* From Monsieur Thiers! 'Peace means order and stability. Citizens of Paris, trade is languishing, demand is falling off, capital is being frightened away. Those to blame must be handed over to justice. Order must be restored at once, fully and unassailably.' Oh là là!

The baker has begun removing the iron bars from her shop door.

WOMEN: Have you heard, Madame Pullard? Business is bad even though there's a war. – How true! It's a week since I had an order for a locomotive. And all my capital has been frightened away by the National Guard and their carryings-on. Hasn't yours?

BAKER: Demonstrations, demonstrations, demonstrations! I should have thought the government's white bread spoke louder than that, ladies.

WOMEN: White bread for order and stability, eh? For paying the rent.

BABETTE: The print's still wet. Seems they're in a hurry.

WOMEN: Wind even before we eat any bread! They can't give us a mouthful without farting out something about order and stability. – Watch your language, citizen. Order! What will Mademoiselle Guéricault say, her being a teacher and not knowing anything about wind? – Leave Mademoiselle Guéricault alone. There's nothing wrong with her. She agrees with what I said and she did her bit with the others when the Cabets and Papa fetched the cannon in from Clichy before the Prussians came. – And do *you* think

Monsieur Thiers only let the Prussians have Clichy because our guns were there?

GENEVIÈVE: Yes, I do, citizen. The Central Committee of the National Guard had reports to that effect.

WOMEN: She's political. – Suppose she is, does that mean she's not telling the truth? – My old man says it was politics took his leg off, not grapeshot. That's why he's political and reads *La Patrie en danger.*

A few government soldiers, among them Philippe Faure, have appeared near the cannon. Babette, still standing by the poster, addresses Philippe.

BABETTE: Oh Philippe, are you back? You're just in time, the bakery's open again.

PHILIPPE: Shush, Babette. I've not come to say hello in there.

He and his comrades busy themselves with the cannon.

BABETTE: What do you want with the cannon?

PHILIPPE: It's going to Versailles. Orders.

BABETTE *calling to the women*: Hey! They're stealing our cannon.

WOMEN: They're doing what? Them and who else?

GENEVIÈVE *hurrying over*: Philippe! You should be ashamed of yourself.

BABETTE: It's the baker's lad. He led them here, he knows his way around these streets.

PHILIPPE: What are you doing out so early? Hold on a minute before you murder us.

GENEVIÈVE: They were giving us white bread, so that we'd give you the guns, like sheep for shearing.

The women run across.

WOMEN: Hey you! Those are ours. They were bought with our money. Our district collected for them.

PHILIPPE: But the war's over.

GENEVIÈVE: Oh so now you want to start a war with us?

PHILIPPE: The guns have to be given up to the Prussians.

WOMEN: Then let the Prussians come and get them. Hands off! You dare touch them, you shit-arses! Fetch the guard from Cabets'!

Geneviève runs to the Cabets' house. Rings the bell. Mme Cabet looks out from an upstairs window.

GENEVIÈVE: Wake Jean! They're taking your cannon. *She runs back.* They're not for the Prussians, they're for Monsieur Thiers. He needs them against us, don't let him have them, citizens!

WOMEN: Hands off that cannon! It's Madame Cabet's cannon.

Jean and François rush from the house in shirt and trousers.

BABETTE: Jean, they've come for the cannon. Philippe led them here.

Noise from the streets nearby, rifle fire and, later, alarm bells.

GENEVIÈVE: There are cannon in the rue du Tabernacle too. It's a raid on the whole quarter. Now we know why they're giving us white bread.

JEAN *calling back*: François, your brother's here, for Thiers.

PHILIPPE *in among the women*: Now, now, ladies. Move aside, will you? I've got my orders.

JEAN: Yes, move aside, let us get at them.

FRANÇOIS *running up with fixed bayonet*: Leave the gun where it is, Philippe, it doesn't belong to you.

BAKER *from inside her shop*: You carry out your orders, Philippe, or I'll not have you back in the bakery.

PHILIPPE: How long have you been in the National Guard?

FRANÇOIS: College is shut. Move aside.

The women step back. François levels his rifle.

PHILIPPE: Put your gun away, kid.

BABETTE: Shoot him.

GENEVIÈVE *flinging herself in front of Philippe*: No bloodshed!

JEAN *dragging her out of the line of fire*: You keep out of it.

PHILIPPE *levelling his rifle*: Put your gun down, kid.

FRANÇOIS: Make one move and I'll fire. Our Father, which art in heaven, Hallowed be thy Name. *Continues to pray, all the while aiming at Philippe.*

WOMEN: So you'd massacre us just because your scabby generals tell you to?

GENEVIÈVE: Oh you poor fools! You can't take the cannon without horses. We'll throw ourselves under the wheels.

PHILIPPE: I'll count to three. One.

MME CABET *coming out of the house with Papa*: Philippe, put that gun down at once. You know very well you've had no education, what are you thinking of, answering your brother back who's studying physics? And I've brought some wine for you all. I'm sure they sent you off without any breakfast.

PHILIPPE *looks round at his comrades, who have not taken aim, and slowly puts down his rifle*: Madame Cabet, you are preventing me from carrying out an order.

WOMEN *laughing, and surrounding him*: That's the way, baker. They can't ask you to shoot your own brother, now can they?

BAKER: You're sacked, Philippe. I don't give employment to traitors.

BABETTE *kissing Philippe*: That's for your treachery.

PHILIPPE: I'm nobody's brother, ladies, and I'm not a baker. I'm under orders.

FRANÇOIS *uncertainly to Genèvieve*: Don't I get anything?

GENEVIÈVE *in high spirits*: Take what you want.

FRANÇOIS: That's not an answer.

WOMEN *in among the soldiers*: How dare you fall on the women when you've no dishonourable intentions? You should be ashamed of yourselves!

SOLDIERS: The war's over. We want to go home.

WOMEN: Oh là là! He wants to go home. And where's home, sonny boy?

SOLDIER: The Auvergne. And soon it will be seedtime. You damn city people never think of that.

WOMEN: Have a drink, sonny boy. – Turn up your rifles. Have you got nothing else that's stiff? – Madame Cabet, give them blankets, they're quaking with cold, loving's impossible.

GENEVIÈVE: This cannon belongs to Madame Cabet. She lives here. You can't take it off her any more than you can her saucepans.

PAPA: Long live Madame Cabet, sole owner of the cannon of the rue Pigalle! *He lifts her up and sits her on the cannon. To the soldiers*: You see, we only needed to talk. *To the women*: Now you've got it back, look after it. Most important, don't let any one of them out of Paris now.

Keep hold of them all. Press them to your breast, or to your breasts, they can't do any damage there.

A worker, Pierre Langevin, comes from the next street, where it has got quieter. He has children with him.

LANGEVIN: *Salut*, Papa! You managed, did you? And no bloodshed?

PHILIPPE *to his comrades*: How can we help it if they don't send us any horses? We can't shove the things through the women without.

PAPA: Everything OK. What about everywhere else?

LANGEVIN: The whole district's awake. No cannons gone so far.

CHILDREN: They tried to pinch our guns at the Moulin de la Galette as well. And they shot two of our people in the rue Lepic.

MME CABET *to the soldiers*: Messieurs, this is my brother-in-law, Pierre Langevin, from the Central Committee of the National Guard.

LANGEVIN: In the rue Granot General Lecomte gave the order to fire, but his men fraternised and he was arrested.

PAPA: Where is he? The swine. It was him who said the Guard should be given a bloodletting. Everyone in Paris knows it was.

LANGEVIN: He was taken to the lock-up.

PAPA: They'll let him escape. If he's not shot in five minutes he'll get away.

LANGEVIN: He'll be brought to justice, comrade.

PAPA: We're justice. *He hurries away.*

MME CABET: Will somebody help me down from this cannon?

LANGEVIN *to the government troops*: And what will you do? So long as you're still armed . . .

ONE OF THE SOLDIERS: Oh shit! Against our own people . . .

The soldiers reverse their rifles.

GENEVIÈVE *to the children*: And you can tear down those silly posters.

They do so.

JEAN: Lift maman down, will you? And then to the Hôtel de Ville again. Arrest Thiers! He must tell us what he wanted the cannon for.

BABETTE: Three kisses for Thiers alive!

C

Eight in the morning. The baker is putting the iron bars back across her shop door. Philippe, standing nearby, is looking sourly at an enormous woman with a rifle over her shoulder pacing up and down in front of the cannon.

BAKER: There'll be disturbances, that's for sure. If they go ahead with the Commune everyone's talking about, there'll be looting. Everything shared out, then they drink their share and share out the rest again. You're a troublemaker yourself and I'm not having you back near my oven. And your brother a young priest! And he's a troublemaker too!

PHILIPPE: He's only in the seminary because there's nowhere else he could go and study.

BAKER: So he's stealing an education from the friars of Saint Joseph! Typical of you people – communards! *Exit angrily into the shop.*

Geneviève comes out of the house next door.

GENEVIÈVE: Good morning, Philippe. How are you feeling now the New Age has begun? *He growls.* Because it has begun. There's an end of violence. We've taken their cannon away.

PHILIPPE: And now you women have got them. A new age, my foot!

Dispirited, he goes into the house where the Cabets and his brother live. Geneviève, in good spirits, pulls on her gloves. Up the street, looking grim, comes Papa.

GENEVIÈVE: Good morning, monsieur. Didn't you go to the rue Granot last night, where they arrested General Thomas? What happened to him?

PAPA: He was shot, citizen.

GENEVIÈVE: Was that right? Who shot him?

PAPA: Who do you think shot him? The people.

GENEVIÈVE: Without a trial?

PAPA: Of course not. After a trial by the people.

GENEVIÈVE: And you were there?

PAPA: Everyone was there who was there. And don't be worrying about the enemies of the people. This is serious. *In an ill humour, he goes into the Cabets' house. Geneviève, the teacher, watches him go, confused.*

4

19 March 1871. Hôtel de Ville. Staircase to the assembly room of the Central Committee of the National Guard. Outside the door sits a National Guardsman, eating bread and cheese and checking people's passes. Papa, Coco and Mme Cabet are waiting. Delegates are arriving for the session.

DELEGATES: If we want to call new elections we must come to some understanding with the mayors of the twenty arrondissements. – On the contrary! We must send in a battalion and arrest them. They are hyenas, they wouldn't be mayors if they weren't. – The main thing is to get an overwhelming majority, all of Paris will turn out to vote if the mayors join us. We must receive them. – For God's sake, no violence! We shan't win Paris by terror. – Who is Paris? *Exit all but one of the delegates.*

PAPA *addressing him*: Citizen of the Central Committee, could you tell citizen Pierre Langevin in there that we have to speak to him? This is his sister-in-law. Why don't they let people in?

COMMITTEE MEMBER: The room is too small, citizen. And don't forget the enemy is listening.

PAPA: It's more important that the people listen. At least leave the door open.

The Committee member goes in and leaves the door open.

VOICE: Urgent motion from the 67th Battalion: 'That in consideration of the hardships suffered by the people of Paris and of their so generously shedding their blood in the defence of the motherland a distribution of a million francs be made in the twenty-two arrondissements, this being money saved by ceasing all payments to officials in the government that has betrayed us.'

CRIES: Carried!

MME CABET: They're getting on with it, aren't they?

PAPA: The most important thing is we march on Versailles.

MME CABET: There won't only *be* white bread, I'll actually have the money to buy it.

PAPA: But if we don't march on Versailles at once, there won't be white bread for very long, Madame Cabet.

VOICE: We continue our discussion of the question of elections. Delegate Varlin.

VARLIN'S VOICE: Citizen Guardsmen! About two o'clock this morning the Government, with the help of a few regular battalions, made an attempt to disarm the capital's National Guard and to seize the cannon whose handing over to the Prussians we had prevented.

CRY: Second attempt to emasculate Paris! The first was foisting a general on us.

Four gentlemen in top hats come up the staircase: the mayors.

VARLIN: Citizens, why was this attack undertaken? To deliver up our country, robbed of her last weapons, to Bismarck's most extreme demands and at the same time to make her solely and helplessly answerable to these demands. So that those who perpetrated the criminal war will get it paid for now by those who bled in it. So that from making good money out of the war they may move to making good money out of the peace. Citizen Guardsmen, the Commune will demand that the deputies, senators, generals, factory owners, estate owners and of course the church, who are to blame for the war, will now be the ones who pay the Prussians their five billion, and that to this end we sell their property.

Loud applause. The mayors have entered the room.

CHAIRMAN'S VOICE: The Central Committee welcomes the mayors of Paris.

ONE OF THE MAYORS: This is the Hôtel de Ville of Paris. You have occupied it by military force. Will you please tell us by what right?

CRY: In the name of the city's people, Monsieur le Maire. Consider yourselves their guests and you are welcome.

Cries of protest.

MAYORS: You know what this answer means? It will be said these people want revolution.

CRY: What do you mean 'want'? The revolution has happened. Look around you.

MAYORS: Citizens of the National Guard, we, the mayors of Paris, are willing to put it to the newly elected National Assembly in Versailles that you wish to elect a new Municipal Council under their authority.

CRIES: No, no, no! An independent Commune!

VARLIN'S VOICE: Not only the election of a Municipal Council but real municipal freedoms, the right of the National Guard to elect its own leaders, the exclusion of the standing army from the whole of Paris. In brief: a free Paris.

MAYORS: That is the red flag. Beware! If you unfurl that flag over the Hôtel de Ville your polling stations will be avoided like plague houses and Paris will spit on your elections.

CRY: The Committee will take that risk. We trust and believe that the people of Paris not only have hands to work with but also eyes to see.

Applause.

MAYORS: And they will see all sorts of things. I for one have no desire to stand for election alongside murderers. *Murmurings.* The Committee did not protest against the murders of General Thomas and General Lecomte.

CRIES: We had nothing to do with it. – I object to the word 'murder'. It was the just execution of murderers by the people of Paris. – Beware of censuring the people, or they will censure you. – No threats! The people joined hands with the bourgeoisie in the Republic of 4 September. – Indeed they did, and that alliance must continue. Everyone must take part in the elections, everyone! Until Paris has voted for us we acknowledge the Government in Versailles as the rightful power of the state. – And what if we do? The National Guard is the nation in arms against the power of the state.

The mayors appear in the doorway.

ONE OF THE MAYORS *calling back angrily into the room*: We note with satisfaction that you are divided even among yourselves.

CRIES *in the room, and murmurings*: We need the entrepreneurs to start up production again. Very well, turn your back on the people to humour the bourgeoisie. The people will withdraw from us and we shall discover that no revolution is possible with the bourgeoisie.

PAPA: That's the truth.

MAYORS: We leave you our sincere good wishes. May you succeed in your task, it is rather too large for us. *Exit.*

CRIES: The bourgeoisie are quitting the room. Good.

PAPA *shouting after the mayors*: Villains!

Langevin and Geneviève come out of the room.

PAPA: Pierre, you must bring a motion at once: people protecting the traitor generals must be eliminated. Shoot them like dogs, straight away, all of them, without trial, or you are lost.

LANGEVIN: What have you got to do with the shootings? Calm down.

PAPA: Me? Nothing. What do you mean? The Committee is dallying.

LANGEVIN: Wouldn't you do better to listen? *He opens the door again.*

RIGAULT'S VOICE: Citizens of the Guard, the right to decide the fate of the country can only rest in the hands of those who are defending it, namely the proletariat, the 200,000 combatants. Their ballot paper is the bullet.

Murmurings.

CRIES: Do you really want to throttle the elections? That means anarchy. Remember it means civil war. And with Prussian batteries from the Bois de Vincennes to the Bois de Boulogne. Unity! The elections are agreed.

GENEVIÈVE: We are divided, that is bad.

LANGEVIN *smiling*: No, it is good, it means movement. So long as it's movement in the right direction. But why have you come?

PAPA: In the 101st we've been talking about the gates not being closed. All night long they've been sending their police, their baggage and their artillery off to Versailles. And that's where Thiers is. We are to tell you that we'll march on Versailles as soon as you give the signal, Langevin.

GENEVIÈVE *quickly*: That would be civil war as well.

COCO: There are 20,000 men with bread stuck on their bayonets camped outside the Hôtel de Ville alone, and fifty cannon have been brought up around the building. You only need shout through the window 'To Versailles!' and everything will be settled once and for all.

LANGEVIN *slowly*: Perhaps. But we need the agreement of France, do we not?

PAPA: Good, then vote. Or don't vote, that's also good. But destroy the enemy while you can, now.

LANGEVIN *hesitantly*: It's hard enough getting the Commune on its feet. Once we're there, Thiers and his henchmen will be a handful of bankrupts in the eyes of France. But I know what you mean, Papa. It's good that you're breathing down our necks. Don't leave us in peace, you are always further on than we are. *He hurries back into the room.*

PAPA: Coco, let's leave it at that. They must know what they're doing after all.

They turn to go. Then they hear the closing speech.

VARLIN'S VOICE: Citizens of the National Guard! The proletariat of Paris, amid the defeats and treachery of the ruling classes, decimated on the battlefields of their own and the Prussian bourgeoisie, weakened by the hunger visited upon them by the Prussian generals and the Parisian black-marketeers, in the early hours of this morning rose up to defend what is left of their shattered *quartiers* and to take their destiny into their own hands. It is the destiny of France. The so-called Government of National Defence, formed by the bourgeoisie after military defeat, has been unmasked and shown to be a Government of National Treachery. Those same people who brought in the Emperor for their adventures and dropped him when he did not deliver the loot, they are now bringing in Herr von Bismarck to defend their wealth against the ones who created it, the proletariat. But the capital of France, declaring the revolt against this gang of adventurers to be legitimate, arms herself now and strides calmly and determinedly to the election of her own free and sovereign Commune and calls on all free Communes of France to gather themselves around her.

Loud applause and cries of 'Long live the Commune!'

GENEVIÈVE: This is one of the greatest days in the history of France.

PAPA: And a part of its greatness will be that nobody can say the representatives of the people wanted civil war. It will be a New Age and there will not have been a bloodbath.

RESOLUTION

1

Whereas you knew how weak we were and made
Laws so we should ever more be slaves
These laws in future shall be set aside
Because we've had enough of being slaves.
  Whereas you thereupon will threaten us
  With rifles and with cannon we hereby
  Resolve from now on we shall fear death less
  Than we fear living wretchedly.

2

Whereas we're hungry and hungry we'll remain
If we put up with being robbed by you
We'll show there's only a pane of glass between
Us and all the good bread we are due.
  Whereas you thereupon will threaten us
  With rifles and with cannon we hereby
  Resolve from now on we shall fear death less
  Than we fear living wretchedly.

3

Whereas there are dwelling-places where you are
While you leave us without a home to go to
We have resolved that now we'll move in there
Because we're sick of slumming it down below.
  Whereas you thereupon will threaten us
  With rifles and with cannon we hereby
  Resolve from now on we shall fear death less
  Than we fear living wretchedly.

4
Whereas there's coal in surplus piled up high
While we are freezing cold without the stuff
We have resolved we'll be the ones that we supply
Because if we do then we'll be warm enough.
  Whereas you thereupon will threaten us
  With rifles and with cannon we hereby
  Resolve from now on we shall fear death less
  Than we fear living wretchedly.

5
Whereas it seems you'll never work out how
To pay the ones who work a decent rate
We'll have the factories in our own hands now
Because there's plenty for us if we throw you out.
  Whereas you thereupon will threaten us
  With rifles and with cannon we hereby
  Resolve from now on we shall fear death less
  Than we fear living wretchedly.

6
Whereas nobody's left who still believes
The government whatever it promises
We have resolved we'll build ourselves good lives
By being the only ones who govern us.
  Whereas you'll listen to what the cannon say –
  No other language will you listen to –
  Well then, we'll have to turn the cannon your way.
  Yes, that will be the best thing we can do!

5

19 March 1871. Gare du Nord. Posters everywhere urging people to vote for the Commune. Crush of bourgeois families, nuns, functionaries fleeing to Versailles.

NEWSPAPER SELLER: Declaration of the Press: Commune elections unconstitutional! Parisians, the following newspapers urge you not to vote: *Le Journal des débats*, *Le*

Constitutionel, Le Moniteur universel, Le Figaro, Le Gaulois – and then during what follows – La Vérité, Paris-Journal, La Presse, La France, La Liberté, Le Pays, Le National, L'Univers, Le Temps, La Cloche, La Patrie, Le Bien public, L'Union, L'Avenir libéral, Journal des villes et des campagnes, Le Charivari, Le Monde, La France nouvelle, La Gazette de France, Le Petit Moniteur, Le Petit National, L'Electeur libre, La Petite Presse.

The tax-collector, among his family, buys the declaration.

TAX-COLLECTOR: What does that mean, 'the Committee is nothing'? It represents 215 battalions. Those people can do what they like. Alphonse, stand up straight. Where's Bourdet with the briefcase? Do I or don't I have a chief clerk in my hour of need?

HIS WIFE: Alphonse, don't slouch. If Bourdet doesn't come you'll have to stay behind, Christophe. Everything's very dear in Versailles, we'll be lost without money. Everywhere will be full.

TAX-COLLECTOR: 'You'll have to stay behind . . .' That's very typical. They can put me up against the wall so long as the money . . .

HIS WIFE: Don't start getting sentimental. You'll wait for Bourdet. Alphonse, stop shrugging your shoulders. *Exit without her husband. He waits.*

Enter Philippe and Jean just as some regular soldiers, led by a functionary, arrive dragging an iron chest.

FUNCTIONARY: Not in the goods wagon, if you please. Those are the registers and the cash boxes from the town hall.

PHILIPPE: It's your mother's fault that I have to go back to the army. How could she pawn François' microscope while he was fighting? It will take all my pay, which I haven't even got yet. And they might court-martial me because of that business with the cannon, and you're to blame for that as well.

JEAN *absent-mindedly*: We had to pay the rent, Philippe. If you bring us twenty francs we can get the things back again. But the most important is that François doesn't find out.

PHILIPPE: His studying gobbles up everything. And if he gets involved in your Commune business the reverend brothers will expel him. A priest and in the Commune! And you can see how wrong your ideas are when you look at him. François wants his microscope, doesn't he? And why? Because it's his property. People want their property, and that's that.

JEAN: Philippe, your head's like a bakery, everything in a mess.

PHILIPPE: Everything's not in a mess in a bakery.

JEAN: Listen. The microscope is a tool of his trade, that's why he wants it. And the lathes in the locomotive works are the tools of our trade, that's why we want them. Got it?

PHILIPPE: Where are you going?

JEAN *thrusts the sack at him that he was carrying for him*: Don't you see, they're taking the cash boxes away. Hey, you there! *To the soldiers dragging the boxes*: Nothing's to be taken away. It's the property of the people. *The soldiers continue, after one of them has given him a kick.* Scum! And no one here to stop them. *Hurries away.*

Exit Philippe, shaking his head. Enter an aristocratic woman with her niece and servants carrying hat-boxes and the like.

NIECE: Who would have thought, Aunt Marie, that the first trains allowed out of Paris would witness such a tragic spectacle! The whole of Paris in flight.

ARISTOCRATIC WOMAN: Not for long. Philine, mind the box doesn't get crushed. There's a Farnaud hat in it.

NIECE: We should have taken the carriage.

ARISTOCRATIC WOMAN: Don't talk nonsense. They'd have unhitched the horses and eaten them. Ah, de Plœuc, how very kind of you. At times like this one learns who one's friends are.

DE PLŒUC: I couldn't let you leave without shaking your hand, Madame la Duchesse.

NIECE: Must you really stay behind? Is it not dangerous?

DE PLŒUC: Perhaps. But the Bank of France is worth the risk, mademoiselle. *To the Duchess*: Might I ask you to hand over the note in this bouquet to Him? *He hands her a bouquet.*

ARISTOCRATIC WOMAN: It will be done. The whole pantomime won't last more than a week. Goodbye for a little while, Henri. *Exit with her niece.*

DE PLŒUC: For a little while, ladies.

The newspaper seller is now selling individual papers. Opposite him a street trader is selling his wares.

NEWSPAPER SELLER: 'Pronouncements of eminent persons' in the *Figaro*! – 'Murders of General Thomas and General Lecomte!' – 'Occupation of the Hôtel de Ville unlawful!' – 'Is the Central Committee in league with the Germans?' – 'Looting in the rue Gras!' – 'Rule of the Mob!'

STREET TRADER *interjecting*: Braces! – Combs from Lyons! – Buttons! – Soap and toiletries, cheap! – Mouth organs! – Belts from Tripolitania!

Soldiers bring in Jean, whose clothes are torn. They are halted by a sergeant of the National Guard and some of his men.

SERGEANT: One moment! What are you doing with him?

SOLDIERS: He was caught trying to climb on the locomotive. A saboteur, sergeant.

JEAN: Listen will you. They're carrying off the cash boxes. You must stop them. You must arrest the whole lot of them.

SERGEANT: Easy, comrade, easy now. We've had no orders to stop the trains. Let him go.

DE PLŒUC: Friends, I am the Marquis de Plœuc of the Bank of France. You say yourselves that the Executive has issued no orders. We do not have a civil war yet, so far as I have heard. And if that is the case the man has committed a crime and must be arrested.

JEAN: Oh? And where was I being taken to? Answer me that.

Nobody speaks.

SERGEANT: I see. You were dragging him off on the train? Let him go at once. *To his people*: Fetch reinforcements.

Exit some of his men. Jean is released. The soldiers creep away. Exit de Plœuc.

SOLDIERS: We were only doing our duty, comrade.

SERGEANT *to Jean*: You were lucky.

JEAN: And you let them go! Look at these posters. I'll tell you something: I voted. But not for your Commune. Your Commune will go under. *He stumbles away.*

6

26 March. Outside the café in Montmartre. Mme Cabet and her little family – Jean, Babette, François, Geneviève – are making themselves at home in the little café, that had been closed. They take down the shutters, roll up the blinds, carry out chairs, hang up white paper lanterns. The waiter in the uniform of the National Guard and the wounded cuirassier in civilian clothes help them. Fast music can be heard from a square nearby. Geneviève comes out of the café with bottles of wine followed by one of the children in Sunday best.

FRANÇOIS *arriving with cane chairs*: This is the Commune, this is Science, the New Millennium! Paris has decided in favour of it!

WAITER: The *patron* decided against it so the waiter has become the *patron*. Make yourselves at home in his café.

GENEVIÈVE: So even the young men of the church salute the dawn. *She places bottles of wine in front of Mme Cabet.*

FRANÇOIS: And the teachers serve the widows with black-market wine. For now the Sermon on the Mount has been set down in paragraphs of the law which begin with the word 'Whereas' and finish in deeds. *He embraces the German soldier who, grinning all over his face, has opened a shutter.* I embrace you, cuirassier, my new brother, deserter from the predatory armies of the anachronistic Bismarck!

MME CABET *who from the start has been sitting on a chair in the middle of the street*: And they've let us off the rent! *Calls out*: Jean! Babette!

FRANÇOIS: Whereas the unjust war that has plagued our country was the work of a minority and whereas it is unjust, unjust, to shift the whole burden of it on to the majority, which is a vast majority of the very poor . . . I've learned it by heart, like my Lavoisier.

JEAN *looking out of the upper window of the café*: Be patient!

FRANÇOIS: And the pawnbrokers give the poor their pawned

belongings back for free, it being the case that life must be worth living.

MME CABET: François, you knew all about it? I'm a thief, everything's so dear. That's why I asked you for the rent, a bit tactlessly, but I wanted to get the things back, you need them of course. Jean! *To the child*: Sit down, Victor. Eat something before you taste the wine. Jean! *The child sits down stiffly. Jean looks out crossly.* I want to speak to Babette. Haven't you finished yet?

BABETTE *somewhat flushed, appears in the window next to Jean*: Maman?

MME CABET: See what wonderful wine we've got, Babette. *Babette laughs and disappears.* She needs looking after, he's very radical, that one.

Down the street come Papa and Langevin. Langevin looks very tired. Papa is carrying a white lantern on his bayonet.

PAPA: Madame, mademoiselle. I bring you your brother-in-law, Member of the Commune for Vaugirard. I dragged him away from work, they're at it like wage-slaves in the Hôtel de Ville.

MME CABET: Have a glass, Pierre.

WAITER: The wine is the *patron*'s, the *patron* is in Versailles, help yourself, monsieur.

LANGEVIN: They've left six thousand sick behind, there's nobody for the street lighting, that's a lot of work.

Jean and Babette raise a red flag out of the window.

PAPA: Ah, raise a glass to Beauty! Loved and feared! Hounded and terrifying! Friendly Beauty, rides in on the storm wind!

MME CABET: Yes, she'll do it. Pierre, Papa, take some of these loaves. And where are the children? The baker opposite brought us bread out on the street when we carried our flag past. Yes, when we carried our flag past, of a certain colour, the baker, the sour-puss, forced these loaves upon us.

GENEVIÈVE: Sit down. I'll sing you an old song.

Margot went to market early.
How loud the drums beat!
She bought meat and celery
And found the butcher grey,

Hair and face gone grey.
'That'll be twenty francs, the meat.'
Tarrabom, tarrabom, tarrabom.
'Pardon me?'
'Five, madame, okay.'
'Ahem.'

Margot went to her landlady.
The drums began to beat.
'Now what do I owe you? Say.'
The landlady went white,
White as death is white.
'It's twenty francs you owe.'
Tarrabom, tarrabom, tarrabom.
'Pardon me?'
'Ten, madame, will do.'
'Ahem.'

ALL *singing together*: Ahem, ahem, ahem.

Across the square come a troop of men and women wearing cockades.

ONE OF THE MEN: Mesdames, messieurs, come along all of you! Monsieur Courbet, the celebrated painter, will be speaking in the Place Vendôme. He will urge the necessity of flinging down Napoleon's Column, cast from the bronze of twelve hundred captured European cannon. A monument to war and an affirmation of militarism and barbarism.

PAPA: No, thank you. We approve of the project and we shall come to see it carried out.

A WOMAN: Then join us for the broth they're serving in the *quartier*.

A man whinnies.

MAN: In memory of five horses, ladies and gentlemen.

FRANÇOIS: Shall we go?

PAPA: I'm happy where I am.

FRANÇOIS: Broth.

MME CABET: Would you like to go? Where are Jean and Babette? Ah, there they are.

PAPA: Monsieur François, you seem to have the makings of a priest.

GENEVIÈVE: No, thank you, we'll sit here a while longer.

The men and women go on their way.

ONE OF THE MEN: Just as you please. The Commune invited you. You did not come. Oh là là!

PAPA: That's freedom.

Jean and Babette have appeared downstairs.

MME CABET: You've been up there too long. I'm cross with you.

JEAN: Maman, you're making Geneviève blush.

MME CABET: I told you, you have to act in accordance with your circumstances.

PAPA: But they are the best, madame, the very best. Paris has decided in favour of life lived how you please. And that's why Monsieur Fritz has decided to stay with us. No more class differences between citizens, no more barriers between peoples.

JEAN: Babette, answer maman, defend me.

BABETTE: Madame, your son will not be rushed. *She sings.*

Père Joseph, when it rains, gets wet
His wife's backside is bare
But she cooks something for him in the pot
By the side of the road in a stolen pot
And before he eats Père Joseph combs his hair.
'Mother, do me something specially fine.
For a poor devil nothing is too good.
Mother, take your time, be the chef, be sublime!
Do me something – wait, some chives in the salad!'

Père Joseph in the Salpêtrière
He has no time at all for the priest
And as though he had money to spare
He sends out for a slap-up feast:
'Warder, do me something specially fine.
For a poor devil nothing is too good.
Friends, take your time, be the best, be sublime!
And don't forget the chives in the salad.'

PAPA: What are we here for, after all? According to my sister, the curé of Sainte Héloise answered that question so: to perfect the self. To do it, he needed quails for breakfast. *To the child*: We live for the extras, my son. We must have them, even if it takes cannon to get them. We do our stint. Then we needn't stint ourselves. Cheers! – Who is the young man?

MME CABET: Victor, bring me a fork will you? *The child goes into the café.* His father was killed with the 93rd, defending the cannon on 18 March. He has started a meat business, rabbits, keep quiet, Jean. I buy something off him now and then, because of his ...

The child comes back with a fork.

PAPA *gets to his feet, raises his glass*: Good luck to you.

The child drinks to Papa. Music from close by. Jean begins to dance with Geneviève, Babette with François, the waiter with Mme Cabet.

PAPA: All going very well, don't you think?

LANGEVIN: Are you happy now?

PAPA *after a pause*: It's what this city wanted, and what it was built for, what it had forgotten under the lash and what it was reminded of by us. – Anything wrong?

LANGEVIN: Only one thing. I sometimes think we'd have done better to attack on 18 March. We put the question: elections or the march on Versailles? The answer was: both.

PAPA: And what of it?

LANGEVIN: Thiers sits in Versailles, gathering troops.

PAPA: Bah, I spit on them. Paris has decided everything. They're old men, half dead already, we'll settle them in no time. And the troops? We'll bring them round to our way of thinking, like we did on 18 March over the cannon.

LANGEVIN: I hope so. They are peasants.

PAPA: To Paris, monsieur.

The dancers come back.

BABETTE: To freedom, Jean Cabet. Total!

PAPA: To freedom.

LANGEVIN *smiling*: I drink to partial freedom.

BABETTE: In love!

GENEVIÈVE: Why to partial, Monsieur Langevin?

LANGEVIN: It leads to total freedom.

GENEVIÈVE: And total, immediate freedom, that's an illusion?

LANGEVIN: In politics.

BABETTE: François, you can dance. What do you dance as? A physicist or a priest, a little priest?

FRANÇOIS: I shan't be a priest. This is a New Age, Mademoiselle Guéricault. I shall study physics and Paris will pay.

BABETTE: Long live sharing! We've got everything, let's share!

GENEVIÈVE: Babette!

BABETTE: I'll teach you to dance cheek-to-cheek with Jean.

She hurls herself on Geneviève.

GENEVIÈVE: I shan't defend myself, Babette.

BABETTE: Then take that and that and that!

They roll on the ground. Geneviève begins to defend herself.

BABETTE: Oh, so you won't defend yourself? But you'll scratch my eyes out, you bitch?

Jean, laughing, has held back François. Papa and the waiter separate the combatants.

MME CABET: You behave as though you'd got wardrobes full of clothes. Oh là là! I was against you going upstairs to hang out the flag. She's a fighter, this one.

FRANÇOIS: A communarde doesn't get jealous.

BABETTE: Made of wood, is she?

GENEVIÈVE: No, she holds on to what she's got. I'm glad there wasn't a bayonet handy, Babette. Good day, Philippe.

Philippe has joined them.

PHILIPPE: Here I am again. I was curious whether I'd find you still alive. According to the Versailles newspapers you are all arrested and murdered. Anyone who doesn't say 'Long live the Commune!' before he goes to sleep is denounced by his own wife and tortured by the communards in the latrines until he confesses everything. That is well known. It is the Commune's Rule of Terror.

They all laugh.

PAPA: This is the first night in history, friends, that here in Paris there'll be no murder, no robbery, no fraud and no rape. For the first time the streets are safe, the city doesn't need any police. The bankers and the lesser thieves, the tax-collectors and the factory owners, the ministers, the tarts and the clergy have emigrated to Versailles. The city is liveable in.

FRANÇOIS: Your good health, Papa.

PHILIPPE: I read about that in the papers too. The orgies! The orgies of the Commune! The tyrants in the Hôtel de Ville have seven mistresses each. It is decreed by law.

BABETTE: Oh Jean's only got two.

FRANÇOIS: And why did you run away?

PHILIPPE: I won't be at their beck and call for nothing. Monsieur Thiers is bankrupt, finished, over and done with. He's stopped paying the army. The soldiers in Versailles are selling their guns five francs apiece.

PAPA: I get my pay.

LANGEVIN: You're your own paymaster, that's the difference.

PHILIPPE: That's the Commune's bad management. They talk about that. I was in the country for a day, in Arles, at home. Mother and Father send their love to you, François. I didn't tell them you've become a communard, a devil that wants everything shared out.

PAPA: I dream of a side of pork. Or trotters.

LANGEVIN: But how did you get through the lines?

PHILIPPE: Nobody stopped me.

LANGEVIN: That's bad. That is the carelessness of the Commune.

PAPA: Pierre, you have too high an opinion of Monsieur Thiers and Herr von Bismarck. Those old men! Welcome, Philippe. So they're finished, are they? Give me a newspaper, Pierre. *Langevin hands him one, he makes a childish helmet out of it, which he puts on.* I'm Bismarck. Jean, you be Thiers, borrow François' glasses. We'll show Pierre what these old men talk about while we're enjoying our little festivities here in Paris.

Papa and Jean strike historical attitudes.

PAPA: My dear Thiers, I've just created an emperor, a dolt be it said in passing, would you like one as well?

JEAN: My dear Herr von Bismarck, I've had one already.

PAPA: I can understand you not wanting another one when you've had one already. That is all very well, but if you don't do as you're told you'll get your emperor back and that's no idle threat. And by the way: would you like a king?

JEAN: Herr von Bismarck, only some of us want a king, a very few.

PAPA: You'll get one if you don't do as you're told. By the way, what is it *they* want, I mean the . . . What's it called, the thing that pays the taxes? That's it, the people . . . What is it the people want?

JEAN *looking around him nervously*: Me.

PAPA: But that's marvellous, I like you just as well as an emperor or a king. So they don't want one of them either? Funny. But you'll do as you're told, won't you? You'll hand the whole thing over even better than they would, the whole of, what's it called, where we are now, yes that's it: France.

JEAN: Herr von Bismarck, I have been entrusted with the task of handing over France.

PAPA: Who by, Monsieur Thiers?

JEAN: By France. I have just been elected.

PAPA *roaring with laughter*: So have we! The Emperor and I have just been elected too.

JEAN *likewise laughing, then*: Joking apart, Herr von Bismarck, I do feel a little insecure. In brief, I can't be sure I won't be arrested.

PAPA: I'll tell you what, I'll support you. I've got five thousand cannon.

JEAN: Then I have only one further wish, Herr von Bismarck. Will you allow me? May I kiss your boots? *Flinging himself on Papa's boots and kissing them.* Oh what boots! Oh how good they taste!

PAPA: Yes, but don't eat them up.

JEAN: And will you promise me, Otto, that with these, with these boots, you'll trample IT down as well?

PAPA: Oh yes, the Commune?

JEAN: Don't speak the word! Don't utter it! You know, for me it's a bit the way Liebknecht and Bebel are for you. *The cuirassier stands and raises his glass.*

PAPA: In the name of God, don't utter those names!

JEAN: But why are you so frightened, Otto? How can you be

of any help to me when you are so frightened? Now I'm frightened too.

They remove the paper helmet and the glasses, and embrace.

BABETTE: Jean, that was good. Seems to me the flag's still not hanging right. Let's go up. *She embraces him.*

FRANÇOIS: I will read it to you after all. *He stands under a paper lantern and reads from the page of a newspaper.* 'Tonight she will drink the wine she owes to nobody. And tomorrow, like an old woman with work to do, Paris will rise and reach for the tools of her trade, that she loves.'

CUIRASSIER *raising his glass*: Bebel, Liebknecht!

WAITER: The Commune!

CUIRASSIER: The Commune!

WAITER: Bebel, Liebknecht!

FRANÇOIS: Teaching and learning!

GENEVIÈVE: The children!

7

a

Hôtel de Ville. Red flags. In the assembly room, while the session is in progress, boards are being hammered up bearing these inscriptions: 1 THE RIGHT TO LIFE. 2 FREEDOM OF THE INDIVIDUAL. 3 FREEDOM OF CONSCIENCE. 4 RIGHT OF ASSEMBLY AND ASSOCIATION. 5 FREEDOM OF SPEECH, OF THE PRESS AND OF THE PROMOTION OF ANY AND EVERY OPINION. 6 FREEDOM OF THE VOTE. *29 March 1871. Opening session of the Commune.*

BESLAY: It is being said against us that we should have been content with the election of the Republic's National Assembly . . .

CRIES: Promoted by Monsieur Thiers! – Against Paris!

BESLAY: But the liberation of the community of Paris is the liberation of all the communities of the Republic. Our enemies assert that we have dealt the Republic a blow. We have indeed! But a blow such as drives a post more firmly into the ground. *Applause*. The Republic of the Great Revolution of 1792 was a soldier. The Commune's Republic will be a worker. And what he needs most is freedom, to turn the Peace to good.

VARLIN: A Republic, fellow communards, that gives back the workers the tools of their trade just as the Republic of 1792 gave the peasants their land and so through social equality brought about political freedom. *Applause*. I shall proceed to a reading of our first legislative acts. Whereas all citizens equally shall hold themselves ready to serve in the defence of our national territory, the standing army is abolished.

CRY: Away with the generals! Away with the paid bloodhounds! Long live the people's army!

CRY: No more class distinctions among our citizens, no more barriers between peoples! We call on the workers in the German armies to shake hands with the workers in the French!

Applause.

BESLAY: Whereas the state is the people governing itself, all public offices shall be held for limited periods only, the holders being elected according to their abilities and always able to be dismissed.

CRY: Equal pay! A worker's pay!

BESLAY: Whereas no people stands higher than the lowest of its citizens, education shall be accessible to all and shall be free of charge and the responsibility of the state.

CRY: Feed the children in school! Education begins with feeding! They can't learn without learning to eat.

Mocking laughter and applause.

BESLAY: Whereas the purpose of life consists in the boundless development of our physical, intellectual and moral being, property must be nothing other than the right of every individual to share, proportionately to his contribution, in the collective result of the work of all. Work must be organised collectively in the factories and the workshops. *Applause.* Those, friends, are our first new laws. They are to be enacted at once. I hereby open this first working session of the Commune of Paris.

b

Ministry of the Interior. Led by a porter, Geneviève and Langevin enter an office. Rain.

GENEVIÈVE: You say not one official has been seen here? Not for a week?

PORTER: None. I should know, I'm the porter.

GENEVIÈVE: How many work here usually?

PORTER: 384 and the Minister.

GENEVIÈVE: Do you know where they all live?

PORTER: No.

GENEVIÈVE: How shall we find out even where the district schools are, where the teachers live, where the money comes from for their salaries? Even the keys have been taken away.

LANGEVIN: We'll have to fetch a locksmith.

GENEVIÈVE: And you will have to go and buy me some oil for the lamp. *She searches in her purse.*

PORTER: Will you be working nights as well?

LANGEVIN: This is the Commune's Delegate for Education.

PORTER: That's all very well but it's not my job to go running after oil.

GENEVIÈVE: Very well, but ...

LANGEVIN: No it's not all very well. You will go and buy the oil. After you've shown the Delegate where the registers are and the maps with the district schools on.

PORTER: I can only show her where the offices are.

GENEVIÈVE: I shall have to ask the cleaning woman. She might have children who go to school.

LANGEVIN: She won't know anything.

GENEVIÈVE: Between us we'll find out.

LANGEVIN: It would be best to build new schools at once then we'd know where they are. Everything has to be done again, from A to Z, it was always done badly anyway. Clinics and street lighting, all of it. How much do your fellow-citizens pay you to carry out your duties, among which fetching oil is not included?

PORTER: Seven francs eighty a day, but it's not my fellow-citizens that pay, it's the state.

LANGEVIN: Yes, there's a big difference, isn't there? The Delegate will direct Education in the City of Paris for eleven francs a day, if that tells you anything.

PORTER: That's up to her.

LANGEVIN: You can go. If going happens to be one of your duties.

The porter shuffles away. Geneviève opens the window.

GENEVIÈVE: He's a poor devil too.

LANGEVIN: Not in his opinion. It was probably a mistake to let him know how low your salary is. Now he despises you. He's not going to kow-tow to a person only earning a few francs more than he does. And kow-towing is the only thing he can learn to do.

GENEVIÈVE: By himself, perhaps. What does he see? Those who had jobs around the Minister and in the ministerial council have all fled because of the low wages and all the civil servants, even the lowest, are abandoning Paris to darkness, filth and ignorance. And we can't do without them.

LANGEVIN: That's the worst thing. Their chief interest consists in making themselves irreplaceable. That's been the way of it for thousands of years. But we shall have to find people who do their work in such a fashion that it can always be done by someone else. The great workers of the future will be the simplifiers of work. Here comes Babette.

Babette arrives with Philippe.

BABETTE: Nobody sees you any more. It says in the *Officiel* that you've been made a minister or something of the sort.

GENEVIÈVE *in a conspiratorial way, showing fear*: Did he tell you where I was?

BABETTE: The porter? Philippe showed him the pistol.

LANGEVIN: I appoint you Assistant to the Delegate for Transport – that's me. The trains on the northern line do indeed depart, but they don't come back. All they do is carry off houseloads of furniture. I shall have to confiscate the assets of the railway company and court-martial their chief executives. That's what it's like in Paris now. Here nobody comes to work, there they go to work to commit acts of sabotage. But why have you come?

BABETTE: You must do something for the bakery workers at once.

GENEVIÈVE: But I'm the Delegate for Education.

PHILIPPE: Then look after us. It says in your newspapers workers must educate themselves. But how can they when they have to work nights? I never see daylight.

LANGEVIN: I believe the Commune issued a decree abolishing nightwork in bakeries.

PHILIPPE: But the master bakers refuse to abide by it. And we don't have the right to strike, we're a vital industry. But the baker can shut up shop when she likes. There's a loaf by the way. *He gives her a loaf of bread.*

GENEVIÈVE: That's bribery. *She bites into it.*

LANGEVIN: If she shuts up the shop we'll confiscate it and run it ourselves.

PHILIPPE: Does it taste good? You can let yourselves be bribed by us, but not by the masters. I'll say it at the guild meeting, or they'll smash the windows in the bakeries tonight. But what's to be done about Babette and Madame Cabet? Their boss Busson, the army tailor, has come back.

BABETTE: But for a pair of trousers he's only paying one franc now. He says the National Guard orders from the firms with the lowest prices.

GENEVIÈVE: Why are you looking at me like that, Pierre?

LANGEVIN: I am studying how you deal with the people, Citizen Delegate.

GENEVIÈVE: They are being economical with the people's resources.

BABETTE: But we are the people.

LANGEVIN *as Geneviève glances at him uncertainly*: Learn, teacher.

BABETTE: If the Commune pays less than the Empire, we don't need it. Jean is on the ramparts getting himself killed, and why? So we won't have to endure that exploitation, that's why.

PHILIPPE: If you won't pay a proper rate for his trousers you're doing the dirty on his own mother. And his girlfriend. You should . . .

LANGEVIN: We should? What's the matter with you?

PHILIPPE: OK, *we* should . . .

LANGEVIN: That's better.

PHILIPPE: So what should we do?

LANGEVIN: Of course, you're not in the union of tailors, are you? That's where prices should be decided. Not in Monsieur Busson's hat factory.

BABETTE: How should we know that?

GENEVIÈVE: I'm trying to organise schools in which the children will learn it.

BABETTE: Where will you get the money for it if you can't even pay a decent price for uniforms?

GENEVIÈVE: The Bank of France is a few blocks away. The difficulties are here. In this place even the cupboards are locked.

PHILIPPE: At least we can break them open, I should say.

LANGEVIN: What, you're a baker and yet you're ready to do a locksmith's work as well? Now I feel more cheerful about the Commune, boys and girls. Perhaps his next sideline will be government.

He has wound up a grandfather clock that had stopped and now gives the pendulum a tap so that it begins to swing again. All look at the clock and laugh.

LANGEVIN: Expect no more of the Commune than you do of yourselves.

8

The office of the Governor of the Bank of France. The Governor, the Marquis de Plœuc, is in conversation with a fat churchman, the Procurator of the Archbishop of Paris. Rain.

DE PLŒUC: Tell His Eminence that I thank him for conveying to me the wishes of Monsieur Thiers. The ten million francs will be transferred to Versailles in the usual way. But what will happen to the Bank of France in the course of the next few days, I cannot say. At any minute I expect a visit from the Delegate of the Commune, and with that my arrest. There are two billion, 180 million here, Monsignore. That is our lifeline. If it is cut these people have won, whatever else happens.

SERVANT: Monsieur Beslay, Delegate of the Commune.

DE PLŒUC *white in the face*: France's hour of destiny, Monsignore.

FAT CHURCHMAN: But how do I get out?

DE PLŒUC: Don't lose your nerve.

Enter Beslay.

DE PLŒUC: Monsignore Beauchamp, Procurator of His Eminence the Archbishop.

FAT CHURCHMAN: May I take my leave?

DE PLŒUC: I assume you need this gentleman's permission.

BESLAY: Give the Captain this visiting card.

The two men bow and the fat churchman leaves.

BESLAY: Citizen, in the Ministry of Finance the safes are sealed. The paymasters of the National Guard battalions stand there unable to open them. But the men must be paid or the Bank will be plundered, whatever I say. These people have wives and children.

DE PLŒUC: Monsieur Beslay, in accordance with the statutes of your Central Committee the employees of the Bank of France formed a battalion. Let me assure you that for more than two weeks they haven't received a penny of their pay either, and they have wives and children too. Now, Monsieur Beslay, you have come through the courtyards and you have seen them there armed, sixty-year-olds among them, and I can assure you that they will fight if the Bank, which is in their care, should be attacked.

BESLAY: Such a fight would last two minutes.

DE PLŒUC: Perhaps only one. But what a minute in the history of France!

BESLAY *after a pause*: The Commune has issued a decree requiring the special battalions to be dissolved and merged with the others.

DE PLŒUC: I knew you would say that, monsieur. *He holds up a scroll.* May I show you a decree out of the archives of the Bank and issued by an older revolutionary body, the Convention, signed by Danton, according to which the employees of large administrative institutions are to be stationed, as soldiers, in their own offices?

BESLAY: Monsieur le Marquis, I haven't come here to shed blood but to secure the means by which the defence of Paris and the reopening of its places of work may be effected and financed by the legally elected Commune.

DE PLŒUC: Monsieur Beslay, please do not think that I for one moment question the rights of the Commune. The Bank of France does not engage in politics.

BESLAY: Ah, now we are making progress.

DE PLŒUC: And what I hope with all my heart is that you of the Commune will recognise the rights of the Bank of France which stands above all parties.

BESLAY: Monsieur le Marquis, you are dealing with men of honour not highwaymen.

DE PLŒUC: Monsieur, I knew that the moment you came in. Monsieur Beslay, help me to save the Bank, which is to say the resources of your country, the resources of France.

BESLAY: Monsieur le Marquis, see us in a true light. We work like coolies, eighteen hours a day. We sleep in our clothes, on chairs. For fifteen francs a day every one of us does three or four jobs that to get done before now would have cost the people thirty times as much. There has certainly never been a cheaper government. But now we need ten million.

DE PLŒUC *pained*: Monsieur Beslay!

BESLAY: Monsieur le Marquis, we haven't collected the taxes on tobacco or on daily provisions but we must pay the soldiers and the workers, we can't hold on any longer unless we do. *De Plœuc maintains a meaningful silence.* Unless by early tomorrow we have six million . . .

DE PLŒUC: Six million. I wouldn't be within my rights to give you one. In your sessions you speak of corruption, you accuse Monsieur Thiers of circumventing procedures to come at money, and now here you are yourself, demanding money from me even though no competent financial body exists. *Despairingly.* Set me up a body responsible for finance, I shan't ask how you do it, but show me a piece of paper I can accept as legitimation.

BESLAY: But that will take two weeks. You are perhaps forgetting that we have the power.

DE PLŒUC: But not that I am in the right.

BESLAY: What funds do you have here?

DE PLŒUC: And you know I have a professional obligation to safeguard the confidentiality of the Bank! Do you, of all people, wish to assault such achievements as the confidentiality of our financial, legal and medical affairs? Monsieur Beslay, may I remind you that you too are dealing with a man of honour? Whatever sides we may seem to be on? Let us work together. Let us consider together how best we may satisfy the needs of our great and beloved city without criminally infringing the infinitely numerous but oh so necessary prescriptions of this venerable institution. I am wholly and utterly at your disposal.

BESLAY: Monsieur le Marquis, for peaceful negotiations I am at *your* disposal.

9

a

Hôtel de Ville. Session of the Commune. Beslay is withstanding vehement criticism. At the same time there is great fatigue.

CRIES: Treachery! – Worse: stupidity! – Shall our communards go hungry while we heed Monsieur the Governor of the Bank of France and his 'necessary formalities'? – Enough negotiations, send in a battalion!

BESLAY: Citizens, if you are not satisfied with my work I shall be more than happy to step down. But remember that the resources of France are our resources too and they must be managed thriftily.

CRY: By you or by the Governor?

BESLAY: I flatter myself that I have won over that perhaps rather pedantic but nonetheless honourable man by touching him in his professional pride and by appealing to his expertise to find us a legal way out.

CRIES: We want no appeals to him, we demand his arrest. –

Why is it necessary to find a legal way out for the people to get their own money?

BESLAY: Do you want bankruptcy? Violate the statutes of the Bank and forty million banknotes are worthless. Currency depends on trust.

CRIES: Whose trust? – The bankers'? *Mocking laughter.* – These are delicate questions. Read Proudhon before you answer them. – We have taken possession of the state and now we must husband it.

VARLIN: For whom? This case illustrates that it is not enough to take possession of the apparatus of the state. It was not made for our purposes. Therefore we must smash it. That must be done by violence.

CRIES: No arrests! Let us not begin the new era with terror! Leave that to the old. – All you are doing is interrupting our peaceful work.

LANGEVIN: On the contrary, we are in the process of organising it.

CRIES: Arrest the Governor of the Bank and then read the newspapers! – The bourgeois newspapers? I read them and can't understand why they have not been proscribed.

BESLAY: Citizens, I move that the issue be discussed in camera.

LANGEVIN: I oppose that proposal. Let us make no claim to infallibility as former governments, without exception, have done. Let us make public all our speeches and our deeds. Let us make the people privy to our imperfections, for we have nothing to fear but ourselves. Accordingly, I shall proceed. I shan't speak of the fact that for 200,000 francs the Delegate for War could buy a thousand cavalry horses from the Germans – they are selling everything – but come back to the question of the soldiers' pay, and include another question in it.

CRY: Don't forget here that 200,000 men and their families live on that pay. The rifle is their trowel or spanner, it has to feed them.

RANVIER: I demand that the military situation be discussed.

LANGEVIN: Instead of paying the army a proper rate and

fetching the money to do so from where it is, namely in the Bank of France, on top of that we stint the piece-rates for the women in the artillery works. I move that we cancel all contracts with suppliers who are using competition to force wages down and that we deal only with workshops that are in the hands of workers' associations.

CRY: One thing at a time!

VARLIN: I support Langevin's motion. *To Beslay*: But I'm also in favour of the immediate occupation of the Bank. For the same reasons.

LANGEVIN: One thing on account of the other.

RANVIER: The military aspect must be discussed as well. Don't you see? Three things, all three of them. Because you have no time. Smash the enemy within today or you will be no match for the enemy outside your forts tomorrow.

CRIES: Where shall we find the strength for all that? Our strength will not suffice.

RIGAULT: We negotiate over the needs of the people. Why do we not listen to their proposals? They wish to participate, everywhere and at once. Why not put our trust in their strength? A strength which to many here is still mysterious and, indeed, suspect. The citizens who stormed the Bastille, declared the Revolution in Paris, protected its first steps, bled on the Champ de Mars, took the Tuileries, annihilated the Gironde, swept away priests and cults, were pushed back by Robespierre, rose up in Prairial, vanished for twenty years, surfaced again under the thunder of the Allies' cannon, sank again into darkness, rose again in the year 1830 and being at once confined, filled the first years of the rule of capital with their strugglings and burst the net of steel in 1848, took the bourgeois republic by the throat four months later and, flung down again, broke out rejuvenated in 1868 and rattled the Empire and toppled it and offered themselves again against a foreign invader and were again scorned and insulted till 18 March when they smashed the hand that sought to throttle them. What could we have against the personal intervention of the people? They demand the immediate taking over of the banks and factories into their control and they demand the fight on all fronts but first and foremost the march on Versailles.

Uneasy murmurings.

CRIES: That means civil war! – Bloodshed! – We hear the word 'violence' too often in this place. Beware!

RIGAULT *holding up newspapers*: Then listen to what is being said on the streets of Paris. I quote *La Sociale*, one of the few newspapers that are for us: 'Citizen Delegates, march on Versailles! You will have the 220 battalions of the National Guard behind you, all support you, what are you waiting for? You have been patient too long. March on Versailles! Put your trust in Paris as Paris puts her trust in you! March on Versailles!' Citizens, let us increase this strength by availing ourselves of it.

Murmurings continue.

CRIES: You quote what you ordered! – They are irresponsible men! – Socialism marches without bayonets!

RIGAULT: But bayonets confront it, citizens. The red flag flies over Marseilles and Lyons, but Versailles is arming rural ignorance and prejudice against them. Let us carry the flame of revolt into the country, burst the iron girdle around Paris and strike terror into the big cities!

Continuing murmurings of unease.

CRIES: Military adventures! – Enough of this! – The Commune rejects civil war! – I move: the assembly resumes its peaceable work and will not be disturbed by the attempts of some all too impatient people to plunge Paris into an adventure. – Agreed, but I move that we suppress the hostile newspapers. I name the following: *Le Petit Moniteur*, *Le Petit National*, *Le Bon Sens*, *La Petite Presse*, *La France*, *Le Temps*. – Look around you and study the principles of this assembly!

Mocking laughter among those around Rigault and Varlin. Meanwhile the Chairman has received a message.

CHAIRMAN: Citizen Delegates, I have received a message which will indeed turn the work of this assembly in a new direction.

b

A lobby in the Hôtel de Ville. Delegates and military personnel are entering or leaving the hall. A newspaper seller is selling the Officiel.

NEWSPAPER SELLER: *L'Officiel*! The Versailles traitors have attacked! Papal zouaves and imperial police have entered Neuilly! Women and children among the wounded! Mobilisation of all citizens between the ages of seventeen and thirty-five! The treacherous Versailles government has attacked!

AN OLD BEGGAR *approaching him*: Have you any bread on you?

NEWSPAPER SELLER: Don't you know begging's forbidden? 'Versailles begins the civil war!'

BEGGAR: Can I forbid my belly rumbling?

Two delegates leave the session.

ONE TO THE OTHER: This attack, undertaken with so few troops, is an act of the purest desperation. Elections in the country have gone badly for Monsieur Thiers.

BEGGAR *catching up with them below*: Messieurs, allow me to show you the balloon just leaving Paris. It is visible above the houses.

DELEGATE: Ah, the 'Sociale'? Has it lifted off?

BEGGAR: With proclamations and declarations, ten thousand of them for the country. The land will be given to the peasants. From the balloon! I'm from the country, I am. I know what's what, I'll show you the balloon.

The delegates look upwards through a window.

BEGGAR: Messieurs, the balloon!

DELEGATE: You're a peasant, old friend?

BEGGAR: From the Auvergne, Saint-Antoine.

DELEGATE: And why are you here?

BEGGAR: Take a look at me, can I still pull a plough? That's for the youngsters.

DELEGATE: So you've come to relatives in Paris, eh?

BEGGAR: They had no room.

DELEGATE: And what's your opinion of the Commune?

BEGGAR: Messieurs, at your service. You want what's best, even though you do want to share everything out. God be with you. The balloon, messieurs, a look at it, that will be ten centimes.

DELEGATE: But why are you against the distribution of the land?

BEGGAR: Well, messieurs, they take it away.

DELEGATE: But not from you. You'll get some.

BEGGAR: Pardon me, messieurs, they take it away. Do I still have my own farm, for example? Ten centimes.

DELEGATE: But your children are on it, aren't they?

BEGGAR: You see?

DELEGATE: But that's because you don't have enough land between you.

BEGGAR: Do you mind if I ask you for the ten centimes for showing you the balloon? It will vanish any minute.

DELEGATE: Do you have a lord of the manor in Saint-Antoine?

BEGGAR: Of course we do. Monsieur de Bergeret.

DELEGATE: And are you fond of him?

BEGGAR: Well, monsieur, he does look after his own.

DELEGATE *shaking his head and paying the money*: An enemy. Owning nothing, he defends ownership, even that of the thief who has robbed him! We shall need years to persuade him. *Exit.*

BEGGAR *showing the coin to the newspaper seller*: Ten centimes, a very good balloon! What fools people are! They could have seen it for themselves.

NEWSPAPER SELLER: 'Women and children among the wounded!' Come here and give over swindling. Take a bundle, stand by the other staircase and shout after me. You'll get a centime a paper.

He gives him a bundle. The beggar repeats the newspaper seller's cries.

BOTH: *L'Officiel.* Mobilisation of all citizens between the ages of seventeen and thirty-five!

C

Night sitting of the Commune. Some delegates are working on papers, others are conferring together, one is giving advice to a woman and child.

CHAIRMAN: Given that it would be unwise for this assembly to intervene in military affairs and despite the uncertain state of the fighting in and around Malmaison, we shall continue with our deliberations. Citizen Langevin.

LANGEVIN: Whereas the first principle of the Republic is freedom; whereas freedom of conscience is the first of all freedoms; whereas the clergy have been complicit in the crimes of the monarchy against freedom, I move that the Commune decree the separation of church and state. – Further to that, I urge the Delegate for Education to require all teaching staff to remove from their classrooms all crucifixes, images of the Virgin and other symbolic objects and to hand over all such objects that are in metal to the Mint.

CHAIRMAN *counting the raised hands*: Carried.

CRIES: We hear complaints that wounded communards are being treated negligently by Catholic nurses. – And what about the plan to have reading rooms in the hospitals? For most workers their time in hospital is the only time they get to educate themselves.

CHAIRMAN *receiving a message*: Citizen Delegates, Battalion Leader André Farreaux, returned from the front, wishes, despite being severely wounded, to appear before you and to make a report.

An officer of the National Guard is carried in on a stretcher.

CHAIRMAN: Citizen Farreaux, I invite you to address us.

OFFICER: Citizen Delegates, Asnières is in our hands.

Excitement. Cries of 'Long live the Commune!' and 'Long live the National Guard!'

OFFICER: Citizens, having been wounded and obliged to leave the fighting, I should like now, with the permission of the Delegate for War, to offer for your consideration certain problems which are hampering your troops in their operations and making even the victories very costly. Our men are fighting like lions, but show precious little interest in being properly armed. Since every battery, drawn from a particular *quartier*, insists on its rights of ownership of its own cannons, we have out of a total of 1,740 cannons only 320 at our disposal for action.

CRIES: Remember the peculiar nature of our army, without precedent in the history of the world. These people cast their cannons themselves, Citizen Officer.

OFFICER: Not on their own account, Citizen Delegate. That may be why they can't deploy them on their own account. Our cannons are being used like muskets or not at all. And everybody wants to shoot but nobody wants to pull a baggage cart. And everyone chooses his own commander and where he wants to go and fight.

VARLIN: What are your origins, Citizen Officer?

OFFICER: Graduate of the School of Artillery at Vincennes, formerly Captain in the Regular Army.

VARLIN: Why are you fighting with the Commune?

ONE OF THE STRETCHER-BEARERS: He's for us.

VARLIN: You know that barely two days ago the Commune decreed the abolition of the rank of general? *The officer says nothing.* I suppose you wish to suggest we put trained officers in command?

OFFICER: War is a profession, Citizen Delegate.

VARLIN: You are doing this with the agreement of the Delegate for War, who has not appeared himself?

OFFICER: Who, contrary to all the rules of the art of war, is fighting in the very front line.

RANVIER: Citizen Delegates, I understand this man to be saying that to put an end to giving orders we must ourselves first learn to give them. Citizen Farreaux, we wish you a speedy recovery. Do not misunderstand the silence of this assembly. Silence does not always mean unwillingness to learn. Our difficulties are great, they have never been encountered before. But they will be overcome. The Commune approves your report.
The officer is carried out.

RANVIER: Citizen Delegates, you have a victory and you have a true report. Use both. You have the troops, the enemy has trained officers. He has no troops like yours. Overcome your well-founded mistrust of people whom until now you have only ever seen on the opposing side. They are not all against you. Add expert knowledge to the Commune's enthusiasm and your victory is certain.

Applause.

d

Session of the Commune.

CHAIRMAN: Citizen Delegates, I interrupt our discussion of the reports on the favourable progress of military operations around Neuilly to read out to you what August Bebel said yesterday in the German Reichstag: 'All the proletariat of Europe and all who have a feeling for freedom in their hearts, look towards Paris. The war-cry of the Parisian proletariat "Death to want and poverty! Death to idle luxury!" will become the war-cry of all the proletariat of Europe.' Citizens, I call on you to rise from your seats in honour of the workers of Germany.

All rise.

VARLIN *calmly*: Long live the Workers' International! Workers of the world, unite!

10

Frankfurt. The opera, during a performance of Norma. *The door of a box opens. Bismarck in the uniform of a cuirassier and Jules Favre in civilian dress emerge.*

BISMARCK *lighting a cigar*: Another thing, Favre – I say, you've gone very grey, haven't you? – Here you are in Frankfurt now signing the peace, but what's happening in Paris, eh? Get that red flag off the town hall, will you? It's been there long enough. I've had a few sleepless nights already over their wretched carryings-on. Damned bad example for the rest of Europe, wants exterminating with fire and brimstone like Sodom and Gomorrah. *Hearkens to the music, audible because he has left the door of the box open.* Altmann is superb! As a woman too, good build. You know – *accompanied in servile fashion by Favre he continues his smoker's perambulation* – you're a funny crew. You coyly refuse our offer of military assistance, but we're to let you have your prisoners, by the back door. I know, I know, it mustn't happen with the help of a foreign power. Like the old song, eh?: 'Oh Theodore keep your hands off me/ Except when no one's there to see.' *Again he hearkens to the music.* Now she's dying. Magnificent! But then that rabble of ours in the Reichstag want us to hand over Bonaparte. No chance. I'm keeping him up my sleeve, to keep you on a tight lead. Ho, ho! I'll hand over the common man and he can bleed the comrades in Paris for you. That will be a surprise. War or no war, we must have order. I'll give the arch enemy a hand, just where she wants it, eh Favre? But we'll have freed you 200,000 men before long . . . And by the way, have you got the pennies to pay for them?

FAVRE: I'm at liberty to tell you now, that was our greatest worry, but it has been settled. The Bank of France. To date we've been able to draw 257 million.

BISMARCK: Well, well. Not at all bad. Another thing: what guarantee have you got that the chums won't fraternise as they did on 18 March?

FAVRE: We've looked out units we can be sure of, people with a peasant background. And besides, the agitators couldn't get at the prisoners-of-war, could they?

BISMARCK: Fine, perhaps we're over the worst. But as I said, I want action. Understand? I've let you delay reparations till after the pacification of Paris. But now be so good as to get a move on. *Hearkening to the music.* Fabulous, the way she does it. And I don't want any accidents, Favre, the first cheque goes to Bleichröder, I trust him, he's my own banker, see he gets his commission, will you? Altmann is excellent.

11

a

Hôtel de Ville.

It is late at night, the hall is empty. Langevin, who has been working till now, is fetched by Geneviève.

LANGEVIN: You complain that there's no money for school meals. Do you know how much Beslay triumphantly brought back from the Bank yesterday, for building barricades? 11,300 francs. What mistakes we are making, what mistakes we have made! Of course we should have marched on Versailles at once, on 18 March. Had we had the time. But the people only ever have one hour. Woe betide them if they are not ready when it strikes, fully armed and able to attack!

GENEVIÈVE: But what a people! I wanted to go to the concert for the ambulance units in the Tuileries this evening. They expected a few hundred, tens of thousands came. I got stuck in a crowd that seemed to have no end. And not a word of complaint!

LANGEVIN: They are patient with us. *Looks at the inscriptions on the wall.* 1. The Right to Life. That's it, but how did we attempt to push it through? Look at the other points. They all look good but what are they in reality? Number 2! Is that also the freedom to do business, to live off the people, to plot against the people and to serve the enemies of the people? Number 3! But what do their consciences prescribe to them? I'll tell you: what the rulers have prescribed to them, since infancy. Number 4! So is it permitted to the sharks on the stock exchange, the polyps in the venal press, the butcher generals and all the smaller bloodsuckers to congregate in Versailles and discharge against us all the 'opinions' guaranteed in Number 5? Is the freedom to lie a guaranteed freedom also? And in Number 6 do we permit the election of deceivers? By a people confused by their schools, their church, their press and their politicians? And where in all this is our right to occupy the Bank of France which holds the wealth that we heaped up with our bare hands? With that money we could have bribed all the generals and politicians, ours and Herr von Bismarck's as well. We should have put only one point on the statutes: *our* right to life!

GENEVIÈVE: Why didn't we?

LANGEVIN: For the sake of freedom, which we know nothing

about. We should have been prepared, as the members of a body fighting for its life, to forgo personal freedom until the freedom of all had been achieved.

GENEVIÈVE: But weren't we anxious not to stain our hands with blood?

LANGEVIN: We were. But in this struggle the hands not bloodstained are the hands chopped off.

b

Session of the Commune. Coming and going of Guards with messages. Now and then delegates leave the session in haste. Every sign of immense fatigue. The busyness subsides as distant cannon fire becomes audible.

DELESCLUZE: Citizen Delegates, you hear the cannon of Versailles. The final struggle is beginning.

Pause.

RIGAULT: In the interests of security I have allowed a delegation of women from the eleventh arrondissement to appear before you to present you, at this juncture, with certain wishes of the people of Paris.

Agreement.

DELESCLUZE: Citizens, you have made me Delegate for War. The seemingly limitless task of making good the damage of war, of converting a national war into a social war, and in addition blows from outside such as Bismarck's handing over 150,000 prisoners-of-war to Versailles, these and other things have not left us time to develop the particular strengths of the proletariat in an area remote and new to them, namely the conduct of war. We have tried all sorts of generals. Those from below, from our own ranks, do not understand the new weapons; those from above who have taken our side do not understand the new men. Our fighters, having just shaken off the tyranny of the factory-owners, will not be commanded as though they were puppets. Their inventiveness and their reckless courage seem to the trained officers to be so much want of discipline. For the relief of Fort Issy our Supreme

Commander Rossel demanded 10,000 men by the next morning. Through personal appeals by various delegates 7,000 were got together. So Monsieur Rossel, wanting 3,000 for his round number, rode off, leaving Fort Issy to the Versailles forces who, herded up in their barracks, are always available. What's more, Monsieur Rossel issues a communiqué to the reactionary newspapers saying that all is lost.

RANVIER: The great surgeon, needed for the operation, who washes his hands in lysol, or, if there is no lysol, then in innocence.

DELESCLUZE: Now we have come to the point where all must be decided, and what will decide it is street fighting. Now we must man the barricades, which military specialists despise. Now the people themselves will fight in person for their streets and for their homes. Citizen Delegates, we shall go into the fight as into a job of work, and we shall do it well. Citizens, should our enemy succeed in turning Paris into a grave it will at least never be the grave of our ideas. *Loud applause, many rise to their feet. Three female workers are escorted in by members of the National Guard.*

DELESCLUZE: Citizen Delegates, the delegates of the eleventh arrondissement.

The meeting comes to order. A few delegates come down to meet the women.

ONE DELEGATE: Citizens, you fetch spring with you into the Hôtel de Ville.

WOMAN: Have no fear. *Laughter.* Citizen Delegates, I have a communication for you. It is brief.

CRY: It's twenty pages long.

WOMAN: Quiet, little man, those are only the signatures, 552 of them. *Laughter.* Citizen Delegates, yesterday afternoon notices were put up in our district urging us, the women of Paris, to be the mediators of a reconciliation with the so-called government in Versailles. We reply: there can be no reconciliation between freedom and despotism, between the people and the butchers of the people. Workers, men and women, belong on the barricades. It was said on 4 September: after our forts, our ramparts; after our ramparts, our barricades; after our barricades, our bodies. *Applause.* We alter that. After our barricades, our houses; after our houses: mines and booby-traps. *Increasing applause.* But having said that, we appeal to you, Delegates of the Commune, not to make a spade out of an axe. Citizens, four days ago the cartridge factory in the avenue Rapp blew up; more than forty women working there were maimed, four houses collapsed. The perpetrators have not been arrested. And why is it only the ones who want to who go to work or into battle? Citizen Delegates, this is not a complaint against you, don't misunderstand us, but as citizens we have grounds to fear that the weakness of the members of the Commune – I beg your pardon, that has been changed – that the weakness of some – I beg your pardon, I can't read it, it has been crossed out – that the weakness of many . . . Citizen Delegates, we couldn't reach agreement on this point. *Scornful laughter.* Well then, that the weakness of some members of the Commune will bring to nothing our plans for the future. You promised to look after us and our children and I'd rather know mine dead than in the hands of Versailles, but we don't want to lose them through weakness. 552 from the eleventh arrondissement. Good day, citizens.

Exit the women.

VARLIN *leaping to his feet*: Citizen Delegates, the wives of the Versailles soldiers weep, so we hear, but our wives do not weep. Will you stand idle and deliver them up to an enemy who has never shrunk from violence? We were told in this place a few weeks ago that no military operations were necessary, that Thiers had no troops and in the eyes of the enemy it would be a declaration of civil war. But our bourgeoisie without a second thought allied itself with the enemy of France to wage a civil war against us and was given troops by him, the captured sons of peasants from the Vendée, rested men, inaccessible to our influence. There is no conflict between two bourgeoisies that could prevent them from at once joining forces against the proletariat of one or the other land. And then we were told in this place: no terror, what would become of the New Age? But

Versailles is practising terror and will butcher us all so that the New Age will never come to be. If we are flung down it will be because we were merciful, which is to say negligent, and because we were peaceable, which is to say ignorant. Citizens, we beg you, at this late stage let us learn from the enemy.

Applause and unease.

RIGAULT: Citizens, if you stopped raising your voices to spare your deadly enemy, you would hear his cannon. *Silence in the hall. The thunder of cannon again becomes audible.* Do not doubt it, he will be pitiless. Now as he makes ready for the copious spilling of this city's blood his spies and saboteurs and agents are among us everywhere. *He holds up a folder.* The names are here, I have been offering them to you for weeks. The Archbishop of Paris does more than say his prayers. The Governor of the Bank of France has a use for the people's money that he withholds from you. Fort Caen was sold to Versailles for 120,000 francs. In the Place Vendôme, in the rubble of the monument of militarism, the exact plans of our ramparts are openly on sale. Our enraged women fling the agents into the Seine. Shall we fish them out? But in Versailles 235 captured National Guards were shot like rabid dogs and they give our nursing sisters to the firing squads. When shall we begin our counter measures?

CRY: Citizens, we have discussed this. We decided that we do not wish to do what the enemies of humanity are doing. They are monsters, we are not.

Applause.

VARLIN: The question 'Inhumanity or humanity?' will be decided by the historical question 'Their state or our state?'

CRY: We don't want any state, since we don't want any oppression.

VARLIN: Their state or our state.

CRY: We cannot except ourselves from oppression if we go over to oppressing. But we are fighting for freedom.

VARLIN: If you want freedom you must first suppress the oppressors. And give up as much of your freedom as is necessary for that end. You can have only one freedom: the freedom to fight the oppressors.

RIGAULT: Terror against terror, suppress or be suppressed, smash or be smashed!

Sounds of great unease.

CRIES: No, no! – That means dictatorship. – Tomorrow it will be us you smash! – You demand the execution of the Archbishop of Paris and you have us in your sights because we oppose it. – All they that take the sword shall perish with the sword.

VARLIN *very loud*: And they that don't take the sword?

Brief silence.

CRY: The Commune's generosity will bear fruit. Let it be said of the Commune: they burned the guillotine.

RIGAULT: And left the Bank alone! Generosity! Citizens, the Commune resolved to adopt even the orphans of the soldiers killed fighting for Thiers. It supplied with bread the wives of ninety-two who came to murder us. Widows belong to no party. The Republic has bread for all who are in misery and kisses for all who are orphaned. And that is right. But where is there action against murder, which I call the active side of generosity? Don't say to me 'Equal rights for those who fight in their camp or in ours.' The people do not fight as wrestlers or traders fight. Or as those nations which take account of the interests of such traders. The people fight as the judge fights evildoers or the doctor cancer. And still all I'm asking for is terror against terror, even though we alone have the right to terror.

CRY: That is blasphemy! Do you deny that the use of violence debases the man who uses it?

RIGAULT: No, I do not deny it.

CRIES: Silence him! Speeches like that discredit us. Look around you. We are not so many as we were in March. Delescluze, you speak to us! Delescluze! Delescluze!

DELESCLUZE: Citizens, you see me undecided, I confess. For so long now I too have solemnly spoken out against the use of violence. 'Disprove,' I said, 'the rooted opinion that justice has need of violence. For once, at long last, let justice prevail by the work of our bare hands. Lies have to be written in blood, truth can be written in ink,' I said. 'In a few weeks the Commune of Paris has done more for the dignity of man than all other regimes in the course of eight centuries. Let us continue calmly bringing order into human dealings and putting an end to the exploitation of man by man,' I said. 'Let us dedicate ourselves to our working people who are useful to all who are not harmful pests. Then the two or three score exploiters in Versailles will see the host of slaves around them melt away like snow in the spring sun. The voice of reason, untainted by anger, will stop our murderers in their tracks, the simple sentence "you are workers like us" will bring them running into our welcoming arms.' That is what I said, and many of you said the same. May I and may you be forgiven if we were deceiving ourselves. I ask those delegates still opposed to reprisals to raise their hands.

Slowly most raise their hands.

DELESCLUZE: Citizen Delegates, you will be issued with arms.

National Guardsmen have entered laden with rifles. They distribute them among the delegates.

DELESCLUZE: Citizen Delegates, we shall continue with the business in hand. The next item is the organisation of a commission for the education of women.

NONE OR ALL

1
Who will deliver you, slave?
Comrade, those deepest below
They are the ones who will see you
They, when you cry out, will hear you
Slaves will deliver you, slave.
  None or all, all or nothing it will be.
  No one can set himself free.
  Guns or chains it must be.
  None or all, all or nothing it will be.

2
You who are hungry, who'll feed you?
Do you want bread for your hunger?

Come to us, we also suffer.
Come to us, let us guide you
We, the hungry, we'll feed you.
  None or all, all or nothing it will be.
  No one can set himself free.
  Guns or chains it must be.
  None or all, all or nothing it will be.

3
For vengeance, where will you look?
Comrade of ours, whom they beat
Join with all they maltreat
We are like you, we are weak.
We are the avengers you seek.
  None or all, all or nothing it will be.
  No one can set himself free.
  Guns or chains it must be.
  None or all, all or nothing it will be.

4
You who are lost, who will dare?
Whoever's too wretched to bear
More must join with those now
Desperate: they're making sure
Today is the day, not tomorrow.
  None or all, all or nothing it will be.
  No one can set himself free.
  Guns or chains it must be.
  None or all, all or nothing it will be.

12

Place Pigalle, Easter Sunday 1871. Jean Cabet, François Faure and two children are working at a barricade. Babette Cherron and Geneviève Guéricault are stitching sandbags. Distant thunder of cannon. Geneviève has been singing a song to the children who are mixing mortar in a wooden bath with shovels bigger than themselves.

CHILD: Would you sing it again, please, mademoiselle.

GENEVIÈVE: Yes, but that's the last time. *She sings.*

Eastertide. Fair on the Seine
For Grandpa and everyone.
All the blue rowing boats down there
Are painted fresh again.
Looking for Easter eggs you hear
Among the trees, from far away
The little children swear
Getting towards mid-day.
At table under the greenery
We tell what fun it's been
And we'll go fishing at Ivry
At Eastertide next year.

CHILD *singing after her*: At Eastertide next year.

SECOND CHILD *to Jean*: Do you and Babette sleep together?

JEAN: Yes.

CHILD: She's going to have a baby, isn't she?

JEAN: Mm. Because she fell in love with me.

BABETTE: You fell in love with me.

JEAN: Whatever. But she started it, let me tell you.

BABETTE: How did I start it? I never said a word. It was you.

JEAN: Yes, I know. But your eyes.

BABETTE: And yours? *To François*: What are you sulking for?

FRANÇOIS: I don't like the way you said 'Philippe has run away'. You have to look at it scientifically, that is dispassionately. I assume the fight seemed to him hopeless, whereas it doesn't to us. Therefore he leaves Paris.

JEAN: Us you mean. Us fighting.

FRANÇOIS: Not us, only the hopeless fight.

JEAN: Unfortunately we can't leave Paris as easily as that. Why? The leaves can't leave the tree. Woodlice can. Philippe's a louse.

FRANÇOIS: I shall have to knock your teeth out, Jean.

JEAN: But dispassionately, if you don't mind.

FRANÇOIS *helplessly*: Oh Jean, we don't know anything. *Pause*. What you are thinking could perhaps be expressed so: Philippe is not an especially brave person because he hasn't learned to think.

JEAN: Good.

BABETTE: Geneviève, if I move in with Jean will you be able to pay the rent on your own?

Pause.

GENEVIÈVE: Yes, Babette.

JEAN: Oh damn it, must you women always be talking about the future?

GENEVIÈVE *softly*: She must, Jean.

FRANÇOIS: It's bad that we are cut off from the country. We can't speak to France.

GENEVIÈVE: They can think for themselves.

JEAN: Babette, that reminds me, we must fetch what we painted. One thing is certain: if they attack, Paris will be their grave, eh François?

They carry on working. Enter Mme Cabet.

MME CABET: Very sorry, I felt a real need to go to early morning mass and last night I stitched four extra bags. Now you shall have your Easter presents.

She hands François a parcel.

FRANÇOIS *opening it*: Lavoisier! Only yesterday I wanted to look up something particular in him.

MME CABET: Oh Jules and Victor, I'm sorry, you should have had yours first. *She gives each of them a bread roll.* Jean, this is a tie, I shortened the flag a bit, Papa was vexed but I did it anyway. I've got nothing for you, Geneviève, but I'll shake hands with you. *She shakes hands with Geneviève.* It's always so embarrassing when you haven't got a present to give, isn't it? And this is for you and really for somebody else, Babette, you know who I mean, don't you? *She gives Babette an Easter egg.* Next Easter he'll have one like that.

JEAN: *She* will.

They laugh.

MME CABET: And now I'd like you to come upstairs with me. There's a drop of wine left.

All follow her except Geneviève. Then when Geneviève also stands up she sees two nuns coming towards her.

FIRST NUN *softly*: Geneviève.

GENEVIÈVE *runs towards the nun and embraces her*: Guy!

GUY: Softly, my darling. Was it very bad?

GENEVIÈVE: But why are you dressed up like this? Seven months!

GUY: Can you take us to your room? Do you live on your own? And can you get me a razor? My blasted beard!

GENEVIÈVE: But why all the secrecy? You're here now and safe. Did you escape?

GUY: No, I'll explain everything, in your room.

GENEVIÈVE: But I don't live on my own any more. Babette's there, she might come in at any moment. I mean, if you don't want anybody to see. Guy, you're not in Paris against the Commune, are you? Not for Thiers?

GUY: Oh so you're still for the International, are you? Despite all the atrocities?

GENEVIÈVE: What atrocities?

GUY: Enough. The time for revolutionary and sloppy humanitarian speeches is over. Now it's serious. The whole of France is sick of your looting and violence.

GENEVIÈVE: So you've become a spy for the butcher Thiers?

GUY: Geneviève. We can't discuss that out on the street. I've been spotted, I didn't want to involve you, my damned beard forced me. After all, we are engaged, or we were, that might be more accurate. You can't let me perish and the sisters of Saint Joseph are involved as well. You're a Catholic, aren't you, or is that over and done with as well?

GENEVIÈVE: Yes, Guy, it is.

GUY: A nice way to treat me! And all out on the street!

GENEVIÈVE: The street is a good place. We are just getting ready to defend our homes on the street.

GUY: That is all utter madness. Versailles is ready to march in, three army corps. And if you hand me over ... *He reaches under his nun's habit for a pistol.*

PAPA *who has arrived with Coco and has witnessed some of the foregoing*: One moment, monsieur. *He levels his rifle at him.* You have some interesting friends, mademoiselle.

GENEVIÈVE: Monsieur Guy Suitry, my fiancé, Papa.

The nun Guy arrived with suddenly runs away.

PAPA: Stop her, Coco. Or him. *To Geneviève*: Explain.

GENEVIÈVE *while Coco chases the nun*: Monsieur Suitry was a prisoner-of-war in Germany. Now he's on business in Paris for Monsieur Thiers.

GUY: Geneviève!

PAPA: Oh. I'm sorry, Geneviève.

COCO *returning*: No breasts, but female. This one goes up against a wall. And then a little visit to the Convent Saint Joseph. *With his bayonet he prods Guy to the barricade.* Turn round.

FRANÇOIS *arriving*: Geneviève, why didn't you come up? What's happening here?

PAPA: Geneviève's Guy has come back. Bismarck gave him back to Thiers so he could come and spy on us here. And the nuns of Saint Joseph mercifully took him in. *To Guy*: Turn round.

FRANÇOIS: You can't do that. You can arrest him.

PAPA: Then he goes off to the Petite Roquette and can eat cutlets with his Eminence the Archbishop. Unfortunately our people in the Commune are trying to be even more merciful than Saint Joseph, till we're all up against a wall. *To Guy*: No, you won't be telling anyone what you've seen in the rue Pigalle.

FRANÇOIS: Nothing rash, Papa.

PAPA: Oh so that's being rash, is it? General Gervaise sells one of our forts to Versailles but I'm being rash, am I? Of course, you people here think I'm in a bit deeper than you are and that explains why I'm not very gentle. *To Geneviève*: There was that certain morning when we met and I hadn't slept, remember?

GENEVIÈVE: Citizen Goule, I have learned in the meantime that the motto must be: 'All for one and one for all'. And even if it was only to defend you I would not leave this barricade.

PAPA *uncertainly*: I think I understand you.

FRANÇOIS: Madame Cabet won't allow it, Papa. Let Geneviève decide, don't do anything in haste. Geneviève, tell them you don't want that. You mustn't think we'll think it's because he's your fiancé. Speak to them, Geneviève. *Geneviève says nothing.*

PAPA: Very well, Geneviève. Go indoors.

COCO: Turn round, you.

Enter Mme Cabet with the children.

MME CABET: Jean and Babette wanted to be on their own. Love, I ask you! Better than stitching sandbags. What are you doing?

COCO: Not a nun, Madame Cabet. Geneviève's fiancé, a spy.

MME CABET: Why's he standing up against the wall? He's not feeling well, you can see that, can't you? *Nobody speaks.* No! Don't do that, not on Easter Sunday. And in front of the children! Not in front of the children! Absolutely not! Hand him over to the police, that's bad enough for Geneviève. You come with me and have a glass of wine. You need it. Now don't do anything stupid here.

PAPA *vexed*: The devil take the lot of you. They'll stamp you out like vermin. Quick march, swine, say thank you to the children, they're the ones who decide in Paris.

He and Coco lead Guy away.

FRANÇOIS *to the children*: Let's get to work.

They begin their work again. Mme Cabet tries to lead Geneviève away but she shakes her head and sits down to stitch sandbags.

FRANÇOIS: There are bad people on our side too. The battalions are even enlisting criminals now.

MME CABET: Yes. Being with us is the only good thing they will ever do.

FRANÇOIS: At the top too. People working for their own advantage.

MME CABET: We get what we get.

FRANÇOIS: I'll have to chop the apple tree down.

MME CABET: Do we really have to? *Enter Jean and Babette.* Jean and Babette, François wants to chop down the apple tree.

BABETTE: No.

JEAN: We'll never make a proper barricade with it in the way. But we'll leave it if you want. *Pats the barrel of the cannon.* Ammunition or no ammunition it's good to have you, whatever the generals say, our own included. *He and Babette unroll a linen banner*: 'You are workers like us'. There's my statement, François. *They hang it over the barricade, the writing towards the attackers.* We have to tell them.

MME CABET: I don't know, Jean, if it's those they had in the army before, from the provinces . . . farm labourers working sixteen hours a day and the sons of debt-ridden grocer women, even the cobblers think they're something better than workers.

JEAN: Perhaps they'll think again when they see the words along with our bullets, maman.

13

Place Pigalle, May, during Bloody Week. At the barricade, ready to fire, stand Geneviève Guéricault, Jean Cabet, François Faure and two civilians. The German cuirassier is dragging a crate of ammunition after Papa into the corner of the wall. A badly wounded woman, a stranger, is lying in a sheltered place. Heavy artillery fire. Rolling of drums, which signifies attacks in neighbouring streets. The apple tree is in full bloom.

FRANÇOIS *shouting loudly*: Langevin and Coco would have been here long ago if they were still alive. It's three days now.

PAPA: Coco's alive. And if Paris can send them home today with bloody noses the whole Versailles rabble will melt away, once and for all.

FRANÇOIS: They are heavily armed. With mitrailleuses. Have you noticed how the New Age always gives its weapons to the hyenas of the Old Age first?

PAPA: On 18 March we'd have cleared out the lot of them in two hours.

FRANÇOIS: What do you think, Jean?

JEAN: As I told you once before, we know nothing.

GENEVIÈVE: At least we're learning now, Jean.

JEAN: As we croak. Much good that will do us.

GENEVIÈVE: It will do some good, Jean. Here they come again.

JEAN: Not yet. What good is knowing to me and you, Geneviève, when we're dead?

GENEVIÈVE: I'm not talking about me and you. I said 'we'. 'We' are more than me and you.

JEAN: I only hope 'we' will be out in force alongside us and behind us now.

It has got rather quieter.

WOUNDED WOMAN *suddenly clear*: Friends, I live at 15 rue des Cygnes, write on the wall, will you, near the door, for my husband, what's happened to me, my name is Jardain.

FRANÇOIS: I will, 15 rue des Cygnes.

WOUNDED WOMAN: We wanted to go on fighting the Prussians because we were told they wouldn't give us back the prisoners straight away. Isn't that right? They had two of mine. Now they are coming back, like that. *She points over the barricade*. What things they must have told them about us! Now I feel bad again. *She sinks back and becomes delirious.*

FRANÇOIS: They have to do it. That's what makes them so raving mad.

JEAN: We ought to carry her indoors.

FRANÇOIS: Not if she doesn't want. She's frightened the house will burn.

JEAN: But she's in the way here.

FRANÇOIS: Not very much, Jean. And she was fighting, wasn't she?

JEAN: Yes, she can handle a gun.

Drums very near.

JEAN: That's in the rue Bac.

Enter Pierre Langevin followed by a child.

LANGEVIN *trying to shoo the child away*: Run along, that's an order, you're only in the way here. *The child moves back, but then halts, waiting for him.* They need reinforcements in the rue Bac.

JEAN *shrugging his shoulders*: Where's Coco?

LANGEVIN *shakes his head, glancing at Papa, then*: Can you spare the cuirassier?

PAPA: *Salut*, Coco. No, he only understands my language. What's happening in the Hôtel de Ville?

LANGEVIN: There's no one left there. They're on the barricades. Delescluze was killed in the Place du Château d'Eau. Vermorel is wounded, Varlin is fighting in the rue Lafayette. The slaughter at the Gare du Nord is such that women are rushing into the streets, boxing the officers' ears and putting themselves up against the wall.

Langevin goes on his way, the child following him.

JEAN: Things are bad, he didn't ask after Mother.

Mme Cabet and Babette bring soup.

MME CABET: Children, you must eat, but there's no chives in it. And why must you wear your kepis? When we've done all we can, they'll only give you away. You'll have to eat with the serving-spoon . . .

Handing Jean the serving-spoon, she collapses.

JEAN: Maman!

FRANÇOIS: From the roofs.

PAPA *roaring*: Take cover! It's only her arm.

He runs out and drags Mme Cabet away, into the house. Babette, stunned, collects up the pan and the spoon. Halfway to the house she also falls.

GENEVIÈVE *restraining Jean*: Jean, you mustn't go.

JEAN: But she isn't badly hit.

GENEVIÈVE: Yes, she is.

JEAN: She isn't.

FRANÇOIS: They're coming. Fire! *He fires.*

JEAN *back at the barricade, he fires too*: You swine! You swine! You swine!

One of the civilians runs away. Papa comes back. Regular soldiers advance from the street on the left, they kneel and fire. François falls. The salvo has torn down the banner. Jean points to it and falls. Geneviève takes the red flag from the barricade and withdraws with it into the corner where Papa and the cuirassier are firing. The cuirassier falls. Geneviève is hit.

GENEVIÈVE: Long live the . . . *She falls.*

Mme Cabet drags herself out of the house and sees those who have fallen. Papa and the remaining civilian carry on firing. From all the surrounding streets regular soldiers advance with fixed bayonets against the barricade.

14

From the walls of Versailles the bourgeoisie watch the end of the Commune through lorgnettes and opera glasses.

BOURGEOISE: My only concern is lest they escape towards Saint-Ouen.

GENTLEMAN: No fear of that, madame. We signed an agreement two days ago with the Crown Prince of Saxony. The Germans won't let anyone escape. Where is the picnic basket, Emilie?

ANOTHER GENTLEMAN: What a noble spectacle! The fires, the mathematical movements of the troops, the boulevards! Now we appreciate the genius of Haussmann in providing Paris with boulevards. There was some discussion as to whether they contribute to the beautifying of the capital. But there can be no doubt now that at the very least they have contributed to its pacification.

Huge explosion. The company applauds.

VOICES: That was the Mairie de Montmartre, an especially pernicious den.

DUCHESS: The glasses, Annette. *Looks through the opera glasses.* Splendid!

LADY NEXT TO HER: If only the poor Archbishop had lived to witness this! It was a little unkind of Him not to swap His Eminence for that Blanqui fellow.

DUCHESS: Nonsense, my dear. He explained it perfectly, with Latin clarity. That worshipper of violence Blanqui was worth a whole army corps to the rabble and the murder of the Archbishop, God have mercy on his soul, was worth two army corps to us. Oh, here He comes himself.

Enter Thiers accompanied by an adjutant, Guy Suitry. The company applauds him, he smiles and bows.

DUCHESS *softly*: Monsieur Thiers, this will make you immortal. You have given back Paris to her true mistress, to France.

THIERS: France, mesdames et messieurs . . . France is you.

Final chorus.

Turandot
or
The Whitewashers' Congress

Translator: TOM KUHN

Characters:

The Emperor of China · Turandot, his daughter · Yao Yel, his brother · The Dowager Empress · Her doctor · A cleaner · The Prime Minister · The Court Tui · The Minister for War · Xi Wei, Chairman of the Association of Tuis · Ke Lei, Dean of the Imperial University · Munka Du · His mother · His two sisters · His secretary · His portrait artist · Nu Shan, Secretary to Xi Wei · Wen, another Tui · Wang, Secretary of the Tui Academy · Gu, Ka Mü, Mo Si and Shi Ka · A Sha Sen, an old peasant · Er Fei, his grandson · A clerk · A waiter · Gogher Gogh, a bandit · Ma Gogh, his mother · Two bodyguards · Turandot's two maidservants · Two Union Tuis · The delegate of the Clothesmakers · The delegate of the Clothesless · A teacher · Si Fu, a pupil · Pupils · A scribe · Shi Me, a young Tui · Meh Nei, leader of a group of young Tuis · The geographer Pauder Mel · An unknown head on the city wall · The hangman · The Tui for General Education · The Tui for Economics · The Tui for Medicine · The Tui for Love-Life · A street-seller · Customers · Qiung, Su and Yao, washerwomen · A swordsmith · Woman at the window · Tuis · Armed men · Bandits · Officers · Soldiers · Members of the Clothesless

The Tuis are characterised by small hats after the style of Tibetan or European priests. The hats differ according to the importance of the Tui, more or less decorative, and of different colours.

I

IN THE IMPERIAL PALACE

A cleaner is scrubbing the floor. The Emperor sweeps in, followed by the Court Tui and the Prime Minister, both in Tui-hats.

EMPEROR: I'm beside myself. It's bad enough to have to hear how the state is being brought to the edge of ruin by mismanagement and corruption. But then to cancel my second breakfast pipe! That's too much! I'm the Emperor of China, I don't see why I should put up with it.

PRIME MINISTER: Your heart, Your Majesty! It was on account of your heart!

EMPEROR: My heart! If my heart is suffering, then it's because people don't take me seriously. Last week they took away two hundred of my racehorses – am I not to go riding any more? I was silent then . . .

PRIME MINISTER: Silent!

EMPEROR: Well, as near as dammit silent. And today I discover that my second pipe has been cancelled. My heart! The revenues are slipping away! They left it to me to choose between the silk monopoly and the cotton monopoly. I was all for silk. But they said, take the cotton. Nobody I know wears cotton, they all wear silk. But all right, I thought, maybe the common people wear cotton, all right, I'll wager on the people. And now I'm bankrupt! *To his brother, Yao Yel, who has just entered*: Yao Yel, I'm abdicating.

YAO YEL: And why, pray, this time?

COURT TUI: China without its Emperor!

PRIME MINISTER: Unthinkable! We'll have to adjust the revenue accounts.

EMPEROR: They shouldn't cancel my morning pipe, if they value me even a little bit.

CLEANER *to whom the Court Tui has been whispering*: Emperor Sir, you mustn't leave us. *She kneels down, in response to a gesture from the Court Tui.* A simple woman of the people, I beg you to continue to bear the burden of the crown.

EMPEROR: I'm moved, but I can't do it, my good woman. I simply can't afford to be Emperor. *To Yao Yel*: And you're to blame, don't contradict me. If I hadn't agreed to transfer the monopoly to you ...

PRIME MINISTER *with a glance at the cleaner*: Your Majesty formally abjured the monopoly, so that no one could maintain ...

COURT TUI: ... that His Majesty had anything to do with business.

EMPEROR: Exactly! So that someone could make a decent profit. And are we making a profit? I demand to see the accounts.

YAO YEL *angrily*: I've heard enough of this. *He pulls the cleaner forward.* What did you pay for the headscarf?

CLEANER: Ten yen.

YAO YEL: When? When did you buy it?

CLEANER: Three years ago.

YAO YEL *to the Emperor*: And do you know what it would cost now? Four yen.

EMPEROR *feels the scarf, interested*: This is cotton?

PRIME MINISTER: Cotton, Your Majesty.

EMPEROR *darkly*: And why do they sell it so cheaply these days?

PRIME MINISTER: Majesty, you'd better know the truth. We've just had one of the most awful years in the history of China. The harvest ...

EMPEROR: So what about the harvest? Has the weather been bad?

PRIME MINISTER: It's been very good!

EMPEROR: So were the peasants lazy?

PRIME MINISTER: They worked very hard!

EMPEROR: So what is wrong with the harvest?

PRIME MINISTER: It's massive! That's the misfortune! There's too much of everything, so nothing's worth anything any more!

EMPEROR: Do you mean to say, I've got too much cotton to get a decent price for it? – Well then, just get rid of it!

PRIME MINISTER: But, Your Majesty, public opinion!

EMPEROR: What? You don't mean to tell me that you, in your great big Tui-hat, are fearful of public opinion? You'd better prepare the text of my abdication! *Exits.*

PRIME MINISTER: Dear God!

EMPEROR *returning*: And I refuse to permit anyone, this time, to do anything which might damage my public standing. *Finally exits.*

PRIME MINISTER: Make me an omelette, but don't break the eggs! Friends, I grew up in the best Tui academy in the country, I'm familiar with all the Tuistic literature, for thirty years I've debated with the leading Tuis every idea which might save China. My friends, there is no solution.

THE DOWAGER *enters, carrying a small tea service*: Now here's a pretty cup of tea. Where's my son?

YAO YEL: Gone. Have they let you . . . *She hurries to the door.* It's dreadful the way the doctors keep letting her escape. The tea is sure to be poisoned again.

COURT TUI: The doctors are always taken in, she mostly seems so sensible.

YAO YEL *sighing*: Sometimes I understand her all too well.

THE DOWAGER *has turned back. To Yao Yel*: You have some at least.

YAO YEL: Mama, you're impossible.

The Dowager makes to leave, disappointed. A doctor rushes in.

DOCTOR: Please, give me the cup, Your Majesty.

He takes it from her. Exit both.

PRIME MINISTER: I give China two years, at most.

2

THE TUIS' TEAHOUSE

Tuis are sitting at small tables, reading and playing board-games. Boards with notices: 'Two minor formulations, three yen', 'Opinions changed. They'll seem like new', 'Mo Si, king of excuse-makers', 'You want to bargain? We've got the arguments', 'Why you're innocent – Nu Shan reveals all', 'Whatever you say – it's the way you say it'. Potential clients, mostly from the country, study the notices.

MO SI: I'd better hurry, I've got some hard wording to finish today. For a cashier in the city bank. About the inflation.

KA MÜ: I'm taking a day off today. Yesterday I sold a cat-gut dealer an opinion about atonal music.

MO SI: For or against?

KA MÜ: Against. I don't just sell opinions off the peg, opinions that'll do for anyone. I only sell tailored stuff. My clients don't want to express an opinion that anyone might have. But I hear your notions for the little man are also selling well, Shi Ka?

SHI KA: Indeed, I've introduced a purchase scheme. You know how I thought of it? The wife of one of my clients was set on getting a baking tray. He consulted me for an excuse. She told him she could get the baking tray by instalments, and he wanted to know if he could have the excuse by instalments too. It might have come cheaper to buy her the tray. Hard times. What's this?

A waiter sets up a notice: 'No service for customers in rags. By order.' A Tui in rags leaves with dignity. Groans.

A TUI: The price of clothes the way it is!

ANOTHER TUI: Soon the little folk won't be able to afford opinions!

QUIET VOICE: Long live Kai Ho.

Laughter.

FIRST TUI: No politics in here, please.

SECOND TUI: So no tea prices here either.

FIRST TUI: Do you really suppose Mr Kai Ho, seditious

agitator that he is, can achieve what the greatest of the Tuis have failed to achieve, to make China a land fit to live in?

SECOND TUI: Yes.

General hilarity.

BUXOM CUSTOMER: What would you charge for a little formulation, about an affair?

MO SI: Up to four yen, depending ...

She sits down next to him. Enter Turandot with the Court Tui. She is not recognised.

TURANDOT: So this is one of the Tuis' most famous teahouses!

COURT TUI: Only for the most lowly, Imperial Majesty. The more important, who maintain the law, write the books, educate our young, in short, those who lead humanity, according to their ideals, from their tribunes, pulpits and professorial chairs, they don't come here. Nonetheless, even these lesser Tuis do their best to lend intellectual support to the population, in all its dealings.

TURANDOT: By telling people what they should do?

COURT TUI: More by telling them what they should say. Why not try it?

TURANDOT *lazily*: So why am I innocent?

NU SHAN: Of what? Ah yes. *He laughs loudly.* Ten yen. *He takes the payment.* Would you demand your ten yen back, Madam, if I were to confess that I don't know why you're innocent, but that you may nonetheless always maintain that you are innocent?

TURANDOT *lazily*: I'm a sensual creature. Hui, explain to the man what my weakness is.

COURT TUI: Here?

TURANDOT: Absolutely.

COURT TUI: The particular personality, of whom we are speaking, simply cannot resist intellectual qualities. A certain kind of elegant formulation arouses her.

TURANDOT: Physically.

COURT TUI: New ways of presenting ...

TURANDOT: ... problems ...

COURT TUI: ... completely enslave her.

TURANDOT: Sexually. – Tell him about the blood!

COURT TUI: The blood rushes to her head at the sight of a domed forehead, an eloquent gesture, at the sound of a well-turned . . .

TURANDOT: . . . sentence.

A WAITER *passes between the tables calling out*: Whitewasher needed for the La Me department store!

Three Tuis rush off backstage.

A TUI *at the next table*: There's only one problem here that's really hard: who's going to pay for the tea?

Gogher Gogh enters, accompanied by a bodyguard who waits at the door.

TURANDOT: Who's that handsome fellow?

COURT TUI: An infamous bandit called Gogher Gogh.

NU SHAN: Not so loud, sir. He likes to call himself a Tui. Although he's failed our lowest grade exam twice . . . You'll hear, he's still studying.

GOGHER GOGH *has joined the Tui with the sign, 'Two minor formulations, three yen'*: Here's your three yen, now listen. I needed money for my studies.

WEN: You'll never get through the exam.

GOGHER GOGH: You mind your own business. In any case, I've finished with school, it's a load of nonsense. But, like I said, I had to have money.

TURANDOT: Why would a bandit want to become a Tui?

NU SHAN: He only became a bandit in order to become a Tui.

TURANDOT: He caught my eye right away.

GOGHER GOGH: For the first exam I took the money from the company till.

WEN *bored*: Borrowed.

GOGHER GOGH: Borrowed. I could only get the money the second time by taking the company's machine-guns and all the ammunition to a pawnbroker.

WEN: To be cleaned. If you need any more you'll have to pay again.

Gogher Gogh fumbles in his pockets for coins.

TURANDOT: Is life so much easier as a Tui, rather than as a bandit?

NU SHAN: There's not so much difference. But he doesn't really live off banditry. Not since the inflation started anyway. He and his gang make their living from protecting the laundries in the suburbs.

TURANDOT: Against what?

NU SHAN: Against attacks.

TURANDOT: By whom?

NU SHAN: By his gang. You see: as long as they pay, they don't get attacked.

COURT TUI *cynically*: Just like the state. Pay your taxes, and you get no trouble from the police.

TURANDOT *enamoured*: Hui! Not in public! Everyone can see us!

GOGHER GOGH: Three yen. I just want one more formulation. How do I explain it to my people?

WEN *pointing to the bodyguard*: You mean people like him over there? Let me think about that.

Sen, a peasant with a white beard, enters with a boy. The Tui Gu leads him to Nu Shan's table.

GU *to the whole assembly*: It's an outrage! This man is from the province of Szechwan. He's been on the road for two months with a small handcart laden with cotton. This morning he was on his way to sell the cotton at Threefinger Market, when they confiscated it!

General protestations.

WEN: And there's such a shortage of cotton, you can pay fifty yen for a neckerchief!

ANOTHER TUI: The mills have long since shut down. For lack of cotton. The Union of Clothesmakers has been threatening trouble if the government won't say where all the cotton has gone.

WEN: Peking is in rags.

GU: Allow me. *He sits down with the old man, the boy remains standing behind him.* What brought you to Peking?

SEN: My name is Sen. This is Er Fei. I've come about studying.

GU: The young man wishes to study?

SEN: No, I wish to study. He has time enough. First of all he can become a sandal-maker. But for myself, I think I'm sufficiently mature, sirs. For fifty years I've dreamt of joining the great brotherhood who call themselves the Tuis

– after the initial letters of Tellect-Uell-In. It is in accordance with their great thoughts that the whole state is governed. They lead mankind.

GU: They most certainly do. And with the profit from the cotton you intended . . .

SEN: To attend a Tui school.

GU *stands up*: Gentlemen! I've just learnt that this old man here, who's had his cotton confiscated by the organs of the state, was intending to use the profit to attend a Tui school! He thirsts after learning, and the state robs him! I have a proposition: let all of us here present adopt the cause of our future colleague.

NU SHAN: There's no point! Everything to do with cotton is determined by the Emperor.

Turandot, responding to a gesture from the Court Tui, gets up and leaves with him.

A TUI: Not by the Emperor! The Emperor's brother!

Laughter.

NU SHAN: There's nothing doing, old man.

A waiter, to whom the Court Tui has whispered something in the doorway, comes up to Sen's table and speaks quietly in his ear.

GU: Gentlemen, something extraordinary has just happened. A benefactress, who would like to remain anonymous, has offered Mr Sen the price his cotton would have fetched on the market. Let's join Mr Sen and celebrate this unexpected opportunity to join our brotherhood!

Several of the Tuis surround Sen and congratulate him.

GOGHER GOGH: You've thought about it long enough. What should I say to my firm?

WEN *gives him his three yen back*: I don't know.

3

IN THE IMPERIAL PALACE

The Emperor is stuffing his second morning pipe. Enter Turandot with the Court Tui.

TURANDOT *lifts up her skirt and shows her father her cotton pants*: How do you like the pants? They're cotton. Hui says it's scratchy. That may be true, but these days it's just so chic, expensive and yet traditional. Go on, say something. When you have a bright idea and I don't say anything, like when you thought up the salt tax, you put on a face for days on end.

EMPEROR: Yes, the cotton prices have been picking up quite nicely. Here, have a brush and make a list of whatever you want. In view of my newly stabilised financial circumstances I can inform you: you may now follow the dictates of your heart in your choice of a husband. At last we can send that Mongolian prince packing. I could never have brought myself to force a husband on you, never. Only in extreme circumstances.

Distant march music.

TURANDOT: When I marry, I'll marry a Tui.

EMPEROR: You're perverse.

TURANDOT *happily*: You think so? When someone says something witty it just goes right through me.

EMPEROR: Don't be indecent. So early in the morning. I'd never permit you to waste yourself on a Tui. Never.

TURANDOT: Grandmama is indecent too when we get chatting. You'd never believe what she says about . . .

EMPEROR: And I won't permit you to talk like that about your grandmother. The Dowager is a great patriot, it says so in all the schoolbooks. In any case, you're too young to be thinking about that sort of thing.

TURANDOT: Hui, am I too young? 'Scratchy!'

EMPEROR: What's that music?

COURT TUI: A demonstration by the Union of Clothesmakers, Majesty.

TURANDOT: That's why I'm so dressed up. I'm going with Hui to watch the demonstration. But there's no hurry. It'll go on for eight or ten hours.

EMPEROR: Why eight or ten hours?

TURANDOT: Until they've all marched passed!

Enter the Prime Minister with a fly-bill.

PRIME MINISTER: Your Majesty might care to take a look at

this leaflet, it was found in front of the La Me department store. The contents are most unedifying. *He reads.* 'Where has China's cotton gone? Must China's sons go naked to their parents' funeral when they die of hunger? The first Manchu Emperor had only enough cotton to make a soldier's tunic. So how much has the last Emperor?' – The style of this vile rubbish suggests the hand of Kai Ho.

EMPEROR: Damn Tui!

COURT TUI: Please! By all means, Sire, give us all a good thrashing, but don't, please, call that filthy rogue a Tui! A troublemaker, with no breeding, who consorts with scum! I beg you . . . I must . . . *He wipes the cold sweat from his brow.*

EMPEROR *listening to the distant music during the following exchange*: No one takes the fellow seriously.

PRIME MINISTER: This fellow, Sire, has managed to stir up twenty million people in the province of Ho. It may please you to take him seriously.

TURANDOT: What's that about a tunic?

COURT TUI: It's the cotton tunic of the first Manchu Emperor, who was himself a peasant. It's hanging in the old Manchu temple, and there's a legend amongst the people: as long as it hangs there on its cord, the people will be bound to the Emperor. A superstition which Mr Kai Ho, who studied in Canton, gleefully exploits.

PRIME MINISTER: And which is believed by millions.

TURANDOT *sings*:

However strong and thick
One day the rope will break
And yet that's not to say
That every thread must fray.

EMPEROR: That's gutter-talk. – What are the likely consequences?

PRIME MINISTER: A new scandal. The Union of Clothesmakers, with its two million members, will band together with the Union of the Clothesless, who number fourteen million. The Clothesmakers don't have any cotton left to make clothes, or clothes for themselves either. There'll be an outcry against the Emperor: 'The Emperor's got our cotton!' and the people will all rally round Kai Ho.

Enter Yao Yel.

YAO YEL *unaware*: Good morning. How sweet is your pipe this morning?

EMPEROR *yells*: Not at all! And where's the cotton?

YAO YEL: The cotton?

EMPEROR *holding the leaflet under his nose*: Look, insinuations and insults, and what is anybody doing about it? I'll abdicate. If this can't be cleared up immediately, with proper explanations, I'll resign, once and for all.

PRIME MINISTER: Kai Ho has uncovered the whole story.

EMPEROR: Incompetence! Indifference! Stupidity!

YAO YEL: Gentlemen, please, could you leave me alone a moment with my brother.

EMPEROR *while all exit except Turandot*: I demand that the culprits be punished, with the full force of the law. The full force.

TURANDOT: That's right, Papa.

YAO YEL: Stop yelling. They've all gone.

TURANDOT *writing furiously*: That's right, Papa. Be polite.

EMPEROR: Where's the cotton?

YAO YEL: I understand that you yelled at the others, but now you have to stop yelling.

EMPEROR *louder still*: Where is the cotton?

TURANDOT: Yes, where is it actually?

YAO YEL: You know the answer to that. It's in your warehouses.

EMPEROR: What? You dare to tell me that? I'll have you arrested!

TURANDOT: Ooh, yes please!

YAO YEL: But you agreed, remember?

EMPEROR: Should I call the guards?

YAO YEL: All right then, we'll put the cotton on the market, is that what you want?

Pause.

EMPEROR: I'll abdicate.

YAO YEL *yells*: Go on then, abdicate, and get yourself hanged!

Pause.

YAO YEL: Call a conference of the Tuis. Promise them something that won't cost you anything, if only they can whitewash the whole business. What do you keep your two hundred thousand whitewashers for? Why do you maintain all those fifteen thousand academies?

TURANDOT: A Tui conference! Now that would be entertaining!

EMPEROR: The Tuis! No one values them more highly than I do. They do what they can, but they can't do everything. What are they supposed to say? The Union of Clothesmakers knows the dirt already.

PRIME MINISTER *enters*: Your Majesty, the delegates of the Union of Clothesmakers – together, unfortunately, with the delegates of the Union of the Clothesless.

EMPEROR: What, they already turn up here together? No Tui conference can help with this.

TURANDOT: Serves you right.

YAO YEL: You'll just have to hand over the cotton.

TURANDOT *still writing*: It serves you right because you're an unintellectual man.

Enter the delegates of the Clothesmakers and the delegates of the Clothesless. Two Tuis follow them.

EMPEROR *bad-tempered*: What is it?

FIRST UNION TUI *before any of the other delegates can speak*: Your Majesty! According to the testimony of the great classic Ka-Me, there is nothing that can withstand the power of the people, if they are united. Your Majesty, the question of the whereabouts of the cotton is a question on which the Union of the Clothesmakers, which I represent, and the Union of the Clothesless, represented by my honoured colleague, have achieved a united front.

SECOND UNION TUI: But not like you think, from above, but from below!

FIRST UNION TUI: That's right, from below. Our leadership is elected from below ... *The second Union Tui laughs.* Only in freedom can freedom be won. *He gets a book out of his briefcase. Turandot applauds.* Ka-Me!

SECOND UNION TUI: Leave the quotations! Whoever heard of an army in freedom winning a battle! *Turandot applauds.*

Since when has discipline been the same as unfreedom? *He also pulls out a book.* What does Ka-Me say?

FIRST UNION TUI: A battle, huh! Violence! That sounds like your Kai Ho talking!

SECOND UNION TUI: And that sounds like your purse talking, the fee your cheating leaders of that union of treacherous treaty-dealers . . .

FIRST UNION TUI: Are you calling me a bought man?

SECOND UNION TUI: Bought by traitors!

The delegate of the Clothesmakers, who came with the first Union Tui, gives the second Union Tui a slap. Whereupon the latter thinks for a moment, then, with his Ka-Me, hits the first Union Tui who hits him back with his own Ka-Me. Enraged, the delegate of the Clothesless slaps the other delegate, and the brawl spreads.

TURANDOT *breathing heavily*: Kick him! – Parry, can't you? – On the chin, yes!

EMPEROR: That's enough of that! *The fighting stops, but the first Union Tui has sunk to the floor.* Let me thank you for your enlightening remarks, and assure you that I concur with your eloquent arguments, especially the last one. Besides, I am much moved by the music that's been playing outside my palace. It seems there's a question of a certain shortage of cotton. However, since you have been unable to achieve total accord, I suggest – *enter the Dowager with a plate of sweet pancakes, which she offers to her son, who – without interrupting himself – declines* – that the question 'Where is the cotton?' should be debated and resolved by the cleverest and most learned men in the land. I proclaim and summon herewith an extraordinary Tui Congress, which will surely be able to explain satisfactorily to the people where it's all gone, all the cotton in China. – Oh, Mama, stop it! And so, good day.

The delegation, with the exception of the unconscious Tui, bows and withdraws, in some confusion, taking the body with them.

EMPEROR: Did I go too far?

PRIME MINISTER: You were admirable.

EMPEROR: I think a Tui Congress will be quite enough for these good folk. They can't even agree amongst themselves.

TURANDOT: I just don't understand what the people want from you this time. In any case, my cotton reserves are exceedingly skimpy. *The Emperor prevents her from showing everybody.*

PRIME MINISTER: Has Your Majesty already thought of a prize for the Tui who can explain to the people where the cotton has gone?

EMPEROR: No. My financial situation is still far from secure. – Leave it, Mama, you know I don't eat cake when I'm smoking.

PRIME MINISTER: Majesty, to answer this question, without compromising Your Majesty's position, will call for the cleverest head in all of China. What can you promise?

TURANDOT *bursts out gleefully*: Teeheeheehee! Me!

EMPEROR: What on earth do you mean, you? I'm not about to gamble my own flesh and blood.

TURANDOT: Why not? You find the cleverest head, and I marry him.

EMPEROR: Never. *Listens.* It *is* a very long procession.

3a

IN THE OLD MANCHU TEMPLE

In a decaying round tower, hanging by a thick rope from the ceiling, an ancient, patched coat. Around it stand the Imperial Family, the Prime Minister, the Minister for War and some of the high Tuis.

EMPEROR: My dear Turandot, this is it, the revered tunic. Your ancestor wore it in battle and, being a poor man, he sometimes had to patch the bullet holes himself, as you can see. Every Emperor wears this tunic at his coronation, because of the old prophecy associated with it. The confidence of the people in their Emperor is indispensable, I'm convinced; you only have to think of all the soldiers who turn out to be somehow related to all the rest of my subjects, or so they tell me. Anyway, in consideration of all this, I am resolved to grant to the one amongst my beloved Tuis who succeeds in restoring the faith of the people in the paternalistic government of their Emperor the hand in marriage of my only daughter. *Ahs and Ohs in surprised applause, Turandot bows.* And as I am led in all things, even material things, by my deep respect for ancient customs, I hereby decree that my future son-in-law should put on this famous coat before the wedding ceremony. So, that's enough of the affairs of state.

4

THE TUI ACADEMY

During the scene change a town-crier calls out: 'Important announcement: the Emperor has promised the hand of his daughter Turandot to the Tui who can tell the people where the cotton's gone.' In the Academy there is much to-ing and fro-ing. A scribe is putting up a notice: 'Emperor's future son-in-law a Tui'. A teacher in a Tui-hat is instructing a class.

TEACHER: Si Fu, tell us the principal questions of philosophy.

SI FU: Are the objects of the world outside ourselves, for themselves, independent of ourselves, or are they in ourselves, for ourselves, and dependent on ourselves.

TEACHER: And which is the correct opinion?

SI FU: No decision has yet been reached.

TEACHER: And which opinion has lately enjoyed the support of the majority of our philosophers?

SI FU: That they are outside ourselves, for themselves, independent of ourselves.

TEACHER: And why does the question remain unresolved?

SI FU: The congress which was supposed to deliver the answer was held, as it has been for two hundred years, in the monastery of Mi Sang on the banks of the Yellow River. The question was formulated thus: Is the Yellow River real, or does it exist only in our heads? However, while the congress was debating this question, there was a thaw in the mountains, and the Yellow River broke its banks and swept the monastery of Mi Sang away, along with all the congress delegates. So the proof that things are outside us, for themselves and independent of ourselves was never reached.

TEACHER: Good. That concludes today's lesson. And what is the most important event of the day?

THE CLASS: The Congress of the Tuis.

The teacher exits with his class. Enter Gu, who is also a Tui, and Sen accompanied by his boy.

SEN: But the Yellow River does exist, surely!

GU: So you say, but can you prove it?

SEN: Will I learn here how to prove things like that?

GU: That's up to you. Which reminds me, I haven't asked you yet why it is you want to study.

SEN: It's such a pleasure to think. And pleasures must be carefully learnt. But perhaps I should also say: it's so useful.

GU: Hmm. Maybe you should take a look around, before you pay the dues and register yourself. Here's a student learning the art of public speaking.

Shi Me, a young man, approaches with Nu Shan, who is a teacher at the Academy. Shi Me climbs up to a small rostrum. Nu Shan positions himself at the wall and operates a pulley arrangement by means of which a basket of bread can be raised and lowered in front of the speaker's face.

NU SHAN: The topic is: 'Why Kai Ho's position is false'. Whenever I raise the bread-basket, then you know you're saying something wrong. Off you go!

SHI ME: Kai Ho is wrong because he doesn't divide humanity into the clever and the not-so-clever, but rather into the rich and the poor. He was excluded from the Association of Tuis because he incited the barge-haulers, crofters and weavers to rebel against the violence which was – *the basket rises* – allegedly – *the basket wavers* – employed against them. So he's clearly in favour of violence! *The basket sinks.* Kai Ho speaks of freedom. *The basket wavers.* But in reality he wants to make the barge-haulers, crofters and weavers his slaves. *The basket sinks.* It is said that the barge-haulers, crofters and weavers don't earn enough – *the basket rises* – to support – in order to live in ease and luxury with their families – *the basket stops* – and that they have to work too hard – *the basket goes on rising* – because they want to spend their days in indolence – *the basket stops* – which is natural enough. *The basket wavers.* The discontent of many – *the basket rises* – of a mere few – *the basket stops* – is exploited by Kai Ho who, as we see, is therefore an exploiter! *The basket drops quickly.* Mr Kai Ho is distributing land in Hu Nan to the poor peasants. But first he has to steal the land himself, so he's a thief. According to the philosophy of Kai Ho – *the basket wavers again* – the purpose of life is to be happy, to eat and drink like the Emperor himself – *the basket shoots up* – but this only goes to show that Kai Ho isn't a philosopher at all, but just a loudmouth – *the basket sinks* – a troublemaker, a power-hungry good-for-nothing, an irresponsible gambler, a muckraker, a rapist, an unbeliever, a bandit and a criminal. *The basket is hovering just in front of the speaker's mouth.* A tyrant!

NU SHAN: Well, there you are, you're still making mistakes, but you have a good heart. Now run along and take a shower, and have a massage.

SHI ME: Mr Nu Shan, do you think I have a chance? I wasn't very good at fudging and only seventeenth in the art of lick-spittling. *Exit.*

GU: Nu Shan! A new pupil! *Nu Shan hurries over.* And by the way, what do *you* think about Kai Ho?

SEN: In cotton country we only hear what the landowners say. He's a bad man, not on the side of freedom.

NU SHAN: Do you like what we teach here?

SEN: It was a good speech. With new ideas. Is it true that Kai Ho wants to redistribute the land?

NU SHAN: Yes, to steal it and then supposedly redistribute it. Can we register you for the Academy then?

SEN: Soon, of course. I'd like to hear a bit more. It's all free for now, isn't it?

Enter Gogher Gogh with his mother, three of his gang and Wen.

MA GOGH: My son would like to take the exam.

SCRIBE: Ah, you again? This is the third time, isn't it? I don't think we have time today. Since the announcement that the Emperor's son-in-law will be a Tui we've had hundreds of new registrations. But why do you want to be a Tui so badly?

GOGHER GOGH: Both my general disposition and my early education have destined me for the civil service.

The scribe looks at him pityingly and, after bowing respectfully to Ma Gogh, he hurries away.

FIRST BANDIT: You've got to understand. You have to get the ammunition back. The inflation will level off and business will pick up again. We've got to raid every new business right from the start, so they get used to the idea of paying for protection.

GOGHER GOGH: I don't want any more shooting. I have other plans.

SECOND BANDIT: OK, but what are they?

Gogher Gogh maintains a grim silence.

MA GOGH: You know you can trust my son.

FIRST BANDIT *uncertainly*: Sure we can.

MA GOGH *points at the notice*: Krukher, a man with education has opportunities, more than ever. I have faith in Gogher.

Enter the great Tui, Xi Wei, with scribes. He sits down.

SEN: Who's that?

GU: That's Xi Wei, Chairman of the Tui Association. He is conducting an examination.

WEN *has stepped up to the examination desk, quietly*: My candidate is here for the third time. In two previous examinations he was asked, both times, what 3 times 5 is. And both times, unfortunately, he answered 25. He has such a steely determination. On the other hand, he's an excellent businessman and a good citizen, and he has a great thirst for knowledge, so permit me to supplicate, Chairman, that the question 'What is 3 times 5?' is asked of him one more time. Intense study has enabled my candidate to take the correct answer, 15, to his heart. *He hands over a purse of money.*

XI WEI *laughs*: Let me consult with my assessors.

FIRST BANDIT: What did you always say that made them fail you?

GOGHER GOGH: 25. And that wasn't right. Because the answer to the question 'what is 3 times 5?' is 15, or so I'm told.

FIRST BANDIT: But it's the right answer if the question is 'What is 5 times 5?'. They'd just better ask the right question. *He pulls a revolver from his jacket, walks over to the desk, shows it to Xi Wei and, after a short exchange, comes back over.* You stick with 25, it's all under control.

WEN *meanwhile, to Nu Shan*: I've paid over five times the fee.

A CLERK *calls out*: Mr Gogher Gogh.

Gogher Gogh steps forward.

XI WEI *with a twisted grin, looking over at the first bandit*: Candidate, what does 5 times 5 make?

GOGHER GOGH 15.

Xi Wei shrugs and lifts his arms. Exits quickly.

FIRST BANDIT: But it was all sorted.

GOGHER GOGH: Of course, if they keep switching the questions . . . It's a scandal, how they cheat a man out of his hard-earned cash. *Loudly*: I demand to be admitted immediately to membership of the Association of Tuis, on account of my carefully considered answer. The examiners were evidently not able to set the correct question for my answer. They're incompetent. As a matter of fact, I should perhaps consider whether I still want to belong to such an association. Everyone knows they're dangerous opinion-mongerers. They'd sell their own grandmothers for a well-turned point of view! They'd better all watch out. I'll be back!

MA GOGH: Come along, you just get cheated here. *Exit with Gogher Gogh, Wen and the bandits.*

SEN: Come along Er Fei. I want to ask something.

GU: So don't you want to register?

SEN: I may already have learnt the better part of what's on offer. I'm just wondering about Kai Ho, that troublemaker, rogue and rapist who wants to redistribute the land. *Exits with the boy.*

4a

A STREET

Streetwalking Tuis solicit clients. Sen and Er Fei. The Tui in rags who was thrown out of the teahouse addresses Sen.

TUI: Care for an opinion about the political situation, old man?

SEN: I don't need one. Sorry.

TUI: It'd only cost three yen, and we can do it while we walk along, old man.

SEN: How dare you solicit me, in the presence of a child too!

TUI: Don't be so stuck-up. It's a perfectly natural urge, to have an opinion.

SEN: If you don't leave us alone I'll call the police. You should be ashamed of yourself. Is this what thinking has come to? The most noble of human activities, and you turn it into a dirty business transaction. *He shoos him away.*

TUI *running off*: Filthy bourgeois!

ER FEI: Leave him, grandfather, perhaps he's just too poor.

SEN: That's an excuse for most things, but not for this.

5

THE HOUSE OF A GREAT TUI

Munka Du, who is being attended to by a barber, and his mother.

MOTHER: But will anybody believe you? Since they know where the cotton really is? My four maids talk about it without the least embarrassment.

MUNKA DU: They'll believe, if they want to. Just as there's always a tennis court for people who want to play tennis, so there's always an explanation for people who want to believe. Mimimimimi. Tennis is a must; belief is a must.

MOTHER: So you don't think there'll be a problem putting this across?

MUNKA DU: Oh, there's a problem all right. It will require a true master. You always need a master to demonstrate that two times two makes five.

MOTHER: Your family expects. Don't go bringing shame upon us.

MUNKA DU: I take exception to that. You know full well that those who fail to deliver a compelling formulation will have their heads cut off. Mimimimi.

MOTHER: Only the second-rate heads will fall.

MUNKA DU: And I suppose they'll only be mourned by the second-rate families! *He stands up briskly.*

The mother pulls a bell. Enter the two sisters of Munka Du, followed by a secretary.

MUNKA DU: Have you brought the quotation?

SECRETARY: I've brought two, a choice. *He hands him two sheets.*

MUNKA DU *with his eyes closed, takes one sheet*: How much?

SECRETARY: Two thousand.

MUNKA DU: That's scandalous.

SECRETARY: The quotations are almost unknown.

MUNKA DU: That may not be such a good thing. *He turns to his family*: Are the creases gone from the back?

MOTHER: Yes dear. Say goodbye to your family now.

MUNKA DU: Mimimimimimimi. My dears. In agony and despair – wait, where's the artist who's supposed to immortalise the scene of my departure for the great competition? *His mother rings. An artist enters. He quickly starts sketching.* In agony and despair, the land looks to its intellectual leaders. What can they tell them? Mimimimimi. Indeed, it is the force of intellect that holds sway over the destinies of the nations, and not political power. Oh, I feel the responsibility weighing on my shoulders. Our lords and masters are going to hear something to remember from me, oh yes. I may perhaps be repudiated ...

ARTIST: Hold the pose, please.

MUNKA DU *holds the pose for a while*: ... but I will not be shaken in my opinion. Mimimimimimi. I may not return to you. But in the annals of history my uncorruptible efforts will live on: to stand by my country in its hour of need and offer it – mimimimimimimimimi – my word, my unambiguous, uncompromising word. *He exits in pomp.*

5a

THE PALACE OF THE ASSOCIATION OF TUIS

The debating chamber.

The first day of the great Tui conference. Sen is introduced to the Imperial Family and to the Congress by Chairman Xi Wei.

XI WEI: It is an honour and a privilege to present to their Majesties, the Imperial Family, and to this great Congress, a guest, whose presence here today must strike us as symbolic. This simple man – *applause* – a mere peasant – *applause* – from cotton country, journeyed with his mule-cart piled high with cotton, here to the capital where cotton was scarce. But with the profit – and this is what is so uplifting about this tale, so beautiful, so exemplary – with his takings, Sen, the man from the north, was resolved to study Tuism! *Applause.* His greatest desire was to set eyes on the great Tuis who inspire and illuminate mankind. *Applause.*

The foyer.

The great Tuis Ke Lei and Munka Du are having a row, in the presence of the Prime Minister. An announcement comes from a huge wooden pipe: 'Attention! The Congress is about to begin.'

KE LEI: I was to be first to speak, that's what I was told. I know it's hard to get the ball rolling, but I accepted, and so I should speak first.

MUNKA DU: I must insist, I am just as content to speak first.

KE LEI: Of course, I don't really want to.

MUNKA DU: I have no wish to impose myself.

KE LEI: But if it's what the people demand, I'll do it.

MUNKA DU: I am ready to accede to the request.

KE LEI: But no one's asking you.

MUNKA DU: And who's asking anything of you?

KE LEI: We all know your game.

MUNKA DU: Your tricks are the talk of the town.

KE LEI: This is beneath my dignity. It's not for my own amusement you know. I . . . *He pulls himself away from Munka Du, who tries to hold him back, and enters the debating chamber.*

PRIME MINISTER: Come along, I'll introduce you to the Emperor for your pains. *They exit.*

At the entrance there's a little struggle going on. Gogher Gogh and two bodyguards are trying to get in.

GOGHER GOGH: I demand to have a turn. You cannot exclude a man of the people! *He is excluded.*

The debating chamber.

XI WEI: Your Majesty, Gentlemen! It is my heartfelt pleasure to present to you our first speaker, our much beloved Dean of the Imperial University, Mr Ke Lei.

THE TUIS *sing the Tui-Hymn*:

By thought we flower!
Knowledge is power.
Yours is promotion
Earth-shaking commotion
Devotion, emotion!
Cometh the hour.

KE LEI: Revered Imperial Family, Honoured Congress! Cotton, *lana arboris*, is the seed-floss derived from the Bombax genus of the Bombacaceae, the so-called cotton-tree, a shrubby plant with narrow finger-shaped leaves and creamy-white blossoms on both trunk and branches. It is a fluffy, fleecy mass which may be spun to produce cloth for the manufacture of clothes, especially for the poorer folk. Honoured assembly, the paucity of this said mass, *lana arboris*, in our market places, and hence the scarcity of cotton cloth, is what brings us here together. So. Let us consider first our nation, our people. And consider it boldly, unflinchingly, without prejudice. From time to time scholars have been reproached for discovering differences, that is to say for believing and maintaining that, amongst the people, there were inequalities, if we may permit ourselves that expression, inequalities, differences of interest and so forth. Now. Permit me to confess that I, irrespective of whether I am reproached for it or not, I share this opinion! Please, I beg you. A forest is not simply a forest, it consists of different trees. And so the people is not simply the people. Of what does it consist, you may ask? Well. We have civil servants, plate-washers, landowners, foundry-workers, cotton-dealers, doctors and bakers. We have officers, musicians, carpenters, winegrowers, lawyers, shepherds, poets and blacksmiths. Not to mention the fishermen, serving maids, mathematicians, artists, butchers, fine grocers, chemists, night porters, glove-makers, language teachers, policemen, gardeners, journalists, ceramic tile-makers, basket-weavers, waiters, astronomers, furriers, fruit-sellers, icemen, newspaper-boys, pianists, flautists, drummers, violinists, accordionists, zither-players, cellists, viola-players, trumpeters, woodwinds, wood-dealers, woodsmen and woodsmiths. And who has not heard tell of the tobacco-workers, metal-workers, forest-workers, farm-workers, textile-workers, building-workers, architects and sailors? Other occupations include the weavers, roof-thatchers, actors, footballers, oceanographers, stone-masons, knife-grinders, dog-catchers, publicans, hangmen, clerks, postmen, bankers, carters, midwives, tailors, mountaineers, butlers, sportsmen and navigators. *Unrest in the audience.* So. Perhaps I have been too exhaustive, too precise, too scholarly. And to what purpose? In order to demonstrate that all these people, different as they may be, are, or let us be circumspect, that an overwhelming majority, the poor, are in one respect all alike, namely that they –

A VOICE: . . . are poor.

KE LEI: Not at all, that they need cheap cotton. They are crying out for cotton! So. We all know, my friends, it is the Emperor who commands the cotton – *muffled disquiet in the audience* – not in terms of ownership, but in terms of decreeing, deciding, disposing – and there is no one who would distribute it more generously, unselfishly, paternalistically than the Emperor. Yet still it is not to be had. Now. If so many people have need of it, must it not be somewhere to be had? Honoured assembly, let me give you my response, again at risk of making myself unpopular: No! Nature, my dear colleagues, is an unruly goddess. We intellectuals are wont to shy away from simple assertions, lest they appear simplistic, lest they seem crude. Well, I shall not be shy. Where is the cotton? Here is my unimpeachable, incorruptible response: the harvest, the harvest has failed. Too much sun, too little sun. Too little rain, too much rain. The detail is still to be determined. But in short, there simply is no cotton to be had – because nothing grew.

He steps down from the rostrum with dignity. The Imperial Family leaves the hall.

XI WEI: Let me thank Mr Ke Lei. The prize judges will broadcast their decision.

The cloakrooms.

The Emperor, the Dowager, Turandot and the Prime Minister. Munka Du stands to one side, waiting.

EMPEROR: Have you spoken to the union representatives?

PRIME MINISTER: Briefly, Your Majesty.

The Emperor looks at him questioningly. The Prime Minister shakes his head.

EMPEROR: That man is making it far too easy for himself. Stupid lies like that won't be enough. Just the opposite. It arouses the people's suspicion that there's something fishy going on. Just five minutes ago we were paying our respects to a peasant who'd carted cotton into the capital! No sense of realities!

At the entrance there has been an exchange. Gogher Gogh is trying to force his way in with two bodyguards.

GOGHER GOGH: I'll remember you, and you. I have a very important communication. *He is removed forcibly.*

TURANDOT: I adore a bit of intellect, but that . . . !

EMPEROR: And the cheek! 'Regardless whether I am reproached for it . . . ' – And 'the overwhelming majority, the poor'! Get rid of the fellow!

PRIME MINISTER: Sire, he won't bore us again.

TURANDOT: Grandmama, it's no fun any more. *She throws herself into the Dowager's arms.* I won't let myself be married off. Not to something like that! *She gives the Prime Minister a kick.* He's the one to blame. I'm the laughing-stock of the whole teahouse. Off with his head! And yours too! *She sobs.* No one cares about me! Off with his head! Off with his head! Off with his head! *She buries her head in the Dowager's bosom.*

PRIME MINISTER *after a short pause*: May I introduce to Your Imperial Majesty the speaker for the fifth day, Mr Munka Du?

Turandot looks up.

The foyer.

Sen, the boy Er Fei, and Gu.

SEN: The man's got it all wrong. There was more cotton this year than last. Where can I find him? I should tell him.

Ke Lei is led past by policemen.

SEN: What's happened? What's he doing with the police? Can't I talk to him?

GU *holding him back*: Better not be seen with him, it could be to your disadvantage.

SEN: Do you mean to say he's been arrested? Just because he doesn't know the truth?

GU: He knows the truth all right.

SEN: So he's been arrested because he lied!

GU: Not because he lied, but because he lied ineptly. You've still got a lot to learn old man.

The cloakrooms.

The Prime Minister is introducing to Turandot Chairman Xi

Wei, who is accompanied by his secretary Nu Shan. Munka Du is with Turandot. From the debating chamber the strains of the Tui-Hymn.

XI WEI: Imperial Majesty, allow me to dedicate this suit of clothes to your revered family. I designed it myself.
Nu Shan takes out of a cardboard box an outfit made of paper, printed with verses.

PRIME MINISTER: In the light of the unsatisfactory progress of the Congress, and in response to the unruly surge of applicants, Mr Xi Wei, the Chairman of the Tui Association, will speak himself, on this, the third day of the Congress.

TURANDOT: Oh, how witty! It's made of paper!

XI WEI: The most noble of fabrics!

TURANDOT: 'Such noble stuff as noble dreams are made on.' *Calls to the maids.* I'll wear it this very day.
A screen is brought, she changes.

PRIME MINISTER *to Xi Wei*: Come along, let's go!
Announcement from the pipes: 'Announcement: the geographer Pauder Mel has set out from the monastery of Tashi Lumpo in Shigatse in order to take part in the Congress.' Applause.

The debating chamber.

YAO YEL: How did it go yesterday?

EMPEROR: Dull. A theologian. All he had to say was: the fewer the clothes, the healthier the man. The sun. You know – Where were you?

YAO YEL: In the country. I tried to burn a couple of bales.

EMPEROR: What on earth for? I won't permit that. Have I no authority?

YAO YEL: How else do you expect to drive the price up?

EMPEROR: Surely not by burning the stuff. What good is a higher price if I've got nothing left to sell?

YAO YEL: You should study a bit of economics, and then we could have a sensible conversation. Let's suppose we have five million bales ... *Xi Wei has entered the chamber. Yao*

Yel continues explaining quietly during the following speech.

XI WEI: Your Imperial Majesties, Gentlemen! At the beginning of this Congress it was basely claimed that China had produced no cotton this year. An insult to the Chinese people. Let me inform you that no less than one and a half million bales were produced. And attend, by what means our people, the most industrious people of the entire globe, produced such prodigious quantities of cotton! We know all about the sweat that was sweated in the rigours of cultivation by the great monasteries and the feudal estates. But think also of the millions of lesser peasants and farmers who work their fingers to the bone on their tiny plots. Let us pay our respects to them, praise be to the smallholder! The heroic producers of clothes for the little man!

Applause.

YAO YEL: Just remember, in case something happens, you've got no head for business: we've got to destroy half of it before we can even start thinking about selling the stuff. All the same, I can't have it burnt. And why? Because it stinks.

EMPEROR: It does not, only wool stinks.

YAO YEL: But it makes an awful lot of smoke.

XI WEI: And now you will ask, and the whole population joins you in asking: so where is it? Where is the cotton? Let me explain: it is vanishing.

Unrest.

YAO YEL: Has he gone mad? Stop the proceedings at once!

XI WEI: And where does it vanish? Where indeed? I can explain that too: it vanishes in transit. *The unrest increases.* Honoured assembly! You suspect terrible wrongdoings, you are justly enraged. But you couldn't be further from the truth in your suspicions. Permit me to regale you with a tale, a new tale of the greatness and virtue of the Chinese people. I refer to the progress made under the enlightened regime of our great Imperial House. Gentlemen, it is not so many years ago, the population of the flat lands were a sorry spectacle. Ghosts in rags, half naked, almost bestial in their nakedness, peopled the villages. Decent clothes, tasteful cloths were unheard of, and scarcely dreamt of.

And today? Gentlemen, the rationalisation of the cotton industry in the hands of a member of the Imperial Family has changed all that. Culture has come to our villages. Culture! *Leaflets come raining down from the ceiling.* The disappearance of the cotton on its way from the fields to the cities can be explained by the steady advance of culture through our land: it is being bought by the people themselves! I don't know what's in these leaflets –

CRIES: Kai Ho's leaflets! Police!

XI WEI: . . . but I do know that it's lies. The truth is: the cotton has all been bought already!

YOUNG MEH NEI *in a group of young Tuis*: By the peasants who have no fields, who have to plough their tiny plots with penknives and plant out cotton in their grandmothers' earwax? *He is dragged off by policemen.* They can't afford cotton clothes!

EMPEROR: He's an ass, this Xi Wei!

PRIME MINISTER: The union representatives are leaving the chamber, taking the leaflets with them.

XI WEI *in desperation*: Silence, please. China stands poised on the brink of an abyss! *He is interrupted by applause. Turandot, followed by Munka Du, has entered the Imperial box. She is wearing Xi Wei's paper costume.* Your Imperial Majesties, Conference! In response to the shortage of cloth, which has been brought about by the growing cultural expectations of the general populace (let me repeat that), I propose that, immediately and without bureaucratic delay, notwithstanding previous decrees, our capital city be permitted to fashion clothes from the most noble of all fabrics, that sacred material by means of which our great thinkers and writers have achieved their immortality, their sublimity: paper!

CRY: And to banish rain!

Laughter. The police seek out the heckler, then the laughers. Renewed applause: Turandot has demonstratively opened her parasol.

ANOTHER CRY: Our labourers will work armed with parasols!

AND ANOTHER: It'd be better to dress yourselves in Kai Ho's leaflets!

The Imperial Family leaves the debating chamber.

The cloakrooms.

YAO YEL: The cotton disappears in transit! Now we only need someone else to blurt out where it really goes, and we can pack our bags!

TURANDOT: And I'm the laughing-stock of the land, yet again! Miserable fool! *She tears off the paper clothes.* There and there and there!

EMPEROR: Don't cause another scandal, I've quite enough with the scandal we've got already. *Exits with Yao Yel.*

PRIME MINISTER: You're the new chairman of the Tui Association.

NU SHAN: I can't do that, I'm his pupil.

PRIME MINISTER: You'll have to settle that with your conscience. *They exit.*

DOWAGER: Off with his head, off with his head, off with his head! *Exits giggling.*

The maidservants, giggling, set up a screen for Turandot. Only the Court Tui and Munka Du remain. Announcement from the pipes: 'The competitors for the fourth day are requested to report in the Grand Chamber.'

TURANDOT *behind the screen*: Munka Du! You'll wait, won't you?

MUNKA DU: I have to report in the Grand Chamber, Imperial Majesty.

TURANDOT: There'll be time for that. There'll be dozens queuing. I want you to speak last.

MUNKA DU: Very well, Imperial Majesty.

TURANDOT: Munka Du! Come to the palace with me today, I'd like to show you something.

MUNKA DU: Imperial Majesty, nothing would give me greater pleasure, but I shall have to prepare for my great speech.

TURANDOT: Hui Zhe, you're still there too, aren't you?

COURT TUI: At your service, Imperial Majesty.

TURANDOT: You may stay. Munka Du, this evening I'll show you a little cotton something.

The maids giggle loudly. The announcement comes over the pipes again.

MUNKA DU: Imperial Majesty, I beg your leave, please let me go and prepare my speech.

TURANDOT: Hui Zhe, go to the Chamber and see how many applicants are still there.

Hui Zhe goes to the Chamber.

TURANDOT: Munka Du!

The debating chamber.

The Prime Minister and the Secretary Nu Shan look up and see the Court Tui approaching.

PRIME MINISTER: This is not good. No one else has come forward, and it's only the third day! Of course there'll still be the speakers from the provinces. Let Mr Munka Du know, he's on first thing tomorrow morning. *To Nu Shan*: And you, get rid of this idiot.

The Court Tui hesitates to go back to the cloakrooms.

The foyer.

Secretary Nu Shan finds his boss, Chairman Xi Wei, completely alone and desolate. At the door, watched over by police, Meh Nei and other young Tuis. On their way out, old Sen and Gu.

GU: And what do you think of the whole affair, my dear Sen?

SEN: The gentleman was very eloquent, but it's not enough, the fields are far too small.

XI WEI: Please, send a message immediately to the authorities, I demand the firmest measures against these young fellows, blatant supporters of Kai Ho, the full rigour of the law, death! *The Secretary gestures to the policemen, and the young men are led away.* Thank you. What have you heard? What are they saying about my speech? The leaflets detracted a little from the effect, don't you think? But the demonstrative appearance of Turandot in my outfit made up a lot of ground, I think. Are they satisfied? *Hoarsely*: Are there any messages for me? No one has said anything, presumably they don't yet know the reaction of the court. Check the abstracts against my speech very carefully before they're published. The heat in the chamber had a bit of an effect on the mood, don't you think? Why don't you say something, man? You've been my pupil for eleven years, I make you responsible for the abstracts. I understand. Tell my sons . . .

The foyer.

The fourth day. The Prime Minister, Nu Shan and the scribe of the Tui Academy. Announcement from the pipes: 'The candidates for the fifth day are to report in the foyer to the Prime Minister's committee.'

PRIME MINISTER: He dares to keep us waiting. Are the entrances all under surveillance, the walls checked, the basements searched?

NU SHAN: The Minister for War took personal control of the operation.

PRIME MINISTER *restlessly*: That doesn't mean much. Only thirty years ago, the man was a member of the Society for Moderate Progress Within the Law. – The geographer of the Tashi Lumpo monastery has announced his candidacy now. But he won't be able to get here before the day after tomorrow. – Have the hooligans from last night been disbarred from the Tui Association?

NU SHAN: They've been executed.

PRIME MINISTER: That's beside the point. I asked if they'd been disbarred from the Association.

Enter Munka Du, in a hurry, with Turandot and her maids. Munka Du clearly hasn't slept much. They bow in greeting.

TURANDOT: Congratulate him, gentlemen, he told me during the night what he's going to say.

PRIME MINISTER: Mr Munka Du, I am sure you understand, after yesterday's events, it has been decided that the candidates, whoever they may be, should be tested for Un-Chinese attitudes.

TURANDOT: He doesn't have any of those.

PRIME MINISTER *bows*: Of course not. *To Munka Du*: You're prepared to submit to this formality? *They sit down.* Do you wet your bed?

MUNKA DU *helplessly*: No.

PRIME MINISTER *to the maids*: Please, don't giggle. It's a question we have to ask. – Are you, or have you ever been a member of the Society of Friends of the Armed Struggle? *Munka Du shakes his head.* The Plague for Human Rights? *Munka Du shakes his head.* Are you for peace, in any form whatsoever? *Munka Du shakes his head.* Do you have dependants or relatives? *Munka Du shakes his head, then thinks better of it, and nods.* In the northern provinces? *Munka Du shakes his head.* Say the name Kai Ho!

MUNKA DU: Kai Ho.

PRIME MINISTER: You're shaking.

MUNKA DU: I'm very tired.

TURANDOT *pushes aside the maids, who have been doing her hair*: That's enough.

She gets up, beckons Munka Du, and exits with him and the maids. The Tui-Hymn is audible, feebly and out of tune.

The debating chamber.

Armed guards all over the place. Enter Munka Du and Turandot. The former makes his way reluctantly to the rostrum, the latter trips nimbly to the Imperial box. She throws off a shawl and sits there, half naked.

EMPEROR: How can you make such a spectacle of yourself!

TURANDOT: Don't complain, it's for your own sake.

NU SHAN: As Chairman of the Association of Tuis, it is my

honour to present to you the supplicant of the fourth day, Mr Munka Du, Professor of the Philosophy Department. *Turandot applauds.*

MUNKA DU: Imperial Majesties, Gentlemen! In this historic hour . . .

A scuffle at the entrance, and four men enter, half naked. They stamp their way to centre stage, singing.

THE FOUR:

Sun and rain, sun and rain
It's all you need to know.
If the cold is in your bones
Kai Ho! Kai Ho! Kai Ho!

The armed guards move in on the four with batons, and drive them out.

THE FOUR *holding up a cotton pennant on a stick*:

If you can't afford a coat
Naked you must go.
There's enough to make a flag
Kai Ho! Kai Ho! Kai Ho!

MUNKA DU *as the four are driven outside*: Imperial Majesties, Gentlemen . . .

YOUNG SHI ME *throws his newly won Tui-hat to the ground and stamps on it*: Let them go free! Or take me too! *He is led away.*

MUNKA DU: In this historic hour . . .

SHI ME *at the door*: What are you doing, the god of the Philosophy Department!? The time for words is past. The power of speech will never clothe their naked bodies! *He is dragged away.*

NU SHAN *furious*: I'll have you struck off, Shi Me!

CRIES: Get on with it, Munka Du! – The Palace of the Tui Association has become a fishmarket. – It stinks a darn sight worse than that.

MUNKA DU *by now grey in the face*: I'll tell you why I'm speaking here, Shi Me, I am speaking because I shall not let anyone rob me of the freedom to speak, wherever I will, and whatever I will. Oh yes, here I stand, to defend freedom, my freedom, your freedom, the freedom of all men.

CRY: And the freedom of wolves!

MUNKA DU *while the policemen seek out the heckler*: Yes!

CRY: And of sheep?

MUNKA DU *while the policemen seek out the heckler*: Yes, of sheep too! I am not of the opinion, I am not of the opinion – *he mops his brow* – I am not of the opinion that one should deprive the naked of cotton for their clothes, but if I were of that opinion, of that opinion, I would wish to be permitted to express it, it, that is the opinion, which I don't share, with anyone. It's not a question of cotton, it is a question of the freedom of beliefs about cotton, which itself is not at issue, which is not our business here. Here, at this hour, it's not a question of business, but a question of opinions. *Unrest.* Opinions are the question, not businesses!

At the door, Gogher Gogh and his two bodyguards have forced their way in.

GOGHER GOGH: So, perhaps a man may express an opinion here, a man who doesn't possess a Tui-hat but who has demonstrated by his deeds that he . . . *He is dragged away.*

CRY: Oppression. They're oppressing the pickpockets!

MUNKA DU: Your Imperial Majesties, Gentlemen! Let us speak no more of cotton, but instead of the virtues which a people needs in order to go without cotton. Not: where is the cotton? That is not the question, but rather: where are the virtues? What has become of that happy spirit of renunciation, the legendary patience, with which the Chinese people has borne so many misfortunes? That eternal hunger, that grinding labour, that rigour of the law?

EMPEROR: He's rambling. And after such a promising beginning!

MUNKA DU: That, Your Majesties, Gentlemen, was – *reading from his notes* – the inner freedom. That, Your Majesties, Gentlemen, is lost.

CRY: What about the outer freedom!

MUNKA DU: Let me pay my respects to the simple folk of former generations who, dressed in rags – for we didn't always have cotton then – who, satisfied with a handful of rice, lived out their lives in dignity, without recourse to begging or to violence. I've heard it said, Kai Ho, you may be sitting here amongst us. *Agitation.* I don't know if that's true. But if you are here, then let me ask you this: what have you done with freedom? You who would enslave the whole world. You demand of everyone that they scream and brawl over cotton, as if there were nothing better!

CRY: Like silk!

MUNKA DU: But I demand of you the freedom to express my opinion, do you hear me? I'm not concerned with the cotton stashed in the Emperor's warehouses, I am concerned with freedom!

Serious unrest.

YAO YEL: Now the cat's out of the bag. These idiots have given the whole game away!

The Imperial Family leaves the chamber.

MUNKA DU: Freedom! Freedom! Free . . .

Singing intones from the pipes: 'Sun and rain, sun and rain / It's all you need to know. / If the cold is in your bones / Kai Ho! Kai Ho! Kai Ho!' – The police move in on Munka Du.

The foyer.

Tuis are jostling in the exit.

CRIES: He's brought ruin on the Association. – He didn't seem himself to me. – That's why he was so vehement. – The warehouses, that was a slip of the tongue. – A slip of the tongue or a slip of the noose.

GU *to the old man, Sen*: Don't be cast down.

SEN: On the contrary, I am uplifted. As they say: the cat is out of the bag, and has spied the rat.

ER FEI: Grandfather, it was a good song.

SEN: Shh! He means the melody, the tune, it was a pretty tune. *Slyly.* You see, I've already learnt something from the Tuis. In the presence of the police, you have to be a Tui.

GU *suddenly throws his Tui-hat to the ground*: I begin to despise my own vocation, old man. *He looks around anxiously, and picks his hat up again, beats the dust off it*: All the same, there's still much wisdom to be learnt here.

SEN: There are many wisdoms. I am for the wisdom which redistributes the fields.

6

BY THE TOWN WALL

A hangman and his assistants are impaling the severed head of Munka Du next to other heads.

HANGMAN: Nothing is more terrible than the reversals of human fortune. Just yesterday Yen Fai and his assistants were setting up the last heads on the west side. They were happy, without a care in the world. They had chosen the west side because the Tibetan caravan was passing by, with the Pilgrims of the Seventh Purification. It was all a great success. The pilgrims proclaimed themselves well satisfied with the spectacle, and Yen Fai's happiness seemed complete. But over night the rains came and a storm blew up from the west, and this morning the whole thing looked a right mess. Heads, good heads, such as it's hard to find in China these days, had become pitiful shadows of their former selves. Yen Fai shouldn't have chosen the west side for such a display. They say the Princess Turandot wept for two whole hours this morning. *They finish their work and move on.* Ah yes, happiness and disaster, they're close cousins for men of our estate.

A MAN'S VOICE *sings in the distance*:

Tell the man who draws the cart
He's soon to die.
Tell him, who'll live on?
The man who's sitting in the cart.
Evening approaches.
A handful of rice
And a fine day
Would draw to its close.

The scribe of the Tui Academy arrives with the boy, Si Fu.

They look at the heads and stop in front of an unfamiliar face.

SCRIBE: That is my teacher, the great light of Chinese grammar. He talked a load of nonsense at the Congress, but now there's no one left who can explain the poems of Po Chu-yi. Oh, why can't they just stick to their own subjects! – There's someone coming.

They exit. Enter Turandot, going for a walk with her maids. Armed guards follow her.

TURANDOT *seeing Munka Du's head*: Dudy! And there's Xi Wei too, the paper-tailor. I suppose I should be wearing mourning, but that would be so off-putting for the other candidates. There are so many heads on the wall; anyone would think our politics was indefensible. Who's that approaching?

FIRST MAID: It's the bandit Gogher Gogh, he's a figure of fun in the Tuis' teahouse.

SECOND MAID: Oh no he's not. The ladies of Peking all swoon over him, he's a real man.

TURANDOT: I see, a handsome fool.

FIRST MAID: It looks as if those two men are following him. Let's go.

TURANDOT: We'll stay right where we are.

Enter Gogher Gogh, looking around anxiously, as if he's running away. When he sees the women he stops. Turandot smiles.

GOGHER GOGH: You're out for a walk.

TURANDOT *laughs*: To buy a chicken.

GOGHER GOGH: That's nice. May I walk with you?

The first maid looks in the direction he's come from, and laughs.

TURANDOT: By all means.

Gogher Gogh's bodyguards approach, looking threateningly at Gogher.

GOGHER GOGH *offers Turandot his arm in a gentlemanly fashion, and leads her past the bodyguards*: You'll need closer protection, miss. There are all sorts of rogues round here.

TURANDOT: Do these gentlemen have some business with you?

GOGHER GOGH: All kinds of people turn to me, failures and outcasts the lot of them.

TURANDOT: Perhaps they just want to ask something?

GOGHER GOGH: I'm sick of questions. I won't answer any more questions, it's a matter of principle.

TURANDOT: Are the questions perhaps uncomfortable questions?

GOGHER GOGH: I've no idea; I won't even listen.

TURANDOT: Ah, a politician! – And what do you think of the conference so far?

GOGHER GOGH: Nothing. This here is the result. I tried in vain to prevent the whole thing, but they wouldn't let me in, just because I'm not as much a scholar as the other gentlemen. And now there's all this trouble. If the state tries to answer every question that's asked, it's bound to come to no good. And why? Because there'll be trouble. That's why. How long do you think you'd put up with your poodle if he trotted up every morning to ask: so where's the pork chop gone? He'd soon seem pretty unattractive.

TURANDOT: There's some truth in that. And what do you think about women?

GOGHER GOGH: The Chinese woman is loyal, hard-working and obedient. But she needs to be managed, just like the people, with an iron hand. Otherwise she'll go soft. *The bodyguards pass by, threateningly.* I'll give short shrift to recalcitrants.

TURANDOT: And what do you make of me?

GOGHER GOGH: You're a mysterious creature, if I may say so. Besides, I believe I must already have had the honour; where have I come across you before?

TURANDOT: I can help you there: it was in a literary setting.

GOGHER GOGH: A nation without literature is no proper cultural nation. But it has to be a healthy literature. I come from a respectable, simple family background. In school I was good at physical education and religious instruction, but I had certain leadership qualities too, from early on. I set up a business with seven like-minded associates; it took iron discipline to make it what it is today. I demand of my followers a fanatical belief: in me. That's the only way I can attain my goals. *To the armed guard*: Arrest those people. *The bodyguards disappear.* Where was it you wanted to go?

TURANDOT *amused*: Well, if you've nothing better to do, in the direction of the Imperial Palace. *To the second maid*: So my judgement wasn't quite right, after all.

They all exit in the direction from which Turandot and her train first came.

THE HEAD OF XI WEI: I fear there'll be rain again tonight.

UNKNOWN HEAD: My main argument was sound, but I acknowledge, in the detail I could have been a little more colourful.

HEAD OF KE LEI: Nothing, nothing grew.

HEAD OF XI WEI: There must be an answer. I think I was quite close last night.

HEAD OF MUNKA DU: If only I'd slept properly, then . . .

HEAD OF KE LEI: It's the Emperor who holds sway – holds sway, an unhappy choice of vocabulary – I needn't have expressed it quite like that.

HEAD OF XI WEI: True scholarship never tires! Of course there's an answer to every question. You just have to have the time to discover it.

UNKNOWN HEAD: We've got time enough now.

HEAD OF KE LEI: You could say, we enjoy a certain sort of freedom here.

The geographer Pauder Mel approaches, in a small carriage pulled by two young Tuis.

YOUNG TUI *shouts*: Clear the road for the great geographer Pauder Mel!

PAUDER MEL: Let's have no excuses, no tiredness! My greatest worry is that the Congress will already be over before I get there. Someone might discover the answer at any moment. And what then?

The young Tuis stop and point fearfully at the impaled heads.

PAUDER MEL: Criminals and traitors! Onwards, my young friends!

7

IN THE IMPERIAL PALACE

The Prime Minister is receiving the delegates of the Clothesmakers and their Union Tui.

UNION TUI: Your Excellency! A precise analysis of the situation reveals ...

DELEGATE *impatiently*: Let me. Our Clothesmakers won't be restrained much longer, that's all there is to it.

PRIME MINISTER: Let me assure you: the Emperor will draw the consequences from the failure of the Great Congress.

DELEGATE *pleased*: That's more like it! As I say, I can't hold my people back any longer.

PRIME MINISTER *leads him out*: You can wait for the decision in the antechamber. I notice, by the way, that the delegate of the Clothesless hasn't turned up.

DELEGATE: They're playing their own politics.

PRIME MINISTER: So you don't see eye to eye with them?

DELEGATE: One thing's certain: you won't see me associating with that fellow any more.

Exits with his Tui. Enter the Emperor and Yao Yel.

EMPEROR: The Tuis are to blame for everything. I only ever wanted what was best.

YAO YEL: And got it too.

Enter the Court Tui, the Minister for War and Nu Shan.

COURT TUI: Majesty, there is no cause for concern.

NU SHAN: The populace is keeping a cool head, Your Majesty.

MINISTER FOR WAR: The city gates are securely in our control, Sire.

EMPEROR: Thank you. Just a moment. What's really happened?

MINISTER FOR WAR: Your Majesty, Kai Ho is getting restless in the northern provinces, he's started to march on the capital.

YAO YEL: Certain ... erm ... stores must be destroyed immediately.

EMPEROR: In that case, I abdicate.

PRIME MINISTER: How?

EMPEROR: How am I going to abdicate?

PRIME MINISTER: No, how can the stores be destroyed.

YAO YEL: Burning won't do. Cotton makes too much of a stink.

EMPEROR: All right, I'm abdicating then.

MINISTER FOR WAR: We can't get the army to do it. There'll be a mutiny.

EMPEROR: I abdicate.

Silence. – The Emperor looks at them in disbelief.

EMPEROR: You can think it over if you wish, but . . . *Since no one is taking any notice, he exits slowly.*

MINISTER FOR WAR: Your Majesty is impossible.

YAO YEL: You don't expect *me* . . . I would never dream . . . against my own brother . . . There's no point even asking . . . So they could say I'd usurped, in the hour . . . Don't press me, I've not the least ambition . . . Perhaps in an extreme emergency, for dynastic reasons, let us say . . . Can I depend on you? Arrest my brother, General. *Exit.*

PRIME MINISTER: Your Majesty!

They all bow and exit.

EMPEROR *enters by another door*: I've been thinking . . . *He sees that they've all left.* This is ridiculous. Is this the way you treat your Emperor? *Drums off-stage. The Emperor rushes to the window.* Why are the guards shouldering arms? Yao Yel! He's . . . Before you know it . . . You have to weigh every word, and in my own house! I must . . . immediately . . .

Enter Turandot with her maids and Gogher Gogh.

TURANDOT: Father, I've brought you one of the most intelligent men I've ever met.

EMPEROR: Have you got any small change?

GOGHER GOGH: Not on me, no.

TURANDOT: What do you need change for?

EMPEROR: I'm going to have to leave. I abdicated, in a moment of absent-mindedness. Yao Yel immediately usurps the throne. Of course it's against the law. The people have to be able to choose their rulers, after all.

GOGHER GOGH *glancing from time to time out of the window*: What's that supposed to mean: the people have to be able to choose their rulers? Can the rulers choose their people? I think not! Would you have chosen this particular people if you'd had the choice?

EMPEROR: Of course not. They're an idle lot, think only of their own good, and they live scandalously beyond our means.

GOGHER GOGH: The people are a danger and a threat to law and order. They're undermining the state.

TURANDOT: Clever, eh? *To Gogher Gogh*: Tell him what you think he should do.

GOGHER GOGH: That's simple. It's just that, unfortunately, I have problems of my own, and they're not so easy to solve. On the other hand, they are connected with yours. To keep it brief, we haven't got much time, the question about the cotton, you mustn't answer it, you must have it outlawed. – The guards, they're leaving!

EMPEROR: I see. Makes sense. It would be a whole lot easier.

GOGHER GOGH: If the guards withdraw I've had it.

TURANDOT: Stop them, forbid the guards to leave, Daddy!

EMPEROR *pacing up and down in excitement*: There's something in what you say. It's the first sensible advice I've had, and you're not even wearing a Tui-hat. I can't stop the guards, not any longer.

TURANDOT: I'd just like to observe, Father, these ideas are Mr Gogh's intellectual property. I know you. Mr Gogh is herewith admitted to the Tui Association's competition, and reserves all rights. I hope you've understood that?

Enter Yao Yel, the Minister for War and the Court Tui.

YAO YEL: There, you see. Why isn't my brother under arrest? Shoot him! Get on with it!

MINISTER FOR WAR *to the Emperor*: There's a mob advancing on the palace. Have you been conspiring with the people?

EMPEROR: Not another one of those questions? And not even the prescribed form of address!

GOGHER GOGH: It's all over. Kru Ki and the others.

TURANDOT: What makes you think you know what the mob wants?

YAO YEL: They want to lynch us, chicken-brain. What else

does a mob ever want?

EMPEROR: He's right.

GOGHER GOGH *suddenly*: I beg you, your attention please. These people, they're excited, they've been incited. As soon as they discover that I'm in here ...

YAO YEL: You mean, they know you?

GOGHER GOGH: They certainly do.

EMPEROR: Then you've got to speak to them, for God's sake man.

GOGHER GOGH: Impossible. If I fall into their hands, I mean, if I appear before them with nothing to show ...

EMPEROR: What does that mean? Promise them whatever you like.

MINISTER FOR WAR: Yes, promise anything.

YAO YEL: Everything!

GOGHER GOGH: That's all well and good. But who am I?

EMPEROR: My dear, good man, I've assessed your proposals most carefully, and I herewith charge you to act according to them, immediately. You have my full confidence. For myself, I'll withdraw to my chambers for a few minutes, and take a little sustenance.

GOGHER GOGH: Your Majesty, I shan't forget this.

Exit the Emperor with Yao Yel, Turandot and the Court Tui. Alarms backstage.

GOGHER GOGH *to the Minister for War*: Excellency, I need your sash. *The Minister doesn't understand.* Your Excellency, lives may depend on your presence of mind. Give me your sash, please. Don't make me humiliate myself kneeling, Excellency. A desperate man stands here before you, and he needs a sash. *He rips the sash off the reluctant Minister and tears it into ribbons.*

Enter the two bodyguards with three other bandits.

FIRST BODYGUARD: Hah, so we've got you?

GOGHER GOGH: Been looking for me, have you? *To the Minister for War*: They've been looking for me. Comrades, China expects ...

FIRST BODYGUARD: Don't joke.

SECOND BODYGUARD: Enough nonsense.

GOGHER GOGH: Quite right, enough nonsense. The time for

jokes has passed. Excellency! Lawless elements, who quite openly seek to damage the property rights of their fellow citizens and shamelessly endanger the sacred order of the state – walk free, while rough but honest, loyal subjects look on unarmed and powerless. In accordance with my Imperial commission, I demand weapons for these men here. From the Imperial arsenals. *He goes up to the bodyguards and formally invests them with the rags of the sash as armbands.* As defenders of the public order, and inspired by your fanatical resolve, you will kick anyone in the guts who dares to rebel. Your reward: twice the normal police wage.

SECOND BODYGUARD: Sure thing, boss.

The Emperor and the others return, drinking from small cups.

EMPEROR: And now?

GOGHER GOGH: Your Majesty, in this historic hour let me present my old brothers-in-arms – and they really are brothers: the Krukher Kru brothers. I've discovered that the mob that was seen in the neighbourhood of the palace turn out to be my own trusted fellow-warriors – who now put themselves at Your Majesty's disposal, body and soul.

EMPEROR: My dear Mr Gogh, I'm moved. But above all it's a question of the Imperial storehouses, they urgently need protection.

GOGHER GOGH: Majesty, give me twenty-four hours and you won't even recognise your capital city.

YAO YEL: What's to happen to the warehouses?

EMPEROR: No questions. *To the Minister for War*: Arrest my brother, General!

Turandot applauds.

YAO YEL: But you'd abdicated!

EMPEROR: Not irrevocably. *Mischievously*: Didn't you issue an order to have me shot?

YAO YEL: Nonsense. There's always a lot of talk when people are excited.

GOGHER GOGH *keen*: Majesty, allow me to carry out your commands, without compromise.

MINISTER FOR WAR *anticipating him*: Imperial Majesty . . .

YAO YEL: You'll make a fine mess of business without my help. *He exits, furious, with the Minister for War, followed by the first bodyguard and two bandits. On the threshold he meets the Prime Minister and Nu Shan. They bow respectfully, then catch sight of the Emperor and bow nervously to him.*

EMPEROR: I have resumed the reins of government, my dear fellow, you'll be hearing from me. At the moment things are happening rather thick and fast.

Behind the Prime Minister the delegate of the Clothesmakers appears with his Tui.

DELEGATE: His Excellency the Prime Minister hinted at this morning's audience that Your Majesty would draw the full consequences of the failure of the Tui Conference.

EMPEROR: Quite right. You're under arrest.

GOGHER GOGH: Follow me. *He sees Nu Shan.* And who is this gentleman?

PRIME MINISTER: Mr Nu Shan, Chairman of the Tui Association.

GOGHER GOGH: A Tui. *Roaring*: You're under arrest! There are, as we all know, dangerous opinion-mongers at work here. To be precise, people with dangerous opinions. I have nothing against it if a man takes money for an opinion. Under my leadership the state will spend even more on opinions. On opinions which suit me. This endless thinking, this way and that, it disgusts me. Just have a bit of decency and respect for the people who know better. *Roaring*: Take him away!

TURANDOT *beaming*: Oh Goghy!

The Dowager Empress comes running in with a jar of ginger.

7a

IN THE COURTYARD OF THE IMPERIAL PALACE

Gogher Gogh addresses his followers.

GOGHER GOGH: It's just been discovered that the Imperial

warehouses are stuffed to the rafters with cotton. Only a few days ago, certain dishonourable wretches were spreading the lie that there was no cotton. They've had their punishment. Equally, the Emperor's own brother, Yao Yel, who'd been stockpiling the cotton behind the Emperor's back, has been arrested and shot. He was going to burn some of the cotton to cover up his crime. But he didn't manage to carry out his monstrous plan. Comrades! A dishonest military clique attempted to persuade the Emperor that your services were no longer needed. And so I find myself, with the approval of the Emperor of course, compelled, as I was in the early years of our movement, to set an example, a beacon visible from afar, from which even the stupidest rogue may recognise that, in the absence of sufficiently energetic protection, no property is secure. To this end, this very night, you will set fire to one half of the warehouses. – Do your duty!

8

THE LITTLE TUI MARKET

On great easels the Tuis are setting up open books. For one yen passers-by may read one page.

GENERAL EDUCATION TUI:

> The poor fool sweats and labours night and day
> But still he can't improve his situation
> All he has to call his own are: troubles –
> And that's because he's short on education.
> The rich man gets to lord it in his palace
> The poor man scrapes a living in a hut.
> It's knowledge always makes the real difference
> And if you've got it – then you'll take your cut.

A very old woman pays a yen and looks into the book. Enter Sen with the boy, Er Fei.

ER FEI: So will I have to be a Tui like him, grandfather?

SEN: We've still got our money.

ER FEI: Can't we buy a frog instead?

SEN: Er Fei, what have you got against the Tuis?

ER FEI: I think they're bad people.

SEN: Look at that bridge over there. Who do you think built it?

ER FEI: The Emperor.

SEN: No. Think again.

ER FEI: The stonemasons.

SEN: Yes. But think one more time. *Pause.* The masons built it, but a Tui told them how to do it. We've only heard how they talk, we haven't yet got through to their real knowledge. There's knowledge on display here. I'm just a bit disappointed how expensive it is. Er Fei, if there's still no sign of progress this time, then, fair enough, they must be driven out with fire and sword. *He walks indecisively from easel to easel.*

Enter four washerwomen, amongst them Ma Gogh.

QIUNG: So, now I've bought it, and that's that. *She shows the Economics Tui a new headscarf.* Cotton.

SU: A millionairess.

QIUNG: Four weeks' pay, but it's worth it. *To Yao*: Everyone thinks it suits me. You think so too, don't you, Yao?

YAO: No. You're too bony for that look.

QIUNG: That's rich, coming from you. You cow, I suppose you're the only pretty one? You think you're pretty?

YAO: No, I'm not pretty either.

MA GOGH: Why do you ask her? You know she always tells the truth.

Qiung laughs loudly.

ECONOMICS TUI: How can we help? What are you young ladies after?

QIUNG: We're from the Almond Blossom Laundry, we're out shopping.

ECONOMICS TUI: Ladies! How can we make a success of business? Take a look in my book, and for just a yen you too can find out what the science of economics has to say about it:

Imagine business isn't going well –
The big fish keep me wriggling in the dark.
Why then I scratch my last remaining hairs out

And ask how I can get to be a shark.
I know what folk endure to earn their bread
And, for their pains, they get it up the butt.
They're good for nothing, or they're good for fleecing –
I know the score – and so I take my cut.

QIUNG: That's something for you, Ma. – She's got her own launderette, and she wants to buy her son a big laundry. You might learn how to make a bit of cash.

MA GOGH: Could you open it at the page where it says something about loans?

MEDICINE TUI: What about your aches and pains? Maybe you're sick and just don't know it? Want to find out what the doctor knows? Just one yen!

Let's say you're wracked by shooting stomach cramps:
The doctor takes one look ... he's seen enough.
The patient staggers out in pain, but first
He pays. Because the doctor knows his stuff.
He knows the Latin names but, more important
He knows the rate for such a painful gut.
Unless you know, you'll ache and ail and sicken
But if you know – why then you'll take your cut.

MA GOGH: I should really take a look in here too. I've got a sore shoulder from the washing. But I'd better see how I can get a proper laundry for my son. But the pain has been quite bad lately.

QIUNG: A woollen shawl would be better for your aching shoulder.

MA GOGH: But that would cost fifteen yen.

Gogher Gogh's second bodyguard enters with two other bandits and Turandot's two maids.

SECOND BODYGUARD: There you are, Mother Ma. And in such an unhealthy part of town. Do you know what we are now? *He points to his armband.* Policemen! Don't worry, it's all the other way around now, from today. Mother Ma, your son has made quite a step-up, he's waiting for you in the Imperial Palace. There, you see.

MA GOGH: Tut, don't you go talking to me in public, Scarface. You'll embarrass my friends.

SECOND BODYGUARD: Mother Ma, these young missies will

be telling their children and their children's children how, once upon a time, they used to know you. Come on, let's go. *He takes hold of her.*

FIRST MAID: My lady, a personality such as yourself, so elevated that it would be improper to address you by name, belongs by the side of her great son.

MA GOGH: Something must have happened to Gogher. I'd better see how he's getting along. *She makes to leave with them.*

FIRST MAID: Permit us, dear lady, to accompany you to the corner, to the sedan chair. The bearers didn't want to enter this filthy market street.

The first bodyguard returns with five other bandits, all carrying torches.

FIRST BODYGUARD: So you found her. Great times, Mother Ma! *Ma Gogh makes a dismissive gesture and goes off with the second bodyguard.* Hey you, say, where are the Emperor's warehouses?

QIUNG: Over Tanners' Bridge. *Exit the bandits.* What's going on? I have a bad feeling. We'd better go home, Su!

SU *has reached the Love-life Tui's stall*: I'll catch you up.

LOVE-LIFE TUI: The mysteries of love! Happiness or broken hearts? How should I behave towards my love?

The game of love has two quite different players
The one adores, the other one's adored.
One partner gives, the other one just takes it
One plays his heart, the other looks on, bored.
So hide your face if e'er you feel it blushing
And keep your pretty, pouting mouth tight shut.
For if you give him leave, he'll have your heart out
And if he knows you love – he'll take his cut.

Come along, miss. Find out the truth, before it's too late. One yen.

SU *pays*: Should I throw myself at his feet, or behave as if I didn't even fancy him?

LOVE-LIFE TUI: The latter, miss, always the latter! *He reads to her in low voice.*

QIUNG: Why do you bother with that rubbish, Su? If the man

who wrote it had understood enough to get himself a girl, he wouldn't have had time to write a book at all.

SEN *who has been standing undecided in front of the Economics Tui's stall*: Ladies, don't make jokes about knowledge. If I wasn't so drawn to this book, I'd certainly make a study of that one. It's my opinion you should never deny anyone a pleasure, and least of all yourself. Why is the young lady laughing? *He smiles at Yao, who was laughing.*

QIUNG *alarmed*: Yao, you're not answering.

SEN: Indeed. You should always answer.

YAO: I'm laughing because, old man, you can't do it any longer anyway.

SEN *laughs as well*: That may be true, but don't tell anybody. If you can't catch the tiger, maybe you can still catch the hedgehog, as they say. And if you don't learn for yourself, maybe you should still learn for others. *Gesturing to the boy.* He's growing fast.

Unrest amongst the Tuis. They all look towards the rear.

QIUNG: Look, something's burning. Over Tanners' Bridge.

SEN: It smells of burning cotton.

TUIS: We'd better move our stalls out of the way. When the fire brigade come they smash straight through everything. – There'll be no fire brigade. – What do you mean?

Gogher Gogh and the Prime Minister arrive, with armed troops.

GOGHER GOGH: That conflagration must have been started by the Clothesmakers and the Clothesless, along with the disaffected Tuis. It's a beacon for the rebel Kai Ho, no question. This calls for rigorous measures. Above all, we must root out the intellectual arsonists. Search through the books, and discover how they undermine the state. *Exits with the Prime Minister.*

FIRST SOLDIER *to the Medicine Tui*: What does it say in this book?

MEDICINE TUI *shaking*: All you need to know about tuberculosis, or broken bones.

FIRST SOLDIER: What? Broken bones? We've had enough of that, broken bones indeed. That's a direct assault on the authority of the police. Arrest him! *He throws the book to the ground and stamps on it.*

SEN *tries to stop him*: Don't stamp on it, it's useful.

FIRST SOLDIER *strikes him down*: You swine! Daring to resist state authority. *To the General Education Tui*: And what's this filth here? Confess!

GENERAL EDUCATION TUI: Knowledge, Officer, sir.

FIRST SOLDIER: Knowledge about what? Anything about cotton, eh?

GENERAL EDUCATION TUI *shaking his head*: That's not a part of general education, Officer.

FIRST SOLDIER: You crooks, you're all in cahoots with the arsonists. Inciting people against the Emperor.

GENERAL EDUCATION TUI: That's only the great Tuis, if at all, and not them either.

FIRST SOLDIER: Did you see anybody come through here with torches?

GENERAL EDUCATION TUI: Some men with armbands passed through.

A bandit with an armband and torch comes from the other direction.

BANDIT: Captain, two Kai Ho supporters have been spotted down at the Tuis' teahouse.

FIRST SOLDIER: Like him here?

The General Education Tui shakes his head in alarm.

FIRST SOLDIER: So, have you seen anyone with torches?

QIUNG *standing in front of Yao*: Not us, no.

YAO: But he's got one over there, Qiung.

QIUNG: That's just a truncheon, like the police have. We'd better go, Yao. Su, we're just leaving.

FIRST SOLDIER: Not so fast! Maybe you've seen someone else round here? Like him?

YAO: Five of them. And that's not a truncheon either.

FIRST SOLDIER: But this is. *He strikes her down and the soldiers drag her off.*

LOVE-LIFE TUI *helps Sen to his feet*: Don't cry little one, he's alive. They set fire to the warehouses themselves, and now they're arresting everyone who saw them do it.

GENERAL EDUCATION TUI: And now they want to ban this

book, by which I make my meagre livelihood. It's rubbish anyway, and not a word against them, hardly a true word in it! The poets, sucking up to their iron fists, the nation's great thinkers, worrying about their salaries! It's all rubbish anyway. Rubbish, stuff and nonsense!

SEN: Don't exaggerate, you made your living from it.

THE SCRIBE *from the Tui Academy comes running, he's bleeding from a head wound*: Oh Su, I've been looking for you for hours.

SU *throws herself in his arms*: Oh Wang! I shouldn't embrace you, I know. He's the one, I'm sorry, I just can't play it by the book.

GENERAL EDUCATION TUI: You're hurt, what happened?

SCRIBE: I'm a scribe at the Tui Academy. Or I was. The Palace of the Tui Association has been stormed by Gogher Gogh's men. They've been incorporated with the police, and they've got new armbands with insignia stamped on them. The Tui Association is accused of insulting the Emperor, because a state secret was revealed at the Great Congress. At this very moment they're burning the three thousand theses about the history of China, just because they mention defeats in the seventh century. Nu Shan has been hanged because he's supposed to have said that Gogher Gogh, who's been Chancellor since five o'clock, didn't know what three times five makes. I'm in danger myself, because I witnessed it all. And it's all because Kai Ho is already in Szechwan.

QIUNG *to the Tuis*: You'd better get rid of your hats.

LOVE-LIFE TUI: Where shall we put them? I live at the other end of town.

ECONOMICS TUI *to Qiung*: Take mine. I live quite a way away.

LOVE-LIFE TUI: I asked first.

ECONOMICS TUI: It's for the life of the mind, my dear.

QIUNG: Give them here, you poor things. *She hides the hats in her skirts.* If my Sun sees me like this he'll think I'm expecting, he'll run a mile.

GENERAL EDUCATION TUI: But the unions won't stand for it. They'll get together now.

Soldiers bring on the delegate of the Clothesmakers and his Tui, in chains.

SOLDIER: We'll teach you to ask the Emperor questions.

DELEGATE: You'll be teaching a lot of people then. *They beat him.*

Bandits bring on the delegate of the Clothesless and his Tui, also in chains.

BANDIT: So, do you still think our leader set fire to the warehouses?

They beat the delegate.

SOLDIER: Hey you! Why don't you come with us to the slaughterhouses: these two should get together.

The bandits turn round, and both sets of captives are led off.

DELEGATE OF THE CLOTHESLESS: *We* didn't know anything about it!

SCRIBE: Where can we go?

QIUNG: To the laundry. Maybe Ma will send someone. They fetched for her from the palace, her Gogher's been made a minister, so perhaps she can save poor Yao. She told the truth again, I couldn't stop her. But we should take the old man too. They can see by his bruises that he's been beaten once, they might just drag him away as a state criminal.

SEN *to the Economics Tui, who is busily ripping pages out of his book*: What are you tearing out?

ECONOMICS TUI: The pages about low earnings.

SEN: Can I buy them off you?

GENERAL EDUCATION TUI *beckons to Sen, in a low voice*: I understand what you're after, old man. But I've got something better for you. *He draws a little book from his pocket.* Don't show it to a soul, it's by Kai Ho.

SEN: I see, yes, I'd like to buy that.

QIUNG: Come with us to the suburbs, old man. You can't read it anyway.

SEN: Others can read it for me. Here's the money I got for my cotton. My journey has been worthwhile.

He gives him the purse and leaves with the girls and the scribe. The Love-life Tui joins them, dragging his book with him. That leaves only the General Education Tui, who is undecided, and the Medicine Tui, who is crouched over his battered book, sobbing.

8a

IN THE COURTYARD OF THE IMPERIAL PALACE

Turandot's two maids enter with a copper bath.

FIRST MAID *sets down the bath*: I'm not crossing the courtyard like this. *She loosens the top of her smock.*

SECOND MAID: If that cow sees you she'll have you whipped.

FIRST MAID: She's so jealous about that bloke!

SECOND MAID: I managed to brush past him on the way to the conference hall, you know, where it's so narrow. And do you know what he said? 'I beg your pardon.' There's manners for you.

FIRST MAID: She says she loves him because he's so clever.

SECOND MAID: She says he's clever, just because she fancies him.

FIRST MAID: That's for sure. There's clever ones as many as fish in the sea, but not so many fine figures.

They take up the bath again and carry it inside.

9

IN FRONT OF THE ALMOND BLOSSOM LAUNDRY

Old Sen is sitting on a barrel outside the laundry, the boy is damping his head bandage. Next to them Qiung is altering a Tui-hat for herself. On the other side, in front of a tall narrow house, a swordsmith is standing directing operations, which proceed invisibly on the first floor. Next to him, a Tui, Ka Mü with parcels of music scores. The district is very poor.

KA MÜ: Sir, they're all masterworks! You must look after them, as I have to go away for a while. This is ancient music. It's endangered because it's not Chinese, and the government we have now . . .

SWORDSMITH: I can't store anything more. I've already had a statue dumped on me, a goddess of justice, two storeys high. We had to break through the roof. Hey, slower there, turn it slowly!

KA MÜ: And this is new music. It's in trouble because it's not 'true to the spirit of the people'.

SEN: That's so unnecessary. The people don't want 'true spirits' anyway.

SWORDSMITH *sighing*: All right, I'll put them in the bedroom. As they're in danger. *He lets him into the house.*

A WOMAN *calls from the upper floor*: I'm sorry, Mr Lü Sheng, you'll just have to stand on your head, the children are so scared of your face.

KA MÜ *comes back out without the packages*: Thank you! Thank you! *He embraces him.* It's for China! *Exits quickly.*

SEN: When I was young like you I always wanted to hear just the one tune that the village carpenter used to play on his flute. These days I want variety in my music, something new all the time.

SWORDSMITH: How can they destroy something that took so much effort! All those little dots!

THE WOMAN *from the window*: Have you heard, they say the forbidden one is just a hundred miles from the capital.

SEN: Not so loud!

Enter Ma Gogh with Yao.

MA GOGH *calls from afar*: Qiung! Su! Good evening, Lü Sheng. So here we are again. *Qiung and Su come out of the house. Embraces all round.* She had the good sense to tell those thieves she worked in my laundry. And the stories she told me got me thinking all right. I couldn't have stood it much longer anyway. Gogher has gone mad, he's in charge now. I was proud of him in his old job, but now I'm ashamed. They wanted me to feel at home in the palace. This morning they brought a copper tub from the museum and set it down on the blue carpet in my chamber, which is that big you could stable fifty mules. And the Prime Minister says: Ladyship, your illustrious son says you only feel at home when you're washing. Please, wash – to your heart's desire! I gave him a kick, but I shouldn't have done that. When he'd gone a servant came in and turned his backside to me, to kick – to my heart's desire. The only sensible person in the whole palace was the Emperor's mother, she told me what she thinks of her son, and gave me a recipe for a special sort of cake. And they all thought she was mad! I made note of the recipe though, for Gogher. Where's my tea? And who's that?

QIUNG: That's Mr A Sha Sen, he's from cotton country, he came to the capital to study.

SEN *apologetically*: They told me I didn't have the head for it, but it seems I do after all, as this bump proves.

SU: What a horrible bruise!

YAO: It's not that big, it'll soon heal.

QIUNG *gives her a hug*: You're so rude, Yao.

The paper window on the first floor rips open and an iron hand pushes through with a huge upturned scale hanging from it.

SWORDSMITH: Careful you idiots!

VOICE *from inside*: There's not enough room for the arm!

SEN: They're stowing away the cultural artefacts, or whatever they call them. At the East Gate I saw a Tui at a temple where there's an invisible god. As we speak, he's probably leading it on a chain to the suburbs, where it can be housed in safety.

Three of the Clothesless come out of the narrow house with large bundles. Suddenly they begin to run.

ER FEI *tugs at Sen's arm*: Soldiers, grandfather!

They all run into the houses. The swordsmith just has time to throw a carpet over the arm of Justice, as two armed men come patrolling down the street. After they've passed by, a street-seller is heard in the background: 'Cotton! Cotton! Cotton for sale! Cotton from Yao Yel's warehouses, the enemy of the state!'. The woman looks out from the upper window. The street-seller comes down the street with a wagon loaded with cotton fabrics, guarded by an armed soldier.

STREET-SELLER: Cotton! Cotton! Cotton, from the burning warehouses of Yao Yel, hanged at the scaffold! Half a year's harvest destroyed by fire! Prices are soaring! Buy now, while you can still afford it! *No one reacts, so he moves on, still calling 'Cotton! Cotton!'.*

WOMAN: You can keep it. We've got nothing to eat and no shoes to wear. Anyway, the forbidden one will take care of everything.

She slams the window shut. Su and her scribe emerge.

SCRIBE: Don't cry too much, a little bit tonight, but then no more tomorrow. Promise me.

SU: Tomorrow too.

SCRIBE: All right. If I'm not back in three weeks it'll be because I've gone a long way round, that's all.

SU: How will you find your way? In those old shoes!

SCRIBE: I know a weaver over on the other side, he's leaving today with three others. And there are thousands of them already. They'll be easy enough to find.

SU: But your shoes are so worn, Wang. What are we to do?

SEN *comes out with the boy and Qiung*: If you could wait a while longer, we could leave together, perhaps.

SU: But you're heading north, whereas Wang's business is here in the neighbourhood. But his shoes are useless, what are we to do about that?

SEN: I see, so his shoes aren't good enough for a little business in the neighbourhood.

QIUNG: But at least he has a warm shawl for his shoulders. *She gives him her new headscarf.*

SEN: Don't stop for every little injustice you see by the wayside, that's dangerous. The river floods the valley, but the dam must be built in the mountains.

SCRIBE: Perhaps you could come with me after all? But I have to leave right away, I'm expected.

SEN: I can't do that, I still have some thinking to do.

SCRIBE: I'm off then, to the Tibetan Gate. Farewell. *He exits to the rear.*

SU: See you tomorrow, Wang! *She goes back into the house. Two of the Clothesless come and knock on the swordsmith's door. The swordsmith beckons them inside.*

SWORDSMITH: I can hardly get to my forge with all this bloody culture. And upstairs there's a terrible draught through the hole in the floor. And here come more of them, no hats on their heads. *He disappears quickly.*

Four Tuis from the teahouse approach: Wen, Gu, Shi Ka and Mo Si.

GU: Still here, Mr A Sha Sen? Is this the blacksmith's place, where we can hide the valuables?

QIUNG: The house is full. Besides, how can you walk around like that, with nothing on your heads? Any fool can see you used to have Tui-hats, and now they're rounding up everyone with a bare head!

WEN: It's terrible. They've closed the teahouse. Wit and wisdom have become homeless beggars.

GU: I have to try. If China loses its art it will degenerate into barbarism. *He knocks at the narrow house.* He's not answering. *He shows the others a scroll.* This is a Pi Jeng. Twelfth century. The hills of the Hoang Ho. Look at the line. Look at that blue. This is what they want to destroy.

QIUNG: Why?

GU: They say, real hills don't look like this. *He shows it to Sen.*

SEN: That's true, hills don't look like that. Not quite like that. But if they looked like that for everyone, we'd have no need of a painting. When I was a child my grandfather showed me what a sausage looks like. This whatsisname, the painter, shows me what hills look like. Of course, I can't see it straight away. But I guess, when I next climb a hill, it'll mean more to me. Perhaps it will be blue, and have such a line as this.

GU: Perhaps it will. But we haven't got time for long discussions. Get the swordsmith! This Pi Jeng is from the Imperial Museum!

SEN: If only it had been ours from the start! It would have been safer then.

MA GOGH *has appeared at the doorway*: I'll hide it for you. Gogher won't get a hold of it. He'd just tear it up. They should have sewn up my womb.

QIUNG: She's the Chancellor's mother, you know.

MA GOGH: There's no call to be afraid. I'll disown him. Give me the picture. He thinks he understands everything, and now he's in charge. It's a bad time for pictures. He thinks he's a painter.

SHI KA: The architects are frightened too.

MA GOGH: Yes, my son's an architect as well.

WEN: We should all have been scientists.

MA GOGH: Possibly not. He's the biggest scientist of all.

MO SI *shows her a globe*: Could you hide the globe as well? The fact the earth is round – it might matter one day.

ER FEI *tugs at Sen's arm*: Grandfather, a soldier!

THE TUIS: He mustn't see us, with our bare heads.

MA GOGH: Give the globe here. *She disappears into the house with the globe and the picture.*

The Tuis run away, with the exception of Mo Si, who has got held up.

SECOND BODYGUARD *looking for something*: And what is this my tired eyes espy? A Tui. Now where have you left your hat? No no, there's no need to be frightened this time. Come here. Clear off, Qiung, you scumbag. *Referring to Sen*: You have some quaint guests here in the laundry.

SEN: I'm a peaceful peasant. Just sitting here doing some thinking. That takes time for me, you know.

QIUNG: Don't you dare go inside. Mother Gogh will smash you over the head with a frying pan. *She sets her new hat at a jaunty angle and goes inside.*

SECOND BODYGUARD *confidentially to Mo Si*: So what's your name?

MO SI: I'm Mo Si, the king of excuse-makers.

SECOND BODYGUARD: That's good. Erm, because we need something, you know, not urgently, but . . . What do you call it, those things you do?

MO SI: A phrase, a formulation?

SECOND BODYGUARD: Right. The boss, right? Is getting married, right? Don't gawp like that, why shouldn't he, with her? Right? But it's just that he can't, right? One smirk on your ugly little face and I'll knock your head off, right? So, what is he to say to her? You come with me, and get it right, right? *He leads him off.*

The Clothesless come out of the swordsmith's with big bundles. One of the bundles falls apart. Guns and swords tumble out. Alarmed, they look at Sen, who just smiles and waves. They pack it all together again and hurry off.

SEN: Er Fei, I'm done thinking. Do up my sandals. The thoughts you can buy here stink. The whole country is governed by injustice, and in the Tui Academy all you get to learn is why it has to be that way. It's true, they can build stone bridges over the widest rivers. But the powerful are carried over them into indolent luxury, while the poor are herded into slavery. It's true, they have medicine. But the few are restored to health so they can commit injustice, while the rest are made fit in order to sweat on their behalf. Opinions are bartered like fish, and thought itself has fallen into disrepute. He's thinking, they say, what mean tricks is he brewing? And yet thinking is the most useful and pleasurable of activities. So what has happened to it? And then there's Kai Ho, I've got his little book right here. So far, all I really know about him is that the fools call him a fool, and the frauds a fraud. But wherever he has been and done the thinking, there are wide fields with rice and cotton, and the people seem to be happy. And if the people are happy when someone has been thinking, then, Er Fei, he must surely have done some good thinking, that's the proof. We're not going home, Er Fei, not yet. Even if I don't survive this new course of study. Good things demand a heavy price.

ER FEI: Will they be rooted out with fire and sword, grandfather?

SEN: No, it's more like with the soil: you have to decide what you want from it, barley or weeds. And act on your decision.

ER FEI *grumpily*: Will there always be Tuis, even when Kai Ho has shared out the fields?

SEN *laughs*: Not for long. We'll all get wide fields to plough and even wider fields to study. And just how we'll get the fields, it says right here. *Sen pulls out his book and flourishes it. They both exit to the rear.*

Qiung comes out of the laundry.

QIUNG *calls after them*: Hey, old man, home is over that way! You're taking the wrong road!

SEN: No, I think I'm taking the right road, Qiung!

10

IN THE ANCIENT MANCHU TEMPLE

Marching up and down, back and forth, small companies of soldiers armed to the teeth, and bandits with armbands. The Prime Minister enters and cross-questions the soldiers.

PRIME MINISTER: Any news of the rebels' positions?

CAPTAIN: Still no news.

PRIME MINISTER: And tested officers were sent with the reconnaissance troops?

CAPTAIN: Indeed, Excellency.

PRIME MINISTER: And dependable agents with the officers?

CAPTAIN: Indeed, Excellency.

PRIME MINISTER: And still no reports?

CAPTAIN: No, Excellency.

PRIME MINISTER: My confidence remains undimmed, Captain.

CAPTAIN: Indeed, Excellency.

Exit the Prime Minister, then the soldiers. Enter the Minister for War and the Court Tui, without his Tui-hat.

MINISTER FOR WAR: Have you heard the latest scandal? They're saying the unmentionable one shot a little Tui. He'd sent him to Her Imperial Highness to explain something and he stayed in her chamber two whole hours. It was something to do with cotton and de-briefing, they say. Hahaha!

The company of soldiers returns.

MINISTER FOR WAR: Repeat your instructions!

CAPTAIN: Said personage is to be arrested immediately after the ceremony.

Exit the Minister and Court Tui, then the soldiers. Enter Gogher Gogh in ceremonial dress, and a company of bandits.

GOGHER GOGH *to the first bodyguard*: Repeat your orders.

FIRST BODYGUARD: Arrest everyone after the ceremony.

GOGHER GOGH: Your brother was on duty with me this morning. Have you spoken to him since? *The first bodyguard shakes his head.* Good. He's gone and shot somebody. Have him quartered, at once, understand? And have the drums beat, so no one can hear what he says.

FIRST BODYGUARD: Right away, boss.

GOGHER GOGH *takes his loyal guard's dagger and conceals it up his sleeve*: I'll be needing this; there's nothing but deceit and treachery in this palace. Another thing: immediately after the marriage you grab the Manchu coat and throw it over me. No one will dare touch me wearing that, except some complete degenerate. I'll make sure that scoundrel Emperor gets the message: you don't just bunk off when danger threatens, and leave me to face the music.

Enter the Emperor with the Minister for War and the Prime Minister, followed by the captain and his men.

EMPEROR: My dear Gogh, I'm a little late, I know. I had to approve some rather stringent measures, you know, the usual thing in such situations.

GOGHER GOGH: Request permission to countersign the measures.

EMPEROR: Beg your pardon? Ah yes, countersign, of course. And there she comes, on cue, the lovely young bride.

Enter Turandot with the Court Tui and her maids. They bow in greeting.

TURANDOT: Papa, I've just met a really nice man, I want to marry him. I don't mean the Tui from last night from the teahouse, he was intelligent as well, and I'm not at all pleased with you for what you did to him, Gogher, there's no need to be churlish. But I don't mean him, it's an officer, he's just explained to me how the palace is to be defended, you see, I consider the situation to be extremely serious, there's no time to lose. So can I marry him?

EMPEROR: No.

TURANDOT: What do you mean, no? This isn't just some passing fancy, it goes much deeper. Because it's all a question of defending ourselves now, every inch. He'd make a very good son-in-law, he knows so much about horses. *An officer enters and tries to communicate with the*

Minister for War, who waves him away because Turandot is speaking. An army without a cavalry, Papa ...

EMPEROR: I can't have the palace defended by horses. Let's proceed to the ceremony.

Exit the officer.

TURANDOT: Papa, that's really very inconsiderate of you. You have to understand, Gogher. It'll hurt for a bit, but life goes on, and after all your war wound healed up all right didn't it. Just do me this one favour, and don't be obstinate. Can I, Papa?

EMPEROR *roughly*: I've already said, no. *To Gogher Gogh*: Of course, if you care to resign and step aside ...

GOGHER GOGH: Your Majesty, Imperial Highness. In this historic hour we stand here, before the shrine of the first Manchu Emperor, in awe and excited expectation. I am a simple man. Not one for speeches. But Your Majesty has entrusted this man of the people with a holy mission, the protection of the throne. And Your Imperial Highness has given me your heart. It is not my part not to justify such trust, all the more as in these difficult times it is, above all, all a question of trust. When Your Majesty's honoured and departed brother, driven by unholy delusion, endangered the honour of the Imperial Family, then I acted with iron determination and took immediate control of the warehouses, and so regained the trust and confidence of the common people.

An officer with a bandaged head comes looking for the Minister of War.

OFFICER: Kai Ho ... at the Tibetan Gate ...

GOGHER GOGH *continues nervously*: I shall now discourse at a little length about the events of last week. The whole business has not just been about cotton, as some people think. There have been those who talked about cotton from dawn to dusk, and tried to undermine the confidence of the people, and they have received their deserts. *At a gesture from the Minister for War the soldiers leave.* It is due solely to my energetic intervention that the Emperor and the people are now united in unprecedented ...

TURANDOT: Papa, I won't do it.

EMPEROR: You just shut up. Mr Gogh, we've received certain intelligences which suggest it might be wise to complete the ceremony as quickly as possible, or else to postpone it.

GOGHER GOGH: Out of the question. I assume responsibility for the protection of your Imperial person, and that of Her Highness.

EMPEROR: Minister . . .

MINISTER FOR WAR: Gentlemen, the situation has clearly deteriorated. *To the Emperor*: I've sent the palace guard to defend the gates.

EMPEROR *while Gogher Gogh's bandits take up positions at the doors*: What? You've sent them away. You had explicit orders . . .

GOGHER GOGH: Hand over the keys! Where's the temple guard?

FIRST BODYGUARD: He must have run away. *He rattles at the entrance door to the temple. It opens.* Not locked!

Cries from outside. The door opens into the inner temple. The Imperial Manchu tunic has disappeared.

FIRST BODYGUARD: Treachery! The tunic has gone.

EMPEROR: Cut down.

PRIME MINISTER: The guard has disappeared: he's stolen it.

GOGHER GOGH: Gentlemen, let us proceed to the marriage ceremony. This little incident is happily of no consequence.

TURANDOT: Perhaps he was cold, Papa.

EMPEROR: But it was a poor coat, all patched up.

GOGHER GOGH: There's few enough these days, even poor quality coats. If you hadn't tried to corner the cotton market! The marriage ceremony, gentlemen!

Drums in the distance. Turandot screams shrilly.

EMPEROR: That was Yao Yel, it wasn't me.

Sounds of jubilation from a great crowd.

SOLDIER: It was the whole pack of you, and you're finished now!

Notes and Variants

THE ANTIGONE OF SOPHOCLES

Texts by Brecht

JOURNAL ENTRIES

16 December 1947

Between 30 November and 12 December finished an adaptation of *Antigone*, since I want to do preparatory work on *Courage* with Weigel and Cas for Berlin and can do this here in Chur where Curjel is working, though I then need a second part for Weigel. On Cas's advice I am using the Hölderlin translation, which is seldom or never performed because it is considered too obscure. I come across Swabian accents and grammar-school Latin constructions and feel quite at home. And there is some Hegel in there too. It is presumably the return to the German-speaking world which is forcing me into this enterprise. As far as dramatic composition is concerned, 'fate' eliminates itself all along the line of its own accord. Of the gods only the local popular deity, the god of joy, remains. Gradually, as the adaptation of the scenes progresses, the highly realistic popular legend emerges from the ideological fog.

23 December 1947

In *Galileo* the moral lesson is of course in no way absolute. If the bourgeois social movement which makes use of him were on the way down, then he could recant without further ado and in that way achieve something very reasonable. (See *He Who Says Yes* and *He Who Says No*.)

In the *Antigone* adaptation the moral decline derives from an enterprise for which the state is not strong enough. It could be poor weaponry, or a bottleneck in food supplies caused by too small a fleet of vehicles, or strategic errors that provide the immediate grounds for the descent into brutality; mishandling of the economy is also adduced as a reason for taking the war option; but that too indicates an enfeeblement.

25 December 1947
Hölderlin's language in *Antigone* deserves deeper study than I was able to give it this time. It is of an astounding radicalism.

'Süss Mahl den Vögeln, die auf Frasses Lust sehn' or:
'So steht es dir und gleich wirst du beweisen, ob gutgeboren ...' etc.

['Sweet dish for the birds that look and lust for food' or
'So it stands for you. And you will prove now whether you are well born ...' etc.]

Then the Swabian popular *Gestus*:

'Und die Sache sei/nicht wie für nichts.'
'Denn treulos fängt man *mich* nicht.'
'Treibt sein' Verkehr er, mit dem Rossegeschlecht.'
'Hochstädtisch kommt, unstädtisch
zu nichts er, wo das Schöne
mit ihm ist und mit Frechheit.'

['And that the matter is/ Not one that does not matter.'
'I won't be caught faithless.'
'He does his trade, with the race of horses.'
'In high civility uncivil he comes
To nothing where beauty is
With him and thuggish pride.']

I wrote the bridging verses in hexameters, largely to test whether I had learnt anything from the *Manifesto*. In fact it is now easier, above all it can be done faster.

25 December 1947
On Christmas Eve Cas and Erika come round. We work on the *Antigone*. First we twiddled the radio knob but the only German station we could find was broadcasting endless lists of names of missing soldiers, and the Nehers' son is missing in the USSR.

4 January 1948
In modelling the set Cas and I stumble on an ideological element of the first order. Should we place the barbaric totem poles with the horses' skulls at the back between the actors' benches, thus indicating the barbaric location of the old poem which the actors leave in order to act (the de-totemised version)? We decide to place the acting

among the totem poles, since we are still living in the totemic state of the class war.

5 January 1948
In *Antigone* the violence is explained by inadequacy. The war against Argos derives from mismanagement in Thebes. Those who have been robbed have to look to robbery themselves. The undertaking exceeds the strength available. Violence splits the forces instead of welding them together; basic humanity, under too much pressure, explodes, scattering everything with it into destruction.

12 January 1948
In Sophocles the Antigone-Creon incident is the sequel to a victorious war: the tyrant (who is simply the ruler), in settling scores with personal enemies who have made victory more difficult for him, runs up against a humane custom and experiences the break-up of his family. In the new version the action starts from the crucial moment where 'very little' is needed for victory and yet the most desperate force has to be employed, i.e. things that are beyond all measure prove to be absolutely essential. This commitment of the last moral reserves fails and hastens the collapse, which in any case had inevitably to follow from the overall constellation. The collapse thereby becomes, as it were, all the more total. The ruling house disintegrates when the son breaks with it (the Megareus-Haemon action repeats the Eteocles-Polynices action, i.e. the elimination of Creon's children follows the elimination of his rival Oedipus' children). Then his tame ideologist, the seer, drops out because he foresees disaster. All that is left for Antigone to do is to help the foe, which is the sum total of her moral contribution; she also had eaten for too long of the bread that is baked in the dark.

18 January 1948
It is no longer adequate just to hold up ancient Greek culture as the ultimate standard; the bourgeois classics were only interested in aesthetics. (Only took an aesthetic interest even in democracy.) *Antigone* in its entirety belongs with the barbaric horses' skulls. Of course, the play has by no means yet undergone the process of thorough rationalisation.

10 April 1948
Everything rises in me when in discussions about the new version I hear *Antigone* being regarded as a moral play. Of course, what with the destruction of Thebes (and of Creon), it does come perilously close to the maxim 'crime doesn't pay', but I still hope that the play shows nothing more (or less) than that enterprises that need too much violence readily fail. This amounts to no more than saying that impractical enterprises are impractical, and would be pretty banal, if it did not give an insight into a special sort of violence, namely the sort which derives from inadequacy, so that violence is seen to derive from stupidity. This brings the moral and the practical together, so that the former loses that sense of being absolute, rigid, enthroned in the supernatural.

It is dangerous to impute a moral mission to art unless you are in a position to see the moral practices of a certain period in relative terms – and who might be capable of this? All the state can do is to come to terms with 'immoral art'. The better the conditions, the easier it is to turn 'immoral art' to advantage. In art the main source of immorality is philistinism.

[*Journals*, pp.377–88. The references are all to the collaborative work in the preparation of *Antigone* for performance in Chur. Brecht and Helene Weigel (who was to play Antigone) were in Zurich, where they ran into Hans Curjel, with whom Brecht had worked on the 'Little' *Mahagonny* in Baden-Baden in 1927 and who was now director of the municipal theatre at Chur. Caspar Neher, Brecht's old schoolfriend, with whom he had worked before 1933 and with whom contact had now been re-established, had recently moved to Zurich as joint chief designer at the Zurich Schauspielhaus. Rehearsals for *Antigone* started in Zurich early in January, under the joint direction of Brecht and Neher, and the team moved to Chur on 16 January 1948. See also Introduction.

With reference to 25 December 1947: the *Manifesto* was Brecht's uncompleted project to recast *The Communist Manifesto* in hexameters. The Nehers' son Georg had been reported missing on the Russian front on 8 April 1943.]

LETTER TO STEFAN BRECHT

Dear Steff,
I'm sending you an adaptation of *Antigone* that I've done for Helli. We're giving a kind of preview for Berlin in Chur, two hours from Zurich. I've used Hölderlin's (relatively faithful) translation from the

Greek; there's something Hegelian about it that you'll recognise and a Swabian popular *Gestus* that you probably won't. (The 'popular grammar' extends even to the ultra-sophisticated choruses.) It's my second attempt, following *Edward*, to develop a heightened stage language from classical elements. The reason for the changes, which obliged me to write whole new sections, is that I wanted to get rid of the Greek *moira* (destiny); in other words, I try to uncover the underlying popular legend. You'll be best able to judge this experiment when you see what has been done with the choruses. – A piece of good news from Sweden: apparently the books are still there: (*Neue Zeit*, Karl Marx, Ilich, [i.e., Lenin], Machiavelli, Montaigne, Aristotle, Hegel, etc.) – If *Galileo* is done again in New York, I'd like you to see it again and write to me about it. And please make sure that Korsch gets tickets. – Just speak to Hambleton or Laughton. – And about the car, you should correspond with Elisabeth Hauptmann (c/o Lorre) directly. She wanted to sell the Buick for you and send you the money, but it seems she can't get very much for it. –

Cordially,
b

Zurich, December 1947

[*Letters*, pp.442–3.]

DRAFT OF A FOREWORD, 1947

Sophocles' *Antigone* is the decided rejection of tyranny in favour of democracy. It is a drama that intervenes polemically in contemporary Greek events: 'If one man owns it that is not a state . . .', 'I'm there to love my fellow-beings, not hate them.' ('I live for love not hatred', l.489.)

The tyrant Creon, who has driven his people into an unjust war, kills Antigone's younger brother Polynices because he has quitted the battle after witnessing the fate of the older brother, Eteocles. In addition, he dishonours him utterly by ruling that his body may not be buried but must be left in the open air to be fed on by the birds. Any among the people who oppose this will be stoned. Antigone revolts against the judgement and intends to bury her brother. She discloses her intention to her sister Ismene. Ismene takes fright and warns Antigone:

ISMENE: Sister, you will be caught in lawlessness.
ANTIGONE: But not in faithlessness.

Ismene beseeches her sister not to attempt an impossible opposition. All will be in vain, nothing can be done against the tyrant. But Antigone thinks otherwise and carries out her intention. Antigone is arrested and sentenced by Creon to a disgraceful death. Disapproval increases among the people. Creon has a mind to have all who oppose him killed. Creon's son Haemon, betrothed to Antigone, sides with her and quarrels with his father. They part after heated exchanges. The blind seer Tiresias warns Creon and prophesies disaster. Creon, urged by the Chorus, now thinks to rescind the judgement, but the disaster has already occurred. Antigone is dead, Haemon has killed himself at her grave. Creon's wife, the mother of Haemon, has likewise killed herself in despair. Cursing himself, Creon collapses.

Brecht increases the contemporary relevance by making the war take an abrupt turn. The victory celebrations were a sham. The enemy meanwhile have regathered their forces and are now advancing victoriously on Thebes. The destruction of the city is inevitable. But Creon, if he must die himself, wishes the city of Thebes to be annihilated with him. And so he defends Thebes senselessly to the death.

Argos, apparently defeated by Creon, summons up fresh energies. The women, the children, all take up arms, and Argos becomes a Stalingrad – the parallel is obvious. A terrible end for Creon's army.

[BFA 24, pp.349–50. This draft emerged in collaboration with Caspar Neher but it was not in fact used.]

ANTIGONE

Come out from the shadows and walk
Before us a while
Friendly girl with the light step
Of one who has made up her mind, a terror
To the terrible.

Girl turning away, I know
You were afraid of dying but
Still more afraid
Of living unworthily.

And you let the powerful off
Nothing and with those confusing the issue
You did no deals nor ever
Forgot an insult and over wrongdoing

There was no covering up.
We salute you.

[BFA 15, p.191. This poem was first published in the programme of the Chur production in 1948.]

MASTERFUL TREATMENT OF A MODEL
(Foreword to the *Antigone-Model*)

1

Thanks to its total moral and material collapse our harrowed and harrowing country has no doubt acquired a vague appetite for novelty; moreover where the arts are concerned it is apparently being encouraged from various quarters to test out new ideas. But since there seems to be a good deal of confusion as to what is new and what is old, while fear that the old will return has become mixed with fear that the new will step in; and since moreover the conquered are always being told in general terms that only morally and intellectually do they need to get rid of their Nazism, artists would be well advised not to rely blindly on the assurance that new ideas are welcome. Yet art can only find its feet by going ahead, and it needs to do so in company with the advanced part of the population and not away from them. Together with them it must stop waiting to be acted upon, and must go on and act itself; it must make a start somewhere in the general ruin.

It is not going to be at all easy for art to regain control of its technical equipment and extend it in new directions. The rapid decline of artistic methods under the Nazis seems to have taken place almost unnoticed. The damage done to theatre buildings is far more conspicuous than that done to the style of acting. This is partly because the former took place with the fall of the Nazi regime, but the latter during its rise. Even today people will speak of the 'brilliant' technique of the Goering-style theatre, as if such a technique could be taken over without bothering what direction its brilliance took. A technique which served to hide the causality at work in society can hardly be used to show it up. And it is high time for a theatre for inquisitive people.

Bourgeois society, with its anarchic system of production, only becomes aware of its own laws of motion in a catastrophe: as Marx said, it is the roof falling in on its head that gives it its first introduction to the law of gravity. But mere catastrophe is a bad teacher. One learns hunger and thirst from it, but seldom hunger for truth and thirst for knowledge. No amount of illness will turn a sick man into a physician; neither the distant view nor close inspection makes an eye-witness into an expert. If the theatre is capable of showing the truth, then it must also be capable of making the sight of it a pleasure. How then can such a theatre be created? The difficulty about ruins is that the house has gone, but the site isn't there either. And the architects' plans, it seems, never get lost. This means that reconstruction brings back the old dens of iniquity and centres of disease. Fevered life claims to be particularly vital life; none steps so firmly as the consumptive who has lost all feeling in the soles of his feet. Yet the tricky thing about art is that however hopeless its affairs may seem, it has to conduct them with complete ease.

Thus it may not be easy to create progressive art in the period of reconstruction. And this should be a challenge.

2

The Antigone story was picked for the present theatrical operation as providing a certain topicality of subject matter and posing some interesting formal questions. So far as the subject's political aspect went, the present-day analogies emerged astonishingly powerfully as a result of the rationalisation process, but on the whole they were a handicap; the great character of the resister in the old play does not represent the German resistance fighters who necessarily seem most important to us. It was not the occasion for a poetic tribute to them; and this is all the more a pity because so little is now done to preserve their memory and so much to make people forget them. Not everyone will necessarily realise that they are not the subject in this case, but only he who does so will be able to summon the measure of strangeness needed if the really remarkable element in this Antigone play – the role of force in the collapse of the head of the state – is to be observed with profit. Even the prologue could only contribute by posing a point of actuality and outlining the subjective problem. The Antigone story then unrolls the whole chain of incidents objectively, on the unfamiliar level of the rulers. This possibility of objectively presenting a major state operation was due precisely to the fact (fatal in another respect) that the old play was historically so remote as to tempt nobody to identify himself with its principal figure. Here too its elements of epic form were a help, and provided something of interest to our theatre on their own account. Greek dramaturgy uses certain forms of alienation, notably interventions by the chorus, to try and rescue some of that freedom of calculation which Schiller is uncertain how to ensure.[1] However, there can be no question, either through the Antigone story or on its behalf, of 'conjuring up the spirit of antiquity'; philological interests cannot be taken into account. Even if we felt obliged to do something for a work like *Antigone* we could only do so by letting the play do something for us.

3

As it is not so much a new school of playwriting as a new way of performance being tried out on an old play, our new adaptation cannot be handed over in the usual way to theatres to do what they like with. An obligatory model production has been worked out, which can be grasped from a collection of photographs accompanied by explanatory instructions. Such a model of course will stand or fall according to the ease with which it can be imitated and varied. Possibly the whole, or certain parts, may give no impression of life when reproduced; in that case the whole or the parts in question must be discarded. A model cannot depend on cadences whose charm is due to particular voices or on gestures and movements whose beauty springs from particular physical characteristics; that sort of thing cannot serve as a model, for it is not exemplary so much as inimitable. If something is to be usefully copied it must first be put forward for copying. What is actually achieved when the model is put to use can then be a mixture of the inimitable and the exemplary.

The idea of making use of models is a clear challenge to the artists of a period that applauds nothing but what is 'original', 'incomparable', 'never been seen before', and demands what is 'unique'. They may realise quite well that a model is not a blueprint, and yet find that their way of going to work gives them no help in the use of models. It is hard enough for them to hurry up and forget the examples of their youth; and now they have learnt to create everything bearing on their parts themselves, entirely from within the resources of the self. What, they will ask, is in any way creative about

---

[1] A dramatic plot will move before my eyes; an epic seems to stand still while I move round it. In my view this is a significant distinction. If a circumstance moves before my eyes, then I am bound strictly to what is present to the senses; my imagination loses all freedom; I feel a continual restlessness develop and persist in me; I have to stick to the subject; any reflection or looking back is forbidden me, for I am drawn by an outside force. But if I move round a circumstance which cannot get away from me, then my pace can be irregular; I can linger or hurry according to my own subjective needs, can take a step backwards or leap ahead, and so forth. (Goethe–Schiller correspondence, 26 December 1797)

the use of models? The answer is that today's division of labour has transformed creation in many important spheres. The act of creation has become a collective creative process, a continuum of a dialectical sort in which the original invention, taken on its own, has lost much of its importance. The initial invention of a model truly need not count for all that much, for the actor who uses it immediately makes his own personal contribution. He is free to invent variations on the model, that is to say such variations as will make the image of reality which he has to give truer and richer in its implications, or more satisfying artistically. The choreographic figures (positions, movements, groupings, etc.)[1] can be treated either slavishly or masterfully; that is, masterfully only in so far as reality penetrates them freely. If the variations are undertaken in the right way they too take on the qualities of a model; the learner becomes the teacher and the model itself changes.

For in truth the model is not set up in order to fix the style of performance; quite the contrary. The emphasis is on development: changes are to be provoked and to be made perceptible; sporadic and anarchic acts of creation are to be replaced by creative processes whose changes progress by steps or leaps.[2] The model was worked out in a dozen and a half rehearsals at the municipal theatre in Chur, and must be regarded as by definition incomplete. The very fact that its shortcomings cry out for improvement should stimulate theatres to use it.

4

Neher's stage for 'Antigone'. Long benches, on which the actors can sit and wait for their cue, stand in front of a semicircle of screens covered in red-coloured rush matting. In the middle of these screens a gap is left, where the record turntable stands and is visibly operated; through this gap the actors can go off when their part is done. The acting area is bounded by four posts, from which horses' skulls hang suspended. In the left foreground is a board for props, with Bacchic

---

[1] Neher's sketches served as the basis for the grouping and the masks, so that the inventors of the model were themselves already, as it were, working to pattern.

[2] The first attempt to use models of epic theatre was made by R. Berlau in Copenhagen. For Dagmar Andreasen's performances of *The Mother* and *Señora Carrar's Rifles* she used photographs of previous productions. Andreasen's Vlassova and Carrar were completely different from the figures created by Helene Weigel. Weigel's could be imitated and also altered. But the performances were a credit to both actresses.

masks on sticks, Creon's laurel wreath made of copper, the millet bowl and the wine jar for Antigone and a stool for Tiresias. Subsequently Creon's battle sword is hung up here by one of the Elders. On the right is a framework with a sheet of iron on which an Elder beats with his fist during the choral song 'Spirit of joy, pride of the waters'. For the Prologue a white wall is lowered on wires. There are a door and a cupboard in it. A kitchen table and two chairs stand in front of it; a sack lies in the right foreground. At the beginning a board with the time and the place on it is lowered above the wall. There is no curtain.

The reason why the actors sit openly on the stage and only adopt the attitudes proper to their parts once they enter the (very brilliantly lit) acting area is that the audience must not be able to think that it has been transported to the scene of the story, but must be invited to take part in the delivery of an ancient poem, irrespective how it has been restored.

There were two plans for the stage. The first was that the actors' benches should as it were represent the scene of the old poem. The screen behind them consisted of ox blood-coloured canvases reminiscent of sails and tents, and the posts with horses' skulls stood in between. The acting area was simply to be brilliantly lit and marked out by little flags. This would have represented a visible separation of the original poem and its secularised version. We became more and more dissatisfied with this plan, until we eventually decided to situate the new part of the story also between the barbaric war emblems. As a third possibility one could cut the Prologue and replace the screens behind the benches by a board showing bomb damage in a modern city.

Costumes and props. The men's costumes were made of undyed sackcloth, the women's of cotton. Creon's and Haemon's costumes had inserts of red leather. Antigone's and Ismene's were grey. Particular care was taken over the props; good craftsmen worked on them. This was not so that the audience or the actors should imagine that they were real, but simply so as to provide the audience and the actors with beautiful objects.

5

As for the style of presentation, we agree with Aristotle in holding that the story is the kernel of the tragedy, even if we disagree about the purpose for which it should be performed. The story ought not just to be a jumping-off point for all kinds of excursions into soul-probing or elsewhere, but ought to contain everything and be the object of all our attention, so that once it has been told the whole thing is concluded. The grouping and movement of the characters has to narrate the story, which is a chain of incidents, and this is the actor's sole task. The stylisation by which his acting becomes art must not in the process destroy naturalness, but has on the contrary to heighten it. Obtrusive temperament or speech of outstanding clarity are to be discouraged. Stylisation means a general elaboration of what is natural, and its object is to show the audience, as being a part of society, what is important for society in the story. Thus the so-called 'poet's own world' must not be treated as arbitrary, cut off and 'obeying its own logic'; instead whatever it contains of the real world must be brought out and made effective. The 'poet's words' are only sacred in so far as they are true; the theatre is the handmaiden not of the poet but of society.

6

To keep the performance subordinate to the story, *bridge verses* were given to the actors at rehearsals, for them to deliver with the attitude of a narrator. Before stepping into the acting area for the first time Helene Weigel said (and in subsequent rehearsals heard the prompter saying):

> But Antigone went, King Oedipus' child, with her pitcher
> Gathering dust to cover the body of dead Polynices
> Which the wrathful tyrant had thrown to the dogs and the vultures.

The actress playing Ismene, before entering, said:

> To her, gathering dust, there appeared her sister Ismene.

Before verse 1 Weigel said:

> Bitterly the gatherer mourned the fate that had come to her brothers.

And so on. Each speech or action that is introduced by such verses comes to seem like their realisation in practice, and the actor is prevented from transforming himself completely into the character: he is showing something. [...]

More makeup than usual was used for the faces, and this too was meant to tell a story: in the case of the Elders, for instance, the ravages left on the face by the habit of commanding, and so forth. As the photographs show, this was not entirely successful.

The tempo of the performance was very fast.

7
The present model is to some extent made difficult to study by the fact that it contains much that is provisional and unintentional; this has to be located and cut out. It includes the entire field of mime on which all the actors apart from Weigel as it were depend for their living. This is a field that brings one up against the almost inextricable tangle of styles of our period of sell-out, which exhibits plays of every period and every country and invents the most disparate styles for them, without having any style of its own. Of course such efforts are a failure, and in a single performance one may find both the resonant pathos and the quaintness which would ruin a play by Aeschylus or Gozzi respectively; quite plainly the actors have completely different aims in view. This unhappy state of things is also bound to affect the proper sphere of the model, that of attitudes and groupings. Generally speaking it is the grouping to which most care has been devoted. Economy in the moves of the groups and figures was intended to ensure that these movements had meaning. The separate constellations, even the distances between them, have a dramatic significance, and at certain moments a single movement of one of the actors' hands may be able to transform a situation. It was also hoped that the inventions of the producers and the actors would be clearly visible as theatrical ideas; this is a field where all standards have been lost, so that no one can any longer distinguish great from small.

In this respect, as in all the rest, the pictures and notes were meant to be studied chiefly for the new beginnings and the differentiations they contain: these needing to establish themselves in the confused and overcrowded zone in which we now produce art that is terminal, finished and generalised.

If the whole experiment is not to be dismissed as unimportant, irrespective of whether or not it is thought to have been properly carried out, then nobody must be put off by the fear that it might mean the sacrifice of all our experience to date. In the theatre, by making things simple we become simplistic. And dancing often reaches a highpoint when someone dances out of line. Working with models need not be pursued with greater seriousness than is needed for any kind of playing. It may reasonably be considered to have something in common with the 'Well-Tempered Clavier'.

BRECHT, NEHER

[*Brecht on Theatre*, pp.209–15, from the *Antigonemodell 1948*, cf. BFA 25, pp.73–81.

In February 1948, during the last stages of the relatively brief rehearsal period in Chur, Ruth Berlau took a large number of photographs of the production; and immediately after the première, she, Brecht and Neher discussed the idea of putting photographs, texts and sketches together into a book. The Gebrüder Weiss publishing house in Berlin was approached, and the book was published the next year. In 1955 the *Antigone-Model* was incorporated into the series of *Model-Books of the Berliner Ensemble* published by Henschel. The idea was to encourage a 'scientific' approach to the theatre, to help the theatre 'regain control of its technical equipment and extend it in new directions', so that future directors, designers and actors would have a clear idea what had worked before; as emphasised in 3 the 'model' is not intended to be prescriptive (although that is what tended in practice to happen, especially in the case of the more popular texts handled like this).

A further fragmentary text in the Brecht Archive adds:

> The book is also intended to help the broader public to acquire a better knowledge of the theatre in general, and to intensify their capacity for enjoyment, as well as for critique. In order to give the book some of the charm of a theatrical production, the photographs are accompanied by a running verse commentary, which reproduces the content of the play.

These are the 'Bridge Verses' which follow.]

BRIDGE VERSES FOR 'ANTIGONE'

But Antigone went, King Oedipus' child, with her pitcher
Gathering dust to cover the body of dead Polynices
Which the wrathful tyrant had thrown to the dogs and the vultures.
To her, gathering dust, there appeared her sister Ismene.
Bitterly the gatherer mourned the fate that had come to her brothers
Both of them killed in the war, the first as a hero, the second
Running away, then slain; but not by the foe: by his own side.
Now she could not persuade her reasoning sister to visit
Their brother's foully ill-used body forbiddenly.
So in the dawning light the sisters quarrelled and parted.

Hearing the war was won, long fought for the fields of grey metal
Next the Elders of Thebes placed victory wreaths on their foreheads

Made of the shining leaves of the green and poisonous laurel
Which can cloud the senses and render the footsteps unsteady.
Outside Creon's house they stood first thing in the morning.
So, coming back from the fray and leaving his army at Argos
There in the dawning light the tyrant found them all waiting.
And he leant on his sword and told them how, over in Argos
Vultures hopped from corpse to corpse; the Elders applauded.
Swiftly they crowned him with laurel. But he would not yet
Yield them his sword. Grimly he gave it his bodyguard.

Railing at Oedipus' son, an example to frighten the people
Next the tyrant spoke of the need for the bloodiest purges
Cleansing his foes from Theban soil, when a runner reported
Terror had not instilled terror: dust covered the hacked body.
Angrily cursing the sentry and all of those who were there, he
Tested the blade of his sword with his thumb to show that he
  meant it.
Pacing with downcast eyes the Elders considered the monstrous
Power of man, who has bent the sea to his keel, and the oxen
Too to his yoke and the horse to his bit, the while often emerging
Monstrous to himself also, as he bends other men to his purpose.

Next Antigone came, brought in for interrogation:
Why had she broken the law? She turned and looked at the Elders.
When she saw they were shocked, she replied 'To set an example.'
Then she appealed to the Elders; the Elders however
Turned to Creon instead. So Antigone told them, 'The man who
Seeks for power drinks salty water, and must go on drinking
Further. I am neither the first nor the last of his victims.'
But they turned their backs. And Antigone told them, 'I warn
  you.'
'You would see us divided,' the tyrant exclaimed, 'and, divided
Why, our city will fall to outsiders.' Coolly she answered:
'That's what you rulers say again and again, and your subjects
Sacrifice all for you, then when their city's been weakened
And enslaved like this it is captured by the outsiders.
Men who bow their heads see earth, and earth shall receive them.'
'Insolence! Would you run down your homeland? You are an
  outcast.'
Then Antigone: 'Who casts me out? That is not home
For me where my head's been bowed. Oh, many are missing
From this city since you took over. Young men and older
Will they ever come back? You started with many, and only
You came home.' At that the tyrant had nothing to answer.

'Idiot,' said the Elders, 'but surely you know we're victorious?'
'She is my enemy,' said the tyrant, 'it gives her no pleasure.'
'Better,' Antigone said, 'and safer, than sitting with you in
The enemy's homes should we be in our rubbled own.'
Coldly the Elders stared, and ranged themselves with the tyrant.
Then from the house next came Ismene, her sister, and told them
'I was the one did the deed.' But Antigone told them, 'She's lying.'
'Settle it,' Creon said as he mopped his forehead, 'between you.'
But Antigone felt herself fainting, and she implored her
Sister to survive. 'It's enough,' she said, 'if they kill me.'
Then said the tyrant, 'When the festivities start in our city
Honouring Bacchus, she shall be buried alive in her tomb.'
And they led her away who had faced and defied the ruler.
Promptly the Elders handed his Bacchic mask to the tyrant
Chanting the choral song: 'You who cloak yourself ready for dancing
Stamp your foot not too hard on the ground, nor yet on the new grass.
Those who provoked you, though, O Victor, now let them praise you.'
To them then there came the younger son of the ruler
Haemon, Antigone's love, commander of the home spearmen
Saying that for Oedipus' child there were murmurings in the city.
Slowly his father spoke of his secret preoccupations
Calling for ruthless force, but the son could not understand it.
So the father wooed him, ignoring the listening Elders
Begging his obdurate son to forget her who broke the law.
But when his son stood firm Creon waved his mask to deride him
Flicking its raffia fringe in his face till the son
Turned and went. The Elders observed it unhappily.

Grimly the victor goes off to the feast
And the Elders, appalled, hear music coming from the city:
The Bacchic dance is parading.
This is also the hour when Oedipus' child in her chamber
Hearing Bacchus afar, prepares for her ultimate journey.
Now he summons his own who, always thirsting for pleasure
Give the peaceable god the joyful answer he calls for.
Mighty the victory, then, and irresistible Bacchus
As he nears each mourner and proffers the cup of oblivion.
Then she'll abandon the mourning robes which her sons' death made her
Sew, and hurry to join the orgy, seeking exhaustion.

When courageous Antigone was fetched from the house of Creon

First she collapsed in the arms of her kindly attendants.
Then the solemn Elders reminded her how she had chosen
Deed and death for herself. She said, 'Are you trying to mock me?'
And went on to bemoan her lot: her difficult youth and
Sombre parents whom she was now on her way to join, manless
And that brother who'd dragged her down to the pit that he lay in.
Then the Elders gave her the dish and the pitcher with wine and
Millet, gifts for the dead, and tried to console her by naming
Saints and heroes who'd died in a grand and dignified manner
Earnestly saying she should accept what the gods had decided.
Then, overcome with wrath, she chided the Elders for cowardice
And when she saw their weakness she found her own weakness had left her.
'Chariots are what you expect,' she cried, 'full of plunder! And chariots
Shall you see coming here to plunder our city! The living:
You are the ones that I mourn.' And her wrath was stifled by sobbing.
And she looked around, saw Thebes as a lovable city
Roofs and hills and hedges, and solemnly bowed in its honour
Saying farewell. Then again she changed from pity to anger.
'You, my city, produced inhuman monsters, and that means
Dust and ashes for you.' To her maids: 'If anyone asks you
Where Antigone went, then say: To the grave, to find shelter.'

Turning away she went, and her step was light and determined.
After her gazed the Elders unseeing, and chanted the chorus:
'She too formerly ate of the tasty bread that was baked
Deep in the shade of the rocks. Nor till her own flesh suffered
And died did she speak up loud in condemnation.'
But the warner cannot have got as far as the pit yet
When the festive city is seized by a terrible knowledge.
For, aroused by the rumours of strife in the house of the ruler
Enter the seer, the blind one. And, mocking, a figure that circles
Round about his path and rattles the mask with its raffia
Fringes above his head, pursuing him over the open
Square, and raising a foot in the dance's insolent measure
Pointing with scornful thumb to show up the old man's afflictions
Cheekily tapping the way with a stick for the tentative gait.
Creon: drunk with his triumph. The Elders look on in silence.

'Foolish old man, you don't seem to like festivities. Why have
You no wreath? Look at us!' And his voice was sharp with resentment.

'Must a blind man,' said the seer, 'be followed by one even blinder?
Know that the gods dislike disputes and crimes against nature.
Ugly now loom the birds that have fed on Oedipus' offspring.'
Laughing, the ruler said, 'Yes, your birds always fly as you want them
Following your slightest whim, a whim that is paid for in silver.'
'Don't offer that to me; what use is silver in wartime?'
Said the seer. 'But the war is over,' the ruler responded.
'Is it over?' enquired the seer. 'For down at the harbour
Fish are still cured for the troops as though they were far from returning.
You are cruel. But why? What follies have you embarked on?'
Silent the tyrant stood and could not think how to answer.

Then the seer got up and left. And mumbling obscurely
Slowly the tyrant started to go. The Elders observed it.
Fear by fear was addressed, they dared to ask him a question:
'What is the news of the war, Creon?' He replied to them, 'Not good.'
Then they came up to him, and the mask of peace he was holding
Holding their own peace masks in their hands as they all approached him
And they argued about the war: was it their war or his war?
'You it was forced me to go to bring you back ore from the Argives.'
'But you told us we'd win.' 'I told you: sooner or later.'
And he prepared to leave. Once more the Elders in anger
Gathered around their king and cried out, 'Bring back our army!'
The army was cause for concern, but their own property more so.
Then he took the mask of peace, which he stuck in the soil there.
'Right, I will send for the army; my eldest shall bring it, Megareus.
Iron shall they have in their hands to smite ungrateful civilians.'

Still there hung in the air the menacing name of Megareus
When a runner arrived: 'Lord, stiffen your lip, for Megareus
Is no more and your army is beaten, the foe is approaching.'
Gasping, he spoke of the battle: the army, split by internal
Strife over Polynices' death, bore its spears with indifference
While the people of Argos like tigers fought for their homesteads.
'Like tigers now they will come,' said the runner. 'And I am glad
I am finished.' He clutched his waist, and with fearful grimaces
Right before Creon's mask of peace he fell heavily earthwards.
At this Creon cried out, cried loudly out as a father.
The Elders exclaimed, 'A tiger-like foe is approaching and Thebes

Jigs in victory. Summon the home spearmen!'
And the Elders tore off the victory wreaths from their foreheads
And they broke their Bacchic staffs and covered the body
Up with wreaths and masks, 'Woe to us!' loudly exclaiming.

Then the ruler remembered his next son, Haemon, the younger –
Commander of the home spearmen – and now to placate him
Hastened away forthwith to grant Antigone pardon.
But the Elders regrouped, their brazen dishes resounding
Drumming to waken the town from its lethal victory junket.
Hollow the brazen alarm interrupted the dances to Bacchus
Till the triumphant strut gave way to a timorous scurry.
Threading her way through the crowds a childish messenger, youngest
Of those maids who had taken Antigone off, now addressed them:
'Dead and done with is Haemon, bleeding there by his own hand!
Seeing Antigone entombed, seeing her hanged there
Straight he fell on his sword, ignoring the pleas of his father.'
Led by Antigone's maids then came to the Elders their awesome
Leader. And in his hands he carried a blood-spattered garment.

'Dead and done with is Haemon. Dead and done with is Thebes.
Since she has failed me she lies now as food for the vultures!'
And to the Elders he showed the bloodstained cloak of the son who
Would not yield him the sword. And anxious now, and pathetic –
Never to learn, he who had led so many went stumbling
Off to the stricken city once more. But behind him the Elders
Followed their leader still, this time to death and destruction.

[*Poems and Songs from the Plays*, pp.189–96; cf. BFA 25, pp.91–159, the *Antigonemodell*, where this text appears as captions to the scene photographs of the 1948 production. And see note above.]

NOTES ON THE ADAPTATION, 1951

1

Sophocles' *Antigone* is one of the greatest works of Western literature. But the question arises whether it is still intelligible to audiences living their lives according to quite different ideas. Mankind, in the view of the ancients, is delivered up more or less blindly to the mercy of Fate. Men have no power over Fate. In his reworking of the play B.B. has replaced that idea with the opinion that mankind's fate is mankind itself. This is a very large alteration which the ancient drama could only bear because, at bottom, it is an entirely realistic text that, with a great deal of practical human insight and political experience, gives shape to a real event whose story the dramatist had inherited, namely the fall of the ruling house of Oedipus. It founders in a savage war of conquest during which such savageries become necessary also against its own people that the part of the ruling house which is in sympathy with the people revolts. This so weakens the house that the enemy, the victims of aggression, are victorious. The tyrant who, to deal with the revolt at home, needs a speedy victory, drives his troops into battle prematurely. Shattered by mutinies, they can no longer withstand the enemy fighting – men, women and children – in the defence of their homeland. Antigone rebels against the tyrant Creon, and the great morality of her act consists in this: that, moved by a deep humanity, in an act of open resistance, she does not hesitate to put her own people in danger of being defeated in a war of aggression.

2

Further alterations of the ancient tragedy consist, for example, in the following:

Thebes' war with Argos is presented realistically. The mineral wealth of Argos is its objective. But this wealth furnishes the people of Argos too with excellent spears. When the struggle becomes very hard indeed and lasts far longer than Creon had calculated, he exerts too strict a discipline on his men and mutinies ensue. Creon has to wage war abroad and at home, and he loses.

The seer Tiresias, who in the original drama shares the gods' gift of prescience, in the reworking is a good observer and for that reason capable of foretelling certain things.

The choruses likewise have been reworked, and new ideas are introduced there also. These choruses, like several other passages in the drama, will scarcely be able to be fully understood at one hearing. Parts of the choruses sound like riddles asking to be solved. But the excellent thing about them is that, with a little studying, they give out ever more beauties. It was not the intention in the reworking simply to remove this difficulty, for overcoming it gives such pleasure – particularly since the work *Antigone* was fortunate enough to have as its translator one of the greatest shapers of the German language, Hölderlin.

First chorus (pp. 17–18)
Human beings, monstrously great when they subjugate Nature, become great monsters when they subjugate their fellow men.

Second chorus (pp. 27–8)
Warning to the despot not to rule too harshly. Those violently robbed of their human dignity rise up and overthrow their oppressors. The Chorus cite as an example the sons of Lachmeus who suffered monstrous wretchedness, even abandoning their womenfolk to a foreign enemy. But they rose up when Pelias struck them, albeit lightly, with a staff, and killed him. The seed of destruction has long been growing in the house of Oedipus, the exhaustion of the oppressed has a limit (it may end). But the fall of the ruling house will drag down many with it (the Chorus mean themselves).

Third chorus (pp. 33–4)
This is a paean to Bacchus, the god of the pleasures of the flesh. His power over human beings is great. Even in war he gets his way. He causes disorder in families, so irresistible is his beckoning to enjoyment. Through him human beings lose all self-control. He even induces them to bow beneath the yoke in the hope of future joys. The wish for pleasure follows the thin-walled ships even into the perils of the high seas. The god mixes the races in outbreaks of joy. But he is unwarlike and a friend of fellowship and understanding.

Fourth chorus (pp. 37–8)
On her way to the place of execution Antigone has scolded the Elders for failing to resist the tyrant and has prophesied that the city will meet with a terrible end. Now the Chorus point out accusingly that she too for a long time put up with injustice. She ate bread baked in servitude, she sat comfortably in the shade of the strongholds of oppression. Only when the violence dealt out by the house of Oedipus rebounded on that house did she awake.

Fifth chorus (pp. 48–9)
The Thebans at the moment of their fall again invoke their patron deity Bacchus. They confess that they have sinned against the peaceful god of joy.

3
Reworkings of this kind are not uncommon in literature. Goethe reworked Euripides' *Iphigenia*; Kleist, Molière's *Amphitryon*. These reworkings do not prevent our enjoying the originals. In the not too distant future, when aesthetic taste and the historical understanding have been properly schooled, such enjoyment will be possible for the broad mass of the population too.

[BFA 24, pp.350–3. Brecht wrote this text, and the 'New Prologue' below, for the first production in Germany, in Greiz, 18 November 1951.]

NEW PROLOGUE TO 'ANTIGONE', 1951

On stage come the actors playing Antigone, Creon and the seer Tiresias. Standing between the others, the actor playing Tiresias addresses the audience:

Friends, the high language
May be strange to you
In the poem from thousands of years ago
That we have learned our parts in here. Unknown
To you is the poem's story that was to the listeners then
Closely familiar. Therefore permit us
To introduce it to you. This is Antigone
Princess of the house of Oedipus. And this
Creon, her uncle and tyrant of the city of Thebes. I am
Tiresias, the seer. This man
Is waging a war against distant Argos, for plunder. This woman
Counters his inhumanity and he destroys her.
But his war, that now has the name of an inhuman war
Collapses on him. Just and unbending
Not heeding her tyrannised country's sacrifices
She ended it. We beg you
Search in your own hearts and minds for similar deeds
In the recent past or for the absence
Of any such deeds. And now
You will see us and the other actors
Entering in turn the small space of the play
Where formerly among
The skulls of the sacrificial beasts of a barbarous cult
In very ancient times humanity
Stood up tall.

The actors step back and the others too come on stage.

[BFA 8, p.242. In Greiz this was susbstituted for the Prelude of 1948, with which we have prefaced the main text of the play.]

Editorial Notes

Hans Curjel, offering Brecht the use of his theatre in Chur in November 1947, suggested several works that might be suitable to stage; and among them Sophocles' *Antigone*, which Brecht chose, having been drawn to it already. Caspar Neher recommended Hölderlin's translation as their working text. It was available in the fifth volume of Hellingrath's critical edition of Hölderlin's works (1913), but had also been published separately and more recently by the Seldwyla Verlag, in Bern. Doubtless Brecht used this edition. But he must have gone elsewhere – perhaps to Hellingrath – for the lines he inserts into *Antigone* from Hölderlin's translations of Pindar's Pythian 1 and Pythian 4 (see below). And the two lines quoted in the 1947 Foreword (above), as though from Hölderlin's *Antigone*, are not in fact from there but from some other, and rather more conventional, version.

Hölderlin's *Antigone* (more or less adapted) had been staged a dozen times before Brecht took it on, and most recently (earlier in 1947) in Basel and Zurich. And in 1949 it would be performed in Salzburg, entire and unaltered, as an opera by Carl Orff. So Brecht's choice of that text, though bold, was by no means unprecedented or eccentric.

The Antigone story itself, because of the issue it treats – individual conscience in revolt against the power and the interests of the state – will always be more or less present in a nation's mind. The times themselves, whenever they press very urgently, seem to demand that it be taken up again. So Hölderlin, translating and writing on the play in 1803, thought it enacted the struggle of a new order, which would be lively and republican, against the old, which was petrified and autocratic. Anouilh's *Antigone*, written (1942) and staged (1944) in occupied Paris, was in Brecht's day another proof of the story's enduring topicality. And no doubt it was that potential which first attracted him. Perennially topical, *Antigone* could in 1947 be made very obviously so. In his draft of a Foreword (1947) and in the Prelude, set in Berlin in April 1945, which he wrote for the first performance in 1948, he confidently asserts the contemporary relevance of his text. But soon after that performance, whilst working on the *Antigone-Model* (1948–9) and before staging the play again in

Greiz in 1951, he backed off from such categorical assertions. For Greiz he replaced the 1948 Prelude with a single speech in which the actor playing Tiresias urges the audience to search in their own hearts and minds 'for similar deeds/ In the recent past or for the absence/ Of any such deeds' – but no more than that.

Antigone's story, always topical in a general way, resisted being harnessed to Brecht's particular politics. If German audiences thought of any deeds similar to hers, it would be Stauffenberg's in July 1944; and of him and his colleagues Brecht disapproved. He might have wished to honour resistance where, in his view, it had most needed to be: in Germany's proletariat. But for that sort of resistance, as Brecht's adaptation makes abundantly clear, Antigone was no model at all. She, like the Elders, is complicit in the ruling class. She does not act against Creon until her own immediate interests are violated. True, she then widens her revolt into one against the war, but not in the wish to shift power from the tyrant to his people. Brecht can and does 'rationalise' the story, removing from it all notions of fate and predestination. But in the end the chief topicality of the subject for him is Creon's crazed violence: the degree of violence necessary to fight an unjust war and control the home population whilst doing so. Creon, like Hitler, learning nothing, drags down the state – which in his view has failed him – in his own catastrophe. The uncertainty over how *Antigone* could best, most topically, be applied results in an adaptation which, for all its power, is in that respect – political applicability – muddled and unsatisfactory. But that failure is more than made up for by success in an endeavour that interested Brecht far more: the theatrical and, as the chief agent of that, the linguistic.

Hölderlin's translation is extraordinary. Disfigured by misprints, riddled with philological errors, radically unconventional in spirit and practice, it excited only ridicule on its first appearance, together with *Oedipus*, in 1804. Public taste and comprehension were more than a century even beginning to catch up. We now see that it is a radically enlivening translation because it goes to the roots of language, word by word, phrase by phrase, cleaving close. And in so doing it estranges the mother tongue.

Brecht delighted in Hölderlin's *Antigone*. Coming back after fourteen years into German-speaking territory he savoured the achievement of a master of the German language. He heard things in the translation that seemed to him familiar – Swabian intonations and turns of phrase and, as he called them, Latinisms – but chiefly what he appreciated in Hölderlin and what he needed for his own purposes was strangeness, estrangement. The German language and a canonical text had been radically estranged. He took over about half of Hölderlin's text into his own, often word for word, often also skilfully and pointedly adapting it. And in the rest of the play, departing from Hölderlin, he homogenised his own language with that highly idiosyncratic base. He does not, as he did in *Saint Joan of the Stockyards* or *Arturo Ui*, ironise or parody the verse, tone and diction of a canonical text. He recognised that after Hölderlin's treatment of it no false pieties still adhered there. Already radically reanimated, its native potency carried over undiminished, the text, far from being a thing to parody, could serve his most serious and contemporary purposes by virtue of its very self. Everything he wanted to say, he could say, either in the given language of the translation or in his own homogenised to it. The whole makes no concessions to a modern audience's powers of comprehension. Indeed, in his Notes on the Adaptation 1951 he signals the difficulty of the text as a great virtue. It repays our involvement, he says, we can learn from it. He offers elucidations of the very difficult choruses; but one of them, the famous 'Monstrous, a lot . . .' actually resists the interpretation he lays on it. And his own interpolations in that mode, particularly when amalgamated with dense strains of language already there, likewise puzzle and resist. There can be no doubt that Brecht intended this effect.

The difficulty – or, better, the linguistic strangeness – of Brecht's *Antigone* not only does not facilitate but must actually hinder any easy application of the story to recent events. Instead, it serves another and for Brecht more important purpose: theatrical. The strangeness of the language – the archaisms, the nervous and contorted syntax, the densely allusive choruses and lyrical laments – all this acts defamiliarisingly, in the interests of Epic Theatre. The staging of *Antigone* (the making a model of it) was a thorough-going experiment in Epic Theatre. The text itself, the very language, is a prime agent in that experiment. Others are Neher's set and, of course, epic acting, for which the Bridge Verses were written as an aid. In the Prelude 1948 the sisters frequently *relate* their actions, and in the play itself Brecht several times slightly alters Hölderlin's text to produce the same effect; for example, in the 'third-person' exchanges between Antigone and Ismene. Brecht was reading Schiller, and having his own views confirmed by him: that theatre, to be effective, must insist on its status as art. Theatre that elides into the realities it seeks to present loses all leverage on them.

Brecht altered Sophocles' plot as it suited him. For example, he made Haemon's brother Megareus more important, at least as a figure off-stage, and excised Eurydice, their mother. He changed the nature of the war being fought against Argos, and the manner and significance of the deaths of Eteocles and Polynices. Brecht's Antigone speaks against the unjust war and in favour of some more humane polity. But whereas in Sophocles, and indeed in most versions of the story, Creon faces her with at least some claim to rightness in his point of view, in Brecht he is wholly in the wrong and does not see his error as he founders.

Brecht followed, cut, adapted and amplified Hölderlin's text for his own direction. And he made some curious 'foreign' insertions into it too. Among the many exemplary instances offered by the Chorus is one of Brecht's own invention: the fate of the sons of Lachmeus. He grafts them, unknown in Greek mythology, on to the established deeds of the bona fide hero Pelias. He fits in (pp.27, 29) three quotations from Hölderlin's Pindar (an even more radical experiment than his Sophocles), adapting the second of them – an image of steering the ship of state – so that its sense becomes quite different in the new context. Much of the terrifying speech in which Creon describes the destruction of Argos (which has not happened, it will happen to Thebes) has its potent source in Goethe's versifying (in 1816) of a prose version (1814) of an Arabic vengeance song by the sixth-century poet and brigand Taabbata Scharran. Goethe quotes it in the 'Noten und Abhandlungen' accompanying his *West-Östlicher Divan*. Brecht borrows five of its stanzas, for his Creon. The perspective on war and atrocity thus opened up is dizzying. To the Greek myth of the wars of Argos and Thebes, in Sophocles' treatment of that myth in the fifth century BC, in Hölderlin's translation and interpretation of Sophocles during the Revolutionary Wars, he adds the East, as Goethe contemplated it, associating Tamburlaine and Napoleon, around the time of Waterloo; Brecht himself, in 1947, thinking of Stalingrad, the flattening of Germany, and unspeakable murder and carnage world-wide. Taabbata Scharran goes perfectly into Creon's voice. All these additions, acts of montage, fit Hölderlin's translation and increase its potent strangeness.

Wherever possible – with the kind permission of Neil Astley – we have used the translation of Hölderlin's *Antigone* which David Constantine undertook for Bloodaxe Books in 2001, modified and adapted to suit Brecht's own. For the rest, an attempt has been made to homogenise, as Brecht did. The intended result is a like strangeness.

Glossary of Mythological Names and Places (for *Antigone*)

Acheron: One of the rivers of the Underworld.
Antigone: Daughter of Oedipus and Jocasta.
Ares: God of war.
Argos: Chief city of Argolis in the Peloponnese.
Bacchus: Dionysus.
Bosporus: Straits joining the Black Sea and the Sea of Marmora.
Cadmus: Founder of Thebes.
Castalia: Sacred spring at Delphi.
Cocytus: One of the rivers of the Underworld. Probably confused, by Hölderlin and so by Brecht, with:
Corycia: A cave on Mount Parnassus.
Creon: Brother of Jocasta, ruler of Thebes after the deaths of Polynices and Eteocles.
Danaë: Daughter of Acrisius, imprisoned in a tower by him and there visited by Zeus in the form of a shower of gold.
Dionysus: God of wine and intoxication, closely associated with Thebes.
Dirce: A nymph, a devotee of Dionysus, who gave her name to a stream near Thebes.
Dryas: Father of King Lycurgus.
Eteocles: Son of Oedipus and Jocasta.
Haemon: Son of Creon and Eurydice, betrothed to Antigone.
Ismene: Antigone's sister.
Ismenus: A stream flowing through Thebes. There was a temple by it in which the ashes of sacrifices were used for divination.
Labdacus: The father of Laius.
Lachmeus, the sons of: Invented by Brecht for a role in a myth he himself invented.
Laius: A king of Thebes, first husband of Jocasta, father of Oedipus.
Lycurgus: A king of the Edonians, a people of Thrace. He was driven mad by Dionysus.
Megareus: Son of Creon and Eurydice.
Menoeceus: Father of Creon and Jocasta.
Niobe: The wife of Amphion, an early king of Thebes. When she boasted that she had more children than Leto they were all killed

by Leto's children, Apollo and Artemis, and she herself in her grief was turned to stone.

Oedipus: Son of Laius and Jocasta.

Pelias: A character in several important Greek myths. Brecht invents another role for him.

Phineus: A king of Salmydessus, his sons were blinded by their stepmother.

Phrygian: Of Phrygia, a district of Asia Minor, here, an epithet of Niobe, who was born there.

Polynices: Brother of Eteocles.

Pontus: The sea, sometimes personified as a son of Gaia the Earth.

Salmydessus: City of Thrace on the Black Sea.

Sardis: Capital of Lydia in Asia Minor, on the gold- and electrum-bearing river Pactolus.

Sipylus: Mountain near Smyrna in Asia Minor.

Tantalus: Famous for his torment, he was a king of Lydia and the father of Niobe.

Thebes: Capital of Boeotia.

Thracian: Of Thrace, in the extreme north-east of Greece.

Tiresias: Blind seer of Thebes, from Cadmus' time into Creon's.

Zeus: Chief of the Greek gods.

THE DAYS OF THE COMMUNE

Texts by Brecht

SOLILOQUY OF AN ACTRESS AS SHE MAKES UP

I shall portray a drinker
Who sells her children
In Paris, at the time of the Commune.
I have only five sentences.

But I also have a walk, a walk up the street.
I shall walk like a person liberated
A person whom no one ever wanted
To liberate, except from liquor, and I shall
Turn around, like a drunk afraid
Of being followed, I shall
Turn around and look at the audience.

I have studied my five sentences like documents
Such as you wash with acid in case, beneath the surface writing
There may be other traces. I shall speak each one
Like an accusation
Against me and all who watch me.

If I were thoughtless, I'd make myself up
Like an old tramp, a drinker
A dissolute or an invalid, but I shall
Walk on stage as a fine woman, destroyed
With yellow skin, once soft, now wasted
Once desirable, now repulsive
So that everyone asks: who
Has done this?

[BFA 14, p.423. This was the poem Brecht wrote for Ruth Berlau when she played the part of Madame Lasalle in the first production of Nordahl Grieg's *Defeat* in Copenhagen in 1937.]

LETTERS TO HELENE WEIGEL

[...] I've just read *Defeat*, don't show it to anyone else, it's astonishingly bad, but I think it can be changed, I've taken lots of notes. Anyway, I now understand Engel's horror. Still, the play has good roles, and they could be made better. I'll cut out the petty bourgeois nonsense and put some life into it, while sticking to the historical facts. [...]

Zurich, 25/26 February 1949

Today, Wednesday, after all sorts of difficulties, Bern has finally sent a re-entry visa, though only for me, nothing for Barbara. In the meantime, I had taken steps, through von Einem in Salzburg, towards getting an Austrian passport. It would be valid for you and Barbara and would at least be a paper to travel with. The prospects are not bad, I should try to keep the line open to as many German-language theatres as possible. Then we could work wherever we pleased. Well, I still need a permit for Barbara and the one Bern has granted me for Munich. If Barbara doesn't get one, I'll go ahead and meet her in Salzburg. I hope the Russian permits are in Bern too, so far we haven't been able to find out. The Commune play is in good shape, I've polished it a bit more and haven't sent it off yet. But now I think it would be better to start with *Puntila*, which is much less controversial; besides the Commune play is an enormous production and if we put it in third place, we could work on it through the season. What about Busch? (Should I try to get Paryla interested?) I have to make sure Steckel can come at the beginning of September, I'll find out in the next few days. (He can definitely come in February.) I think we could also get Seyferth for Puntila, and I believe Engel would be glad to have him. (In my opinion Steckel would be better.) Please ask Engel and let me know what you think. Otherwise Seyferth would come in February, and then it would be for the Commune play in the dual role of Thiers and Bismarck. – The information about the actors is being sent to you. – Also the figures on travel costs. – [...] Tell her [Ilse Kaspriowiak] everything is all right. Of course you can't say anything definite about which play is to be done first, until you've read the Commune play. But you know the subject, and of course I've stuck scrupulously to the truth, which as we know is not to everyone's liking. Hirschfeld has read it; he spoke of it with great enthusiasm, but advised me to run it third, and possibly with an Ensemble augmented by the Deutsches Theater.

I kiss you
b

Zurich, 21 April 1949

[...] The play is finished in rough draft, time enough to polish it in

Berlin. I'll send it off at the beginning of the week, to be re-typed by Kaspriowiak: don't show it to Engel until you have a clean copy, that's important I think. I'll have to go over it again for the language, and scenes 7–11 need more dash (and documentation). – It's been a lot of work. [...] If only I weren't detained here; so far I haven't wasted any time, I've been able to do the play, I had Cas here for it, now we're working on the sets, which will be beautiful, I think. Oh yes, another thing: Hauptmann should ask old Duncker for literature, he's the one who compiled the 1871 book. What I especially need is *Documents historiques contemporains* (Collection de la Revue de France): *Les 31 scéances officielles de la Commune* (1871).

b

Zurich, April/May 1949

[*Letters*, pp.459, 468–79. These are three of a whole series of letters to Helene Weigel and others, in the early months of 1949. They show Brecht trying, in the midst of worries about visas for himself and his daughter Barbara, to set up an opening season at the Berliner Ensemble. See also Introduction.

Weigel was the Intendant of the new Ensemble and so responsible for organising productions. Gottfried von Einem, a young Austrian composer, was a director of the Salzburg Festival, with whom Brecht was negotiating, both about artistic projects and for Austrian papers. Erich Engel had been a co-director of *Mother Courage* at the Deutsches Theater in January and discussions were underway for further collaborations. Leonard Steckel had directed *The Good Person of Szechwan* and *Galileo*, and played both Galileo and Puntila at the Zurich Schauspielhaus; he was to play Puntila in Berlin (the play with which the Ensemble opened on 8 November). Karl Paryla and Wilfred Seyferth were other members of the Zurich company. Kurt Hirschfeld was deputy director and another of the important contacts there; he had played a major part in the Brecht premières in Zurich during the war, and was credited as the director of the Zurich *Puntila* when Brecht himself had been unable to get a work permit. Ilse Kaspriowiak was Brecht's secretary at the Berliner Ensemble. Caspar Neher (Cas) was to design most of the Berliner Ensemble's early productions, including *The Days of the Commune*. Hermann Duncker was the author/editor of *Pariser Kommune 1871* (Berlin: Neuer Deutscher Verlag, 1931), Brecht's main historical sourcebook for the play.

At around the same time Brecht wrote to Elisabeth Hauptmann who, recently returned from the United States, had been installed on the board of the Ensemble as dramaturg, asking her to hunt out further material:

> About the Commune:
> Documentation of mistakes.
> The different tendencies among the communards.
> Were any big businesses threatened?
> What about war profits?
> What business connections were there with the victorious Germans?
> Food prices. Black market.
> Bureaucracy in the Commune.
> Did the courts sabotage the Commune?
> What about the students?
> Jokes and anecdotes.
> The journalists.
> Attitude of the Goncourts. Of Zola.
> Is there anything by Maupassant? Baudelaire?
> Attitude and role of England.
> Did the Church agitate? What was the attitude of the lower clergy?
> Were some of them favourable?
> Were there shifts of mood?
> Songs in the cabarets?
>
> (*Letters*, p.473)

Later in the year he wrote to both Duncker and another Marxist historian, Albert Schreiner, sending them copies of the typescript and asking them to check on the historical accuracy of the play (*Letters*, pp.480 and 486).]

NOTES FOR THE PRODUCTION

1 The language is full of gallicisms. The lively, fast and physical manner and the elegant gestures of the French will have to be worked on; especially in the representation of the workers.

2 A deal of spite, but no caricatures!

3 For the women buying bread, play the vulgarity with relish.

5 One might show how Jean Cabet climbs up on to the back of the locomotive, argues with the stoker, gets physical with him, gets thrown off by the soldiers, etc. That sort of thing provides the *spectaculum magnum* people want.

6 The whole scene needs to be light, quick, the big city takes a huge deep breath, with noises from all over the place.

7b (Ministry of the Interior) Langevin watches Geneviève 'governing'.
8 Beslay should be played *tragi*-comically.
9c (Night session of the Commune) The Commune *learns* from the enemy class.
11b (Last session of the Commune in the play) All the speeches, even the passionate ones, are dragged out, by people who are dog-tired; their gestures are slow, drunken with sleep.
12 From time to time the conversation sticks, and the jolly tone becomes uncertain.
After 14 the revolve turns, and the whole ensemble steps forward through a basic set (the flags on the houses are raised, the barricade has gone) and sings the final chorus.

NOTES ON 'THE DAYS OF THE COMMUNE'

1 The population of Paris (in the National Guard) defends the capital and demands weapons, bread and proper leadership in battle, while the bourgeoisie wheels and deals and sabotages.
2 Thiers in Bordeaux sues for peace with the Germans, since otherwise France, and in particular Paris, would slip from the grasp of the bourgeoisie.
3 Thiers has secured peace and distributed bread, but his seizure of the guns of the National Guard gives rise to mistrust among the people.
4 The central committee of the National Guard decides to take up arms against Thiers, the bourgeoisie and their bourgeois peace, they announce elections for the Commune.
5 The flight of the bourgeoisie from Paris at the prospect of elections.
6 Overwhelming majority for the Commune. Paris celebrates.

THE STAGE SET

The basic set consists of a podium stretched into a gentle oval curve, and behind it the historical map of a besieged Paris in 1871, with the positions of the guns and barricades. The squares (in 1, 6 and 3 and 12 – the last of which has neither baker nor café, as if the barricade was projected across the entrance to a street) can be developed into the grand assembly hall of the Commune (4, 7, 9, 11). The houses in the long perspective of streets (12 and 13) are painted on thin flags which can be dropped down from the flies. The interiors (2 and 5 and 7a and

8 and 10) are set up inside the semi-circle of the podium. Two of them (2 and 10) have an architectural view as back-drop, which covers up the map of Paris. They are all built up of single, separable elements of furniture and the like, window, door, table, safe, grandfather clock, etc. For scenes 4, 9a and 14 the revolve is turned so that the back of the podium can be used. On the half-height curtain the words 'The Days of the Commune'.

[BFA 24, pp.354–5. All of these notes date from 1949 when Brecht was planning to stage *The Days of the Commune* as his first production at the newly founded Berliner Ensemble. All the numbers refer to the scene numbers (although 5 and 7a are not really what we would understand as 'interiors'). The final chorus was never completed.]

Editorial Notes

Unlike *Antigone*, which appears to have had an exceptionally straightforward genesis amongst Brecht's works, the archival material, notes and letters relating to *The Days of the Commune* betray Brecht's concern that the play might not work, might not make proper use of its complex historical material, or might turn out too unwieldy on stage.

In Svendborg in 1937, when Brecht was working on his Spanish Civil War play *Señora Carrar's Rifles*, he encountered the Norwegian Communist Nordahl Grieg's play, *Nederlaget* (*Defeat*), which had enjoyed a surprisingly successful première in Copenhagen earlier that same year (with Ruth Berlau in the minor role of Madame Lasalle). The tale of the Paris Commune of 1871 had some application to the current situation in Spain, where 'bourgeois' forces were defeating the left-wing republic with the assistance of foreign troops. Margarete Steffin produced a rough translation and, with Brecht's support, it was published in 1938 in the Moscow-based exile journal *Das Wort* (The Word) – despite Brecht's misgivings about the play, which he may not have read very carefully at this stage. When Grieg visited Svendborg that same year, Brecht apparently gave him a dressing-down about his misunderstanding of Marx's classic essay on the Commune, *Civil War in France*. Anyway, the translation was taken up again in 1947 in Berlin by the Henschel publishing house. In 1948/49 Brecht's initial plan was for a production of Grieg's play at the Schiffbauerdamm Theatre in Berlin. For a nation in defeat, struggling between restoration and wholesale social change, both of them sponsored by competing foreign powers, an account of the historical events of the Commune could now be read as a rather different sort of political cautionary tale. He talked to Erich Engel and Erwin Piscator as potential directors, and even drew up cast lists. But on re-reading the play, on the way to Zurich where he was looking to recruit actors and others for the new Berliner Ensemble, he decided it was impossible: 'Now I understand why the Danish king and the gentlemen in their dinner jackets applauded when the communards lay dying' (Ruth Berlau, *Brechts Lai-Tu*, Darmstadt/Neuwied, 1985, p.220). Instead he resolved to re-work the material into his own account of the Commune.

Nordahl Grieg (born 1901) studied briefly in Oxford, lived for two years in Moscow, and worked as a journalist and playwright in his native Norway for most of the 1930s, except for a visit to Spain. He escaped to Britain after the Nazi occupation of Scandinavia, and died when the Lancaster he had joined as a war correspondent was shot down over Berlin in December 1943. *Defeat* was conceived in response to Grieg's own experience of the defeat of the Left in the Spanish Civil War. The action begins in March 1871 and involves an alternation of scenes between representatives of various sectors of the people, the Commune delegates and Thiers and his ministers (there is no Bismarck scene). It is broadly Naturalist in style, but with an operatic conclusion: a raggle-taggle band of communards and children huddle in a churchyard, awaiting their execution by advancing government soldiers; a musical accompaniment of an aggressive drum beat is eventually overcome by the freedom motif from Beethoven's Ninth Symphony (see extract below). Brecht inverts this whole operatic finale, and gives us a coda in which a group of bourgeois spectators turns the brutal ending of the Commune into a 'sublime', 'immortal' spectacle, which they can enjoy (through opera glasses) from the safety of the fortifications of Versailles. It is a scathing comment on Grieg's dramatic concept. Brecht also intended a musical finale, but presumably with a bitterly ironic tone.

In fact, his play borrows a generous handful of motifs, scene outlines and characters (and some of its structure of alternating settings) from Grieg's text. One scene in particular bears a resemblance: Grieg's Act Two, scene 8, in which the Governor of the Banque de France meets first a secret envoy of the Versailles government and then Commune delegate Beslay, corresponds closely to Brecht's scene 8. In general, ideologically the two plays are rather similar; the opposition between them is, above all, one of dramatic conception. Brecht cuts out Grieg's pathetic gestures and sentimental deaths, introduces more differentiated class conflicts and interests (the student/seminarist, the National Guard soldiers and the profiteers), develops the action around the baker's, and hugely expands the role of the women. Above all, he introduces the documentary elements and the scenes of the meetings of the Commune, which are totally absent from Grieg. He turns the loose four-act structure into a carefully managed sequence of episodes and dialogues.

In Zurich Brecht worked closely with Caspar Neher, who designed the set and did individual scene sketches, and with Berlau, who gathered historical accounts and documentation from the Zurich Central Library. His main sources (as well as Grieg's play) appear to have been:

Prosper Lissagaray, *Histoire de la Commune de 1871* (Brussels, 1876; and the German edition of 1877);
Hermann Duncker (ed.), *Pariser Kommune 1871. Berichte und Dokumente von Zeitgenossen* (Berlin, 1931);
Les 31 Scéances-Officielles de la Commune (Paris, 1871);
Karl Marx, *Der Bürgerkrieg in Frankreich. Adresse des Generalrates der internationalen Arbeiterassoziation* (1871);
Vladimir Iljitsch Lenin, *Über die Pariser Kommune* (Vienna/Berlin, 1931);
Journal Officiel (*Réimpression du Journal officiel de la Commune*, Paris, 1871);
Sergei Akhrem, *Das war die Diktatur des Proletariats: die Pariser Kommune* (Moscow, 1932).

These are works which Brecht himself lists, or which feature in his library. Altogether, there is a considerable amount of quotation from them, especially in the scenes of the sessions of the Commune itself; and there are odd sentences from other sources strewn throughout (including a fragment of Baudelaire's 'Crépuscule du Matin' at the end of scene 6). In this procedure of documentary montage and quotation Brecht's play much resembles Büchner's *Danton's Death* which, interestingly, was the other play he was considering for the new Berliner Ensemble (see Introduction). In addition, his papers include maps of Paris and environs in 1870/71.

There is music too. Rather than harnessing Beethoven's Ninth to his cause, Brecht's first inclination was to go back to French sources. However, his plan to incorporate ballads by Eugène Pottier in translations by Erich Weinert was eventually rejected. Instead, the play features two of Brecht's own songs of the 1930s ('None or All' and 'Resolution'), documents of a quite different conflict aptly transposed to this new setting, as well as several new songs, for which Hanns Eisler was once more prevailed upon to provide settings.

In April 1949 Brecht wrote to Helene Weigel that the new version was already finished, but it is clear that he was still uncertain about it. He even suggested that the title page might offer a fictitious attribution as cover: 'after the French of Jacques Malorne'. After he returned to Berlin he continued to seek the advice of historians (Duncker and Schreiner), and he kept postponing a production: at first because the subject matter was too controversial, then because it was unsuitable for a middle-class audience and, very possibly, because of opposition from the Party authorities. In 1952 in the documentation volume of the Berliner Ensemble *Theaterarbeit* (Theatre-Work) the play was announced as a project for the forthcoming season, and a sketch of one scene was published alongside designs for the stage set; in 1954 a further series of extracted scenes appeared in the journal *Neue Deutsche Literatur* (as well as in an unauthorised Italian translation); and in 1956 further scenes were published in *Theater der Zeit* and *Neues Deutschland*.

Early in 1956 Brecht at last commissioned Manfred Wekwerth and Benno Besson (two young colleagues at the Berliner Ensemble, the latter recruited from Zurich) to direct the première of *The Days of the Commune* in Karl-Marx-Stadt (Chemnitz). He first checked with Henschel whether there was a copyright problem with respect to Grieg's original play and its German translation, but they assured him there was a minimal overlap and suggested he offer the Grieg heirs a share of two per cent. According to Wekwerth, Brecht then proposed another thorough re-working of the play, in order to develop the political turning points more clearly. But Brecht died (in August 1956) before any more work was undertaken; and the play was published in the *Versuche* (*Experiments*) series before the end of the year. There it carried a prefatory note:

> The play *The Days of the Commune* was written in 1948/49 in Zurich, after reading Nordahl Grieg's *Defeat*. Some features and characters were borrowed from *Defeat*, but in general *The Days of the Commune* is a kind of riposte. It is the twenty-ninth Experiment. Collaborator: R. Berlau.

Despite all the discussion, it was still virtually the same as the fair copy of 1949 (on which our text is based). After the première, Wekwerth and Joachim Tenschert undertook a thoroughgoing revision, and justified their massive changes with reference to Brecht's alleged intention to revise the play himself. It is their 'Berliner Ensemble rehearsal script' which has previously appeared in English (as *The Days of the Commune*, translated by Clive Barker and Arno Reinfrank, Methuen, 1978). Even a fleeting comparison will make clear quite how much they changed. Hence the decision of the present editors to revert to Brecht's own text.

From the Last Scene of Nordahl Grieg's *Defeat*

[*A group of communards, women and children have taken refuge in a churchyard. There they hear the advancing government soldiers, represented by march music, and await their execution.*]

DELESCLUZE *stands up*: Now they are coming.

The deep, rhythmical music comes nearer. Through it can be heard the motif from Beethoven's Ninth Symphony.

ROSE: They'll kill us now.

[. . .]

Driven by the music, they go back step by step towards the wall.

DELESCLUZE: At last! No more fear, no more defeat, no more imprisonment. Now I'm protected by death, I can stand, looking at the sky, remembering, hoping . . . There is nothing more to be done.

LUCIEN: Thank you, Pauline.

PAULINE *takes his hand*: Thank you, too.

GABRIELLE: Delescluze, there's still something we can say.

DELESCLUZE: To whom?

GABRIELLE: To those who kill us. Come, children: we'll tell them of the future, of our irreconcilable hope.

MAURICE: How shall we do that?

GABRIELLE: They'll see it in our smile.

MAURICE: What shall we smile at?

We feel, now, that the advancing soldiers have come to a halt.

LUCIEN: Now we've just got to stand quietly, and not worry. Now they've come on a bit. Good. Now it's all right.

The shadow of the firing party's rifles falls on the wall. A roll of drums. Darkness. At the same instant, the Beethoven motif frees itself from the drums, and rings out in clear, magnificent harmony. Curtain.

[This is the final page of the play (Act Four, scene 3) in the English translation by Eleanor Arkwright, London: Gollancz, 1944, p.87.]

Chronology of the Paris Commune

Brecht's play is set in the period from 19 January to the street battles between 21 and 28 May 1871.

1870

19 July: France declares war on Prussia. In August French defeats follow in quick succession.

2 September: Surrender of Napoleon III to the Prussian army, after the Battle of Sedan.

4 September: Insurrectionary demonstrations in Paris. Proclamation of the Republic. Formation of the provisional Government of National Defence.

18 September: Prussian armies complete the encirclement of Paris.

31 October: Demonstrations against an armistice. Battalions of the National Guard (a citizens' army dating back to the Revolution, now augmented by part of the army which rejected the Government of National Defence) occupy the Hôtel de Ville. Demands for a Commune.

27 December: Prussian artillery begins to bombard Paris.

1871

18 January: Wilhelm I proclaimed Kaiser in a ceremony at Versailles.

19 January: French sortie, failure and heavy losses around Buzenval.

22 January: Violent demonstrations against the armistice.

28 January: Paris capitulates to the Prussians.

8 February: Elections to a new National Assembly. Overwhelmingly monarchist and conservative, it convenes in Bordeaux, with Adolphe Thiers as Chief Executive.

15 February: Formation of the Central Committee of the National Guard, for the defence of the Republic. The National Guard seize cannon that would have gone to the Prussians.

26 February: In Versailles, Thiers and his Foreign Minister Jules Favre, as representatives of the Government of National Defence, sign the ceasefire which the Germans have imposed.

1–3 March: Token occupation of Paris by the Prussians.

10 March: National Assembly transfers its seat to Versailles, ends the remission of rents, stops paying the National Guard.

18 March: Abortive attempt to seize the cannon from the National

Guard. Revolt. Central Committee of the National Guard takes charge in Paris. Generals Thomas and Lecomte are shot. Exodus of Government troops and functionaries to Versailles.

26 March: Elections in Paris.

28 March: Inauguration of the Paris Commune.

29 March: Opening session of the Commune. First decrees: Abolition of the standing army, remission of rents. Later decrees include: separation of church and state; destruction of the Vendôme Column; abolition of night work for bakers; restitution of pawned possessions; confiscation of abandoned factories and their transformation into worker co-operatives; abolition of the rank of general; fixing of government and civil service salaries at a rate no higher than that of a skilled worker.

2 April: Start of military operations between Paris and Versailles, Commune does badly. Paris again besieged and bombarded.

3 April: Many captured communards are shot by Versailles forces.

5 April: In retaliation the Commune decrees that hostages may be taken. Archbishop of Paris arrested.

6 April: Burning of the guillotine in the Place Voltaire.

30 April: Municipal elections in the rest of France, big gains by moderate republicans.

10 May: Treaty of Frankfurt: France to pay war costs and cede Alsace-Lorraine.

21 May: Versailles troops enter Paris.

21–28 May: Bloody Week. The Commune executes 63 hostages. In the street fighting, 873 Government soldiers and about 3,000 communards are killed. After the fighting, Thiers' troops kill another 20,000.

Only in 1873 do the last German troops leave French territory. Despite various monarchist movements and plans for a restoration, by 1879 the French Republic is secure.

TURANDOT

Texts by Brecht

JOURNAL ENTRIES

12 May 1942
At Horkheimer's with Eisler for lunch. Afterwards Eisler suggests a plot for the *Tui-Novel*: the story of the Frankfurt Sociological Institute. A rich old man (Weil, the speculator in wheat) dies, disturbed at the poverty in the world. In his will he leaves a large sum to set up an institute which will do research on the source of this poverty. Which is, of course, himself. The activities of the institute take place at a time when the Emperor too would like to see a name given to the source of the evil, since popular indignation is rising. The institute participates in the deliberations.

20 August 1953
Buckow. *Turandot*. Also the *Buckow Elegies*. 17 June has alienated the whole of existence. Despite their pathetic helplessness and lack of direction, the workers' demonstrations have shown that this is the rising class. It is not the petty bourgeois who are taking action, but the workers. Their slogans are confused and powerless, foisted on them by the class enemy, and there is no strength in their organisation, no councils have been set up, no plan has been formed. And yet here we had the class in front of us, in its most depraved condition, but nevertheless the class. The important thing would have been to use this first encounter to full advantage. This was the point of contact. It came not as an embrace but as a slap in the face, but it was contact nonetheless. – The Party had reason to be alarmed, but it didn't need to despair. After the whole historical development it could not in any case expect the spontaneous agreement of the working class. There were tasks it had anyway, in the circumstances, to carry out without that agreement, indeed even against the workers' resistance. But here, however ill-timed, was the big chance to win over the workers. For this reason I did not find the terrible 17 June simply negative. The moment I saw the proletariat – nothing would lead me to make ingenious excuses or allowances here – exposed to

the class enemy again, to the capitalism of the Fascist era in renewed strength, I saw the only force that is capable of coping with it.

13 September 1953
When I look at *Turandot* now – she stands right outside German literature and seems, as single persons often do, shaky on her pins. If I were wholly a comedy writer, which I almost am, but only almost, then such a work would have relatives grouped around it, and the clan would be able to assert itself.

As for the 'message' of the work, there's nothing simple about it. Like Molière's *L'Avare* in this respect. He is ridiculing the avarice of an age in which the bourgeoisie has recently discovered how to put money to productive use. Avarice has become quite impractical, stands in the way of making money and is thus ridiculous (and also earns the laughter of the feudal class which is generous and does not stint with the product of the labour of the oppressed classes). And yet avarice is of long standing. Basically, as the compulsion to save, as the aim of productivity, as the bad side of capitalism, throughout its career. (And is, if captured at the right time, a really deeply rooted bad quality.) – In *Turandot* the will to formulate, to think unproductively is captured at a time when the (capitalist) mode of production does not permit productive forces to develop any further; it presents itself as impractical, therefore ridiculous. And it will carry on like this for a while, until the intellectuals are no longer outside and in opposition to the rest of the population, and the whole population, on the contrary, has been intellectualised.

[*Journals*, pp.230–1 and 454–6. These notes, from two quite different stages of Brecht's life – in 1942 he was in California, in 1952/3 in Berlin – give some impression of the various impulses behind the *Turandot* adaptation, and the constructions which might be placed on it. For the reference to 17 June, see Introduction.]

ADDITIONAL SCENES FROM THE 'TURANDOT' COMPLEX

THE TUI AND THE WASHERWOMEN AT THE RIVER

Amongst the women washing clothes by the river a Tui sits, cautiously washing his toes.

TUI: A pretty sight, ladies, a splendid subject for a painter. The colour contrast, the laundry and the bare arms, the charming movement, the light. Ah, I love these fleshly sights!

WASHERWOMAN: Yes, we like them too. But we don't often get to see them, you know.

TUI: Ah. That's not quite what I meant. Is the water cold?

SECOND WASHERWOMAN: You can see for yourself, look at our hands. You see how red they are, and how calloused the skin is? But you can dip your toes in all right.

The Tui sits down so that they cannot see his feet.

TUI: I wasn't asking on account of my feet, but to know if it is cold for you.

WASHERWOMAN: Uhuh. But you can dip them in, no worries.

TUI: There's no hurry. How does Xi-Fu put it? 'Hurry is the wind that brings the scaffolding crashing down.'

ANOTHER WASHERWOMAN: What's going to come crashing down if you just wash your feet?

The washerwomen laugh. A supervisor approaches.

SUPERVISOR: What's so funny? You don't get paid for jokes. The other day some linen got torn again. I'll have it deducted from your pay, just so as you know. You there, come to my hut after you knock off, I want a word with you.

A WASHERWOMAN: Yes sir.

The supervisor exits.

ANOTHER WASHERWOMAN: See that, he thought it a pretty sight as well.

TUI: What do you mean?

WASHERWOMAN: You heard, he told her to come and see him in the hut.

ANOTHER: He ripped my 'linen' too the other day, but you don't get paid any more for it.

TUI: But ladies, you don't have to put up with that. That's a clear transgression, 'Transgressions are harmful,' that's what Mi-di expressly says.

SECOND WASHERWOMAN: And he should know. *To the woman who was addressed by the supervisor*: You're a bit eager, I'd say.

WASHERWOMAN *answering*: And I suppose you're not?

SECOND WASHERWOMAN: The other day you smiled at him, I saw it quite clearly. He promised me the place by the basket.

WASHERWOMAN: Well, he didn't promise me anything, but he's cut my pay three times in a row.

TUI *has his toes in the water, triumphantly*: The water isn't cold at all! Ladies, I must make a confession: I'm a poet by profession. I should like, if you have nothing against it, to try to sweeten your labours a little by reciting a poem, that is to say, if you can contribute a couple of yen to the costs of having it printed. The poem is called: 'The Ballad of the Triumph of Woman'.

WASHERWOMEN: I heard a really nice ballad recently. I could spare a yen, if it's any good. Last spring there was someone collecting money in advance out on the bleachery, but then his poem turned out to have only one verse. Let's do it like this: we'll pay one yen after each verse, until there's no more money left.

TUI: Agreed, but the refrain counts as a verse.

WASHERWOMEN: Oh no. We're not having any of that. Either we do it our way, or not at all. And it's got to have rhythm, so we can do the washing to it, otherwise we're not paying.

TUI *sighing*: All right. You drive a hard bargain. *He sings the ballad. When he's done*: So that's it, nothing more? Many thanks, ladies, and good evening. *Exits.*

A WASHERWOMAN: He could have done it for nothing just as well.

SECOND WASHERWOMAN: That sort won't wash their feet for free you know.

THE TUI AND THE PORTER

A porter is groaning under the weight of a column. A Tui follows close at his heels.

TUI: Dear friend, do you know what it is you're carrying?

PORTER: Must be at least eight stone, sir.

TUI: A particularly fine example of a column, choice marble, not that modern hollow stuff.

PORTER: Not a bit of it, sir.

TUI: Wouldn't you like to learn a thing or two about such an outstanding work of art, my good man?

PORTER: What do you mean? Uh, it's heavy.

TUI: Indeed, it is also no light thing to teach a person a genuine artistic sensibility. I could do my best, of course. But then I don't know if you can afford the ten or twenty yen it might cost, what do you say?

PORTER: What is it that's supposed to be costing me?

TUI: Well. I could tell you something about the great artistry of this capital. You probably haven't had a closer look at the capital at all, am I right?

PORTER: Yes, I'd like to know something about the capital. But I don't have ten yen.

TUI: Do you have five?

PORTER: I could give you three, if you could say a bit about the capital.

TUI: Are you interested in the historical angle, my friend?

PORTER: Everything. But you'll have to talk quickly, the thing weighs a ton, and if I set it down I'll never get it back on my shoulder. You're far too weak to help me. The money's here in my pocket.

The Tui takes it out of his pocket.

TUI: Well now, the capital dates from the seventh century, it's from the school of Wang-ho, and shows the famous overlapping intersections, but the decoration doesn't employ any animal or human motifs. Good evening. *He walks away quickly.*

PORTER: Hey! You haven't told me anything about the capital! Stop, stop!

THE BLANKET TUI

At a street corner there's a small shop with a window display of blankets. A Tui is talking to a passer-by, a poorly dressed man. He has his stall, a market umbrella, set up opposite the blanket shop between the houses.

TUI: Would you care to buy a blanket, my good man?

MAN: Yes, I could do with a blanket, mine's old and too short.

TUI: Well let us have a look at this display here together. What do you say to these blankets?

MAN: Too short.

TUI: They are, aren't they? Too short! They're all made too short. To save on cloth. I'll wager you can't think how to cover your feet if you want to pull a blanket like this up to your chin. It's a scandal.

MAN: It certainly is.

TUI: And do you know who's to blame when you shiver?

MAN *looking around nervously*: I don't want anything to do with politics.

TUI: That's just what I say too. *Loudly*: I'll tell you who's to blame, my good man. I shan't guard my tongue; there'll be no dark secrets in my heart. That hushing-everything-up, that keeping-your-head-down, that's not my style. Should I tell you who's to blame, or not?

MAN: You can tell me, but it wasn't me that asked.

TUI *yelling*: You!

MAN: What?

TUI: You're to blame!

MAN: How come?

TUI *triumphant*: Because you can't draw your feet in! *Eagerly*: That surprised you, eh? You would never have thought it was so easy, would you? I can tell you, this simple solution cost me years of contemplation until I'd grasped it. Without this brainwave I would never have been able to set up my stall here.

MAN: Why? What do you sell at your stall?

TUI: Instructions.

MAN: For what?

TUI: Instructions for the use of the blankets. Oh yes, I know you're thinking, all right, I just buy myself a blanket, and that's that. You don't look any further. And when that cold draught comes whistling round your feet, then you're taken all unawares. And what's the reason for the cold draught?

MAN *suggests*: Because the blanket's too short.

TUI: Rubbish. The blanket's just as long as any other blanket in this town. In the price range you can afford. Just buy yourself one of my little instruction leaflets – I can let you have one for a mere twenty yen – and you'll feel no more draughts. Look, this blanket will cost you eighty yen. A longer one would cost – *he measures him with a glance* – a man of your height at least a hundred and fifty yen. The short blanket and the instructions, and no more draughts, would cost a mere hundred yen. Is that a deal, or what?

MAN: So what's in your instructions?

TUI: You get a little diagram, how to arrange your legs; and then of course you have to practise.

MAN: But isn't it uncomfortable?

TUI: Only at the beginning. After a few years you won't want to lie any other way. You won't be able to. If someone was to give you a longer blanket, you'd just cut the end off.

MAN: Well, I have to have a blanket.

TUI *pushing him into the shop*: That's for certain.

After a while they come back out. The Tui gives the man, in exchange for twenty yen, a piece of card with a drawing on it, and takes the blanket from under his arm. With a nail he bores a little hole in one corner of the blanket.

TUI: And now you see what I've done here. That's the trick. You put your big toe through this hole, and that's how you hold the blanket down. Even if you have a restless night you'll never shake it off. And the beauty is, the trick can be repeated no less than four times: if your hole rips, you still have another three corners to make a fresh one.

[BFA 9, pp.193–6. Brecht's *Turandot* is unfinished; we cannot be sure what else, of the substantial material in the archive, should be counted as belonging to the play. These three scenes are the only additional ones which Brecht actually completed. They might possibly have found a place in the play, or they may be conceived as quite independent sketches. Elsewhere Brecht talks of another 'sequence of small plays' (see below). There are similarly independent versions of Ke Lei's performance in scene 5a, entitled 'The Tui and the Audience', and of the 'Tuis Soliciting Custom' in 4a (BBA 559/124 and 125).]

TWO SONGS FROM THE 'TURANDOT' COMPLEX

BALLAD OF THE EMPEROR

As things stand, we shouldn't be complaining
Seems we could afford a little laugh
Those who take the strain on our behalf
Show every sign that they'll continue straining.
All the years it's been this way
No one ever shouted Ho!
Where precisely does it say
How it's been it has to stay?
Just maybe, maybe
Things won't always be just so.

SONG OF THE PARTICULARITY OF THE LIMESIAN TUI

Elsewhere of course it may not be like that
It's only what I know that I can speak
All men are creatures of their habitat
Perhaps our Tuis here are quite unique.

I can only speak of what I know
All men are creatures of their habitat
But one thing that I'm confident I know:
Our Tuis here are very much like that.

They bicker heatedly like grand pretenders
And marvel how intelligent they are.
Like the emblem bolted to the fender
Which always likes to think *it* drives the car.

[BFA 15, pp.273–5. These are among the songs that may have been intended for the play.]

PREFACE TO 'TURANDOT'

At the beginning of the summer in which I wrote the play in question, a terrible event had shocked every intelligent person in the Republic. Since the end of Hitler's war, which had led to the Soviet occupation of this part of Germany, socialist measures like the expulsion of the war-mongering Junkers, the nationalisation of many factories and the admission of workers' and peasants' children to higher education had effected a powerful change in the way people live. They had not succeeded, of course, in effecting an equally great change in the way people think. There were many reasons for this. First of all, the economic system had to be transformed at a time when the economy had been weakened by the war. Hitler's regime had exhausted the last reserves of national prosperity, and the economic restoration, tackled conscientiously and ingeniously by workers and peasants, also suffered initially from the necessity of making amends for at least some of the monstrous devastation which the German people had perpetrated during their invasion of the Soviet Union under Hitler's regime: this country too had reached the limit of its resources.

Furthermore, the socialist measures were new; those who were putting them into practice had little or no experience in such matters, every step was an experiment on virgin territory, even with Russian support. Everywhere, mistakes were made, people were harmed or had their feelings hurt, expensive detours or expensive short-cuts were taken, again and again decrees took the place of persuasion.

A revolution had not taken place; not even in the last days of battle had the population risen against a regime which had plunged them into misery and crime. The German proletariat, disunited, weakened by unemployment, terrorised by a militarised petty bourgeoisie, formed underground fighting troops which achieved the superhuman but did not go beyond passive resistance. Many of its best leaders were murdered. Towards the end of Hitler's war, the bombing raids on the cities also annihilated new organisations which might have been able to seize power during the collapse. Whatever measures for reconstruction were instigated, they were undertaken for the majority of the population but not by them.

It is, particularly in the chaos of military defeat, in a highly civilised system with a high degree of division of labour, impossible to do without a state apparatus, but difficult to establish an entirely new one. So, under the new commanders, the Nazi apparatus once more set itself in motion. Such an apparatus cannot be imbued with a new spirit through control from above; it needs control from below. Unconvinced but cowardly, hostile but cowering, ossified officials began again to govern against the population.

[BFA 24, pp.409–10. This foreword to *Turandot* was written in late summer 1953 at Brecht's summer retreat in Buckow at the same time as his *Buckow Elegies.* (Compare also the *Journal* entry for 20 August 1953.) It represents arguably the most significant of Brecht's statements on the workers' uprising in East Berlin on 17 June 1953, and suggests surprising ways in which he may have thought his work on the play relevant to current events. In particular, Brecht identifies bureaucrats and civil servants as a reactionary force within the GDR undermining the project of East German Socialism. At first sight the essay may not seem to have much to do with the play, but in fact this context was crucial for Brecht. The connections he establishes between the Nazi regime and the GDR bureacracy, and the fact that the GDR was *not* the product of a popular revolution such as that which concludes the play, provided the urgent justification for revisiting the old *Turandot* project.]

NOTES

The stage must be transformed quickly; the scenes 'A Street' and 'In the Courtyard of the Imperial Palace' can be played in front of the small curtain. The buildings must be weightless, poetic and realistic suggestions.

The Whitewashers' Congress will work best on a revolve, so that the stage can move smoothly between vestibule and cloakroom, without a curtain.

The Tuis are characterised by small hats after the style of Tibetan or European priests. The hats differ according to the importance of the Tui, more or less decorative, and of different colours.

The costumes can be mixtures, based on the Chinese.

The performance must be quick.

[BFA 24, p.410. Typescript of summer 1953.]

'TURANDOT' AND THE INTELLECTUALS

The play *Turandot or The Whitewashers' Congress* is part of a substantial literary complex which for the most part consists still of plans and sketches. It includes a novel, *The Downfall of the Tuis*, a volume of stories, *The Tui Tales*, a sequence of small plays, *Tui Farces*, and a little volume of treatises, *Lickspittling and Other Arts*.

All these works, which have occupied the author for decades, are concerned with the abuse of the intellect.

[BFA 24, p.411. Summer 1953. Brecht had been putting together material under these headings since the 1930s, but not all of the works listed here are identifiable. See also the Introduction.]

REMARKS ON 'TURANDOT'

I devised the plan to write a *Turandot* play back in the 1930s, and during the exile period I did some preliminary work towards a novel, *The Golden Age of the Tuis*. Above all after writing *Life of Galileo*, in which I had portrayed the dawning of an age of reason, I wanted to portray its evening, the dusk of that variety of reason which, at the end of the sixteenth century, had launched the capitalist age.

[BFA 24, p.411. Summer 1953.]

TUI SKETCHES

Point of view

1 The people doubly cheated. Tui-thinking is wrong (damaging or useless). The solution: Thinking is wrong.
2 The Tuis of the Potsdam Republic: You saw where you got by thinking! The Tuis of the Weimar Republic: You'll see where you get with not-thinking! (The thought of distinguishing between correct and false thinking is missing.)
3 The Tuis in exile then cry out: Things are so bad, because we are gone and H is there! Those who remain, the fully adapted fellow travellers: Things are so good, because we and H have stayed and the others are gone!

The End: The people have fallen amongst the most corrupt and scoundrel Tuis. The Idea triumphs, the *Volk* dies a miserable death.

Definition
A Tui is someone who can hold a head to Eugen.
Tuis are the intellectuals of this age of markets and commodities.

Mongers of the intellect. [. . .]

Tui Congress

The battle of the orators Barbusse and Gide
Gide gracious, Barbusse even more gracious, so Gide hates Barbusse and speaks like Christ.
Barbusse goes out to the toilet and sharpens his teeth with a file (with which he otherwise sharpens his sentences).

Six days of speeches
The trainers. The boxes. Women admirers. The illustrators. Massage.

The resolution is expected to proclaim freedom of speech (unfree for the last time). The world-resolution.

Next door an assembly of pig merchants. Their applause penetrates the hall.

The Kaiser wishes to protect his property (by increasing it). But this is not to happen in a completely crass way. Force should not be employed, and if it is, it mustn't be recognised. Also the images of the good Kaiser must not be harmed, the patriarchal defender of cultural values and of wise, humble comportment. A willing compliance is called for, at least from the soldiers who, as we know, are related to the other subjects.
Only when the Tuis fail will naked force be employed.

The guilt of the Tuis: they associate culture (ethics, art etc.) with property. If it gets serious (an emergency) property will sacrifice both them and culture. Then they'll be between two stools, in banishment.

[BFA 17, pp.153, 156–7. Brecht wrote a great many short prose sketches and outlines like this, as well as several longer stories. For the most part they were probably intended to become part of a so-called *Tui-Novel*, the fragments of which occupy 150 pages in the German collected edition. These extracts, just a sample of the material from the relevant folders, date from the mid-1930s.

Eugen was Brecht's first given name. His rather obscure definition, 'Tui ist, wer dem Eugen den Kopf reicht', may be a variation on the German saying 'jemandem (nicht) das Wasser reichen', which is more or less equivalent to '(not) holding a candle to someone' – in which case he is ironically acknowledging himself to be a Tui.

On Barbusse and Gide, see Editorial Notes.]

Editorial Notes

Like so many of Brecht's projects, the *Turandot* play suffered from a very long and often interrupted process of genesis. Or perhaps benefited. The richly allusive nature of the text is of course a product of the various contexts in which, successively, its material was to be made to function: as a parody of aspects of the collapse of the Weimar Republic and the Nazi assumption of power (Gogher Gogh and his bandits, the warehouse fire etc.), as a satire of the German anti-Nazi exiles and their colleagues who gathered at the two International Congresses for the Defence of Culture in 1935 and 1937 (see below), of the inability of the Communists and Social Democrats to unite against Fascism (the Clothesless and the Clothesmakers), or of the Frankfurt School 'intellectuals' (Munka Du has some caricatural traits of Theodor Adorno, and compare *Journals*, pp.230–1), of the survival of a bureaucratic caste of civil servants in the young GDR, of Stanislavsky's theatre theory (*Journals*, p.18) or of the performance of cultural leaders of the GDR at the Stanislavsky conference in mid-April 1953. And so on. There are even veiled references to the exchanges of such Marxist critics as Kurella and Lukács in the so-called Expressionism Debate of the 1930s, or of Erpenbeck and others in the new Formalism debate of the 1950s, to the McCarthyite anti-Communist witch-hunts (the interrogation of Munka Du), to the Chinese Civil War in 1948 (Kai Ho has aspects of Mao Tse-tung), to the controversy in the GDR about the value and function of the bourgeois cultural heritage (scene 9) and, much more sensitively, to the workers' uprising in East Berlin in June 1953 (see 'Preface to *Turandot*', above). Scene 9 appears to engage with the cultural politics of all three: National Socialism, the Stalinist Soviet Union and the GDR. These various contexts are fleshed out in several of the essays from the 1930s and 1950s on cultural matters collected in *Brecht on Art and Politics* (see especially pp. 157–62 and 327–31, and compare Introduction).

The first plans and drafts for a *Turandot* play date from around 1930. Brecht had known the Turandot story for some time: his personal library contains a copy of Carlo Gozzi's *Turandot* (1762) in Karl Vollmoeller's translation (Berlin, 1911) with a handwritten note 'Bert Brecht 1925'. In May 1932, on a visit to Moscow, he attended a performance of Gozzi's tragicomedy, done up as a grotesque farce by

Evgeni Vakhtangov. In a newspaper interview in 1935 Brecht reported that he was working on a comedy, 'in which I portray how bourgeois ideologues market the ideological opinions favoured at the time by the bourgeoisie' (*Deutsche Zentral-Zeitung*, Moscow, 23 May 1935, cf. BFA 9, p.398). In the course of the 1930s these sketches were expanded with a view to a whole complex of literary projects about the 'Tuis'. This was Brecht's word, a syllable play on 'Tellekt-Ual-In', to describe 'the intellectuals of this age of markets and commodities'. (Possibly he was also aware of the kinship of his neologism to the Chinese words, more generally rendered as 'Dui' and 'Tuan', and meaning, respectively, a team and an association.) The other parts of the *Tui*-complex (see '*Turandot* and the Intellectuals' and 'Tui Sketches', above) were to remain fragments. The main thrust of these writings was the satirical debunking of the role of the intellectuals in the failure of the Weimar Republic and their feeble response to Nazism and Fascism. For example, in letters to friends after the 1935 International Congress for the Defence of Freedom in Paris (a huge event with leading cultural representatives from thirty-seven countries) Brecht remarked that he had collected quite a lot of material for his *Tui*-project:

> We have just rescued culture. It took 4 (four) days, and then we decided that we would sooner sacrifice all else than let culture perish. [. . .] We proceeded at once boldly and with caution. Our brother Henricus Mannus submitted his passionate oration in favour of free speech to the Sûreté before delivering it. A slight incident attracted notice. Towards the end, brother Barbussius devoured brother Andreus Gideus whole on the open rostrum. The episode ended tragically, for I'm told that an onlooker committed suicide out of boredom.
>
> (*Letters*, p.208)

The traces of these impressions of Heinrich Mann, Henri Barbusse and André Gide's contributions to the Congress are still fresh in scene 5a of our text of *Turandot*.

The experience of exile in the United States, and above all the experience of the Hollywood film industry, did not help to progress the plans, although there are some sketches from 1944. In April 1942 Brecht noted in his *Journal*,

> It is impossible to show up the sale of opinions here, where it is nakedly practised. The comedy of those who think they are leading but are in effect being led, the Don-Quixotry of a consciousness which labours under the illusion that it is determining social existence – all that only applies to Europe.
>
> (*Journals*, p.222)

And it was not until the summer of 1953, when Brecht was back in Europe, living in Buckow, outside Berlin, that a full draft of the play was worked out. Taking up the plans and fragments from the 1930s, which had already situated the action in an economic crisis of overproduction, Brecht now added the revolutionary activity of Kai Ho to the mix of the plot. But the immediate context of the political and cultural laundering and fixing of the GDR (of which Brecht and Eisler had very direct experience, see Introduction) also forced its way into the play. As in the *Buckow Elegies*, it was the continuities between the Nazi past and the Communist present that most disturbed him. The following summer, after a brief experience of the play in rehearsal, Brecht returned to the project and thoroughly re-worked it once more, especially developing the role of A Sha Sen. It is on a typescript of August 1954 that our text is based.

As well as the Gozzi version of the story, it seems that Brecht also went back to the pseudo-Persian tale of Prince Kalaf and Princess Turandot, which may have been available to him in a German edition of *The Thousand and One Days*, based on selections from *Les milles et un jours: contes persans*, possibly by (or translated by) François Pétis de La Croix (Paris 1710–12), and to further later translations-cum-adaptations by Friedrich Schiller (from 1802) and by Waldfried Burggraf (1923), both of which are in Brecht's library. The broad outlines of the plot of the traditional tale of *Turandot* will be familiar to many people from Puccini's last opera of the same name (left unfinished at his death in 1924 and premièred at La Scala in 1926); there is, however, no evidence that Brecht was aware of this version, also based on Gozzi's play. Unlike Schiller, the twentieth-century German and Russian versions Brecht used tend to downplay the heroism of Turandot and emphasise her capriciousness, but Brecht is the first to make her foolish, rather than frighteningly intelligent. From Gozzi onwards, all the dramatic workings of the story introduce the stock *commedia dell'arte* characters of Pantalone, Tartaglia, Brighella and Truffaldino, which Brecht rejects. Later versions tend to emphasise the comedic touches and characters. Burggraf's 'sages', who interpret the suitors' answers to the puzzles, are already satirical caricatures. And there are other motifs and turns of plot which Brecht has clearly borrowed from his many sources. The story of the old man and his son (A Sha Sen and Er Fei) seeking socially useful arguments from the philosophers' academy seems to be borrowed from Aristophanes' *Clouds*. Brecht's play has, typically for him, wandered a long way from any of his many models.

The archive contains five main typescripts of *Turandot* and a bundle of other material, the function and place of which are not always clear.

It is not possible to reconstruct an entirely coherent text, nor a clear process of revision which might make sense of all the fragments. Generally speaking, the plans and drafts from the 1930s and other earlier phases of the composition tend to emphasise the parody of the Hitler regime and the attitudes of the anti-Fascist exiles. For example, it is suggested that the Clothesless and the Clothesmakers will only make common cause in Gogher Gogh's 're-education camps'. In early versions the Clothesless themselves are associated literally with nakedness, and there are several jokes about half-naked characters on stage.

Above all, the ending of the text seems unsatisfactory. One other version has the Emperor and Gogher Gogh making moves each to arrest the other, until they realise that the soldiers and bandits, who might carry out their orders, have all disappeared. At one early stage, it seems, there was to be an additional closing scene, 'The Washerwomen Give Shelter to the Leader of the Clothesless', in which Sen presents the Manchu cloak to Kai Ho. This was to be followed by the 'Ballad of the branches and the trunk' (*Poems*, pp.206–7), a song which dates back to the years of *Round Heads and Pointed Heads*. Yet another variant, under the heading 'Emigration', sees the Tuis as severed heads trying once more to discover the solution to the problem of the missing cotton.

A note on the names

Brecht followed all his predecessors and set the story of the wilful and beautiful princess in China, but the only name he borrowed from his sources was that of Turandot herself. For the rest, names like Gogher Gogh and Krukher Kru seem to go right back to the sorts of games Brecht was playing in the 1920s (e.g. Galy Gay in *Man equals Man*); others too (Pauder Mel and Munka Du) have nothing at all Chinese about them. Some may well be syllable-plays on the names of the objects of Brecht's satire (as in the long prose text, *Me-Ti*), but if they are, no one has been able to decode them. A few seem to be simple careless *chinois* gestures: Yao, Su and Wang. It is just possible that a handful of the names are intended to allude to Chinese words and proper names, but it is not possible to discover any clear references. We have preserved a hotch-potch similar to Brecht's, but have modified some of the names: to make them more easily recognisable or pronounceable in English, or to make them look more like appropriate transliterations from the Chinese. We have generally used transliterations more or less suitable to Brecht's historical context, hence Peking, Po Chu-yi (not Beijing, Bo Ju yi), Hoang Ho (for the Yellow River) and Shigatse (rather than Xigazê).

These are the names which have been modified, or for which it seems possible to suggest some paths of association.

Brecht's names	*English text*	*Possible associations*
Eh Feh	Er Fei	'Er' could be the Chinese character for 'son', or for a second child
Fi Jej	Hui Zhe	
Gogher Gogh	Gogher Gogh	Brecht mentions a ballad of 'Goger Gog, the tin soldier' in 1920, but no such work has survived. The figure has much in common with Hitler
Gu	Gu	Chinese: a surname, can also mean 'ancient' (see Wen)
Hi Wei	Xi Wei	possibly derived from Hermann Weil, the businessman who financed the foundation of the Frankfurt Institute for Social Research
Jau Jel	Yao Yel	
Kai Ho	Kai Ho	clear allusions to Mao Tse-tung
Ka-Me	Ka-Me	play on Karl Marx
Ki Leh	Ke Lei	
Kiung, Su and Yao	Qiung, Su and Yao	Qiung can mean 'poor', but these are all Chinese names
Krukher Kru brothers	Krukher Kru	hints of Gregor and Otto Strasser, early associates of Hitler
Ma Gogh	Ma Gogh	'Ma' is also Chinese for 'mother'
Me Neh	Meh Nei	

Munka Du	Munka Du	possible references to Adorno, but unclear where the name comes from
Wen	Wen	Chinese: 'literary', 'cultured' (there was a Gu-Wen 'archaising' literary movement), but also a name

All other names are spelt as in Brecht's text and have no obviously relevant associations.